ON CHARACTER BUILDING

"Nearly all studies of characters and characterization in the canonical gospels that have appeared since the publication of *On Character Building* are indebted to John Darr's sophisticated construction of the rhetorical interplay between an ancient text and a culturally literate first-century reader's initial encounter with that text. Given the ongoing interest in the study of New Testament texts as literature, this volume retains its influential voice on methodological matters pertaining to characterization. This reprint edition will help ensure that Darr's work continues to receive a deservingly wide readership for years to come."

Frank Dicken

Associate Professor of New Testament, Lincoln Christian University (Lincoln, IL)

"In a period when narrative approaches to the NT Gospels were developing and becoming influential, John Darr's *On Character Building* appeared as one of a few early works to focus on Luke-Acts. The book is significant for its sophisticated yet accessible approach to characterization in general, as well as the numerous insights given into both characters and literary themes in the narrative of Luke-Acts. I am delighted that the volume will remain in print!"

Dr. Joshua L. Mann

ON CHARACTER BUILDING

the reader and the rhetoric of characterization in luke-acts

JOHN A. DARR

WIPF & STOCK • Eugene, Oregon

Wipf and Stock Publishers
199 W 8th Ave, Suite 3
Eugene, OR 97401

On Character Building
The Reader and the Rhetoric of Characterization in Luke-Acts
By Darr, John A.

Softcover ISBN-13: 978-1-7252-8356-5
Hardcover ISBN-13: 978-1-7252-8357-2
eBook ISBN-13: 978-1-7252-8359-6

Publication date 10/22/2020
Previously published by WJK, 1992

This edition is a scanned facsimile of the original edition published in 1992.

To Kathe

CONTENTS

SERIES PREFACE

New currents in biblical interpretation are emerging. Questions about origins—authors, intentions, settings—and stages of composition are giving way to questions about the literary qualities of the Bible, the play of its language, the coherence of its final form, and the relations between text and readers.

Such literary criticism is rapidly acquiring sophistication as it learns from major developments in secular critical theory, especially in understanding the instability of language and the key role of readers in the production of meaning. Biblical critics are being called to recognize that a plurality of readings is an inevitable and legitimate consequence of the interpretive process. By the same token, interpreters are being challenged to take responsibility for the theological, social, and ethical implications of their readings.

Biblical interpretation is changing on the practical as well as the theoretical level. More readers, both inside and outside the academic guild, are discovering that the Bible in literary perspective can powerfully engage people's lives. Communities of faith where the Bible is foundational may find that literary criticism can make the Scripture accessible in a way that historical criticism seems unable to do.

Within these changes lie exciting opportunities for all who seek contemporary meaning in the ancient texts. The goal of the series is to encourage such change and such search, to breach the confines of traditional biblical criticism, and to open channels for new currents of interpretation.

—The Editors

ACKNOWLEDGMENTS

At the heart of this study lies the simple observation that when we read Luke-Acts, we both "build" the characters of the story *and* undergo a certain character building of our own. As I struggled to produce this book, I discovered that *writing* about characterization (widely held to be among the most enigmatic and frustrating of all literary phenomena) can also be a character—and community—building exercise.

Without the encouragement, guidance, and support of many persons and institutions, this book would not have been completed. Financial backing came from the American Academy of Religion, which awarded me a Research Assistance Grant for 1989-90. The Theology Department of Boston College has proven to be a fertile environment for my research; students and colleagues alike have been a source of affirmation and insight. Pheme Perkins and Tony Saldarini deserve special thanks for their support and scholarly input. I am grateful also to the Literary Aspects of the Gospels and Acts Group of the Society of Biblical Literature for their constructive critique of some of what appears here. Conversations with Abraham Smith and Shawn Kelley have stimulated my thought as well. Graduate students James Ernest and Ron Marr helped with proof-reading and compiling indexes. Dianne Couts, Richard Darr, and Ann and Fred Pfisterer provided timely assistance also.

Readers familiar with biblical scholarship will recognize my enormous debt to Mary Ann Tolbert, who guided my initial steps into the complexity of literary theory. My editor, David Gunn, may well have spoiled me for working with any other editor; his patience, energy, and common sense know no bounds.

Finally, I dedicate this book to my wife, Kathe, whose skill as scholar, editor, and writer is evident on every page.

—JOHN A. DARR

INTRODUCTION

Some of the most vivid, enduring, and effectual characters in all of Western literature appear in Luke-Acts. Who can forget Mary entrusting her newborn son to a manger, the shepherds of Bethlehem "keeping watch over their flocks by night," young Jesus teaching the teachers in the temple, the risen Lord walking to Emmaus with followers who fail to recognize him, or Saul, bound for Damascus, and "breathing threats and murder against the Lord's disciples?" Etched indelibly on our collective unconscious, these and other evocative characters have inspired numerous artists—playwrights, painters, and sculptors—over the centuries.

Our knowledge of how these familiar characters are generated and how they function in their larger narrative world is severely limited, however, because—with the exception of a few recent and preliminary studies—biblical critics have largely neglected the subject of Lukan characterization.[1] How is distance (the level of identification between reader and character) controlled? What devices give a personage depth and individuality? Are figures illustrative (typed/symbolic) or more realistic? What roles do characters play and how are such roles recognized by the reader? What contemporary literary stereotypes and social conventions are evoked? How do characters contribute to the discourse or rhetoric of the work? These and other such *literary* questions have seldom been formulated or posed, much less answered, by interpreters of Luke-Acts.

Reasons for this odd lacuna are, of course, rooted in the peculiar evolution of biblical studies over the last two hundred years. The historical critical methods which completely dominated the field until recently were simply not designed for interpreting the gospels and Acts as integrated narratives. Rather, they were developed in order to reconstruct the *prehistory* of these stories (Tolbert 1989:21-27) and thereby to shed light on the development of early Christianity. In all its basic forms (source, form, and redaction criticism), the process is essentially one of detection through dissection: one disassembles the text into the blocks of material (sources, forms, redactional glosses) from which it was ostensibly cobbled, and then analyzes these discrete pieces for clues about origins, environments, and stages of development.

The historical critical methods were well-designed for their specific tasks, and they have greatly increased our understanding of earliest Christianity. However, our fixation with them has, to a great extent, blinded us to the insight that each New Testament narrative evokes for its audience a unique narrative world—an ordered whole in which elements mutually condition and illuminate one another—to be studied on its own terms. Fragmenting the text has meant fracturing the narrative's larger patterns of character, plot, rhetoric, irony and suspense. Such literary phenomena "get divorced from the very terms of reference that assign to them their role and meaning: parts from wholes, means from ends, forms from functions" (Sternberg 1985:2). In short, historical methods were not designed to analyze characterization, and, in fact, have tended to obstruct our perception of this and other literary features of New Testament narrative.[2]

Characters and characterization are clearly literary topics. To address them properly, therefore, one must utilize a literary critical methodology. But what sort of literary approach should one employ? The vast labyrinth of modern literary theory should give pause to even the most adventurous and knowledgeable critic. Theoretical and methodological questions have slowed the fledgling literary critical movement in gospel studies. As Stephen Moore's recent review of that movement fully and convincingly documents, many of the studies that have appeared thus far exhibit little theoretical depth or sophistication. Indeed, the order of the day has been a kind of shallow eclecticism, borrowing bits and pieces from various hermeneutical models with little regard for their systemic integrity or philosophical underpinnings.[3]

Another obstacle confronting the would-be literary critic of Luke's writings is the "environmental displacement" of the text (Jackson 1989:37-62). That is, interpreters must find appropriate ways of dealing with the chronological and cultural *distance* that separates us from the origins of this Greco-Roman narrative. What literary conventions constrained and enabled its first reading or hearing? What social norms and values does it presuppose, and how might a knowledge of these illuminate its rhetoric? Most literary critics of the New Testament have been very hesitant to ask these kinds of historical (or "extratextual") questions, preferring instead to adopt the ahistorical, "text-in-a-vacuum" approaches encouraged by formalist methods such as structuralism and the New Criticism. This position is well-summarized in the popular maxim, "Every poem should be treated as though it were contemporary and anonymous." The situation is little better among the postmodern critics, for they tend to view a text as submerged in a morass of "pure textuality" that largely obliterates its distinctiveness, effaces its boundaries, and negates its otherness. In both cases, the critic feels free (even *obliged*) to ignore or downplay the significance of the cultural framework within which the story was shaped and first read. But the loss of historical perspective means the loss of vital interpretive clues to New Testament narrative.[4]

The flight of gospel literary critics from history is hardly surprising given (1) the longstanding and suppressive hegemony of historical criticism within the field, and (2) strong ahistorical currents within secular literary theory. As often happens in such cases, however, the movement away from a previous methodology has been exaggerated, and thus is subject to modulation. The familiar argument that literary critics of New Testament narratives should abandon the historical task in general (and not just the peculiar kind of historical criticism associated with traditional biblical scholarship) is unwarranted and ultimately untenable. Evidence of the latter is unwittingly provided by the very scholars who argue against the relevance of the text's original cultural environment, for, almost without exception, they continue to appeal to what is surely that ancient culture's most unique aspect, its language.[5] Few, if any, scholars would be willing to abandon the Koine texts for *Today's English Version*. This strong reticence to take leave of the Koine, however, constitutes a tacit acknowledgement of the principle that a text's original cultural setting or "context of conventions" (linguistic, social, literary) remains pertinent to critical interpretation of that text.[6]

In summary, a methodology for interpreting Lukan characters must be both *theoretically sound* (consistent, coherent, grounded in the best of literary theory) and *text-specific* (geared to the narrative's cultural idiosyncracies).[7] In the present study, I propose an approach that meets these criteria. More specifically, I develop and demonstrate a reader-response (or pragmatic) model attuned to the Greco-Roman literary culture of the first century. Furthermore, my goal has been to make this approach accessible to a broad range of persons who study the gospels and Acts (seminary students, clergy, biblical scholars), not just literary theorists. My argument builds from the general to the specific, from theory to praxis. Chapter 1 lays out critical premises, addresses some basic issues, defines the salient terms and concepts of audience-oriented theory, and locates this approach in relation to others. In Chapter 2 the focus narrows to characterization in Luke-Acts, and specific guidelines and procedures for interpreting *dramatis personae* in this ancient narrative are established. Chapters 3-6 demonstrate and extrapolate the method by applying it to several Lukan characters.

Treatments of John the Baptist, the Pharisees, and Herod the Tetrarch illustrate this new approach. This sampling is broadly indicative of characterization in Luke-Acts in that these figures (1) represent the three basic categories of characters in the narrative (based on plot function and degree of description), and (2) are continuing characters (they appear or are referred to in numerous episodes over a wide swath of narrative in both Luke and Acts). Aside from Jesus, Paul, and perhaps Peter, John is the most fully developed *protagonist*; we encounter him, or references to him, in every major section of the story, even in the ministry of Paul late in Acts (19:1-7). The Pharisees are secondary though important figures who provide an excellent example of the ways in which group characters develop and function. Herod is essentially a tertiary character, neither a simple background figure (such as the crowds), nor as frequently and fully dramatized as either the Pharisees or the disciples.

John, the Pharisees, and Herod represent the broad strata of characters in Luke-Acts, but they certainly do not demonstrate all aspects of Lukan characterization. And, since theory and practice are (or should be) mutually informing, the model fashioned herein will undoubtedly evolve as further literary studies of characters in Luke-Acts are undertaken. And yet, the theoretical framework I have constructed is designed to accommodate certain additions with minimal readjustment. There will surely be advances, for example, in our understanding of the social and psychological factors that bear on reading. Although my interpretations focus largely on the reader's "cognitive" moves, the audience-oriented theory that I have developed here could easily be adjusted to account for these other factors as well. In short, the present work is not the full and final word on Lukan characterization. Rather, it is designed to serve as a methodological entree to this exciting new field of research.

1

READING READERS READING LUKE-ACTS: A PRAGMATIC APPROACH

INTRODUCTION

What distinguishes literary theories from one another is how they define and address fundamental issues like the status of the text, the roles of author, audience, and critic in the production of meaning, the nature of reading and interpretation, and whether (or to what extent) cultural context controls the way we process a piece of literature. My approach to characterization is notable because I focus not only on the role of the author and features of the text, but also and especially on how audience and critic participate in the generation of literary characters. More specifically, I have designed my interpretive model with two very important, but almost universally disregarded, realities in mind: *readers "build" characters, and critics "build" readers*. Much of the following methodological discussion, therefore, is devoted to exploring and explaining the nature, relationship, and broader implications of these dual constructive processes.

CRITICAL PREMISES

Four premises undergird this theoretical model. First, texts are stable, but schematic, linguistic entities. Second, all texts function rhetorically; they are what some scholars call motivated discourses, webs of literary structures designed to evoke certain responses (cognitive, ideological, emotional) in a reader. Third, meaning inheres in neither text nor reader alone, but is produced in and through their interaction. And last, the writing, reading, and interpretation of texts do not occur in a vacuum, but rather are conditioned and enabled by cultural context(s). In this light, "the meaning" of Luke-Acts is the result of both intention (the rhetorical patterning of the text) and convention (the repertoire of cultural knowledge a reader brings to the text); and the means by which it is produced is the dialogical process called reading.

BASIC ISSUES AND DEFINITIONS

Because approaches such as this one are designed to elucidate how a narrative works when an audience engages it, they are labeled *pragmatic*, or *functionalist*.[1] They are also (somewhat broadly) grouped under the rubric of reader-response criticism. But there is actually a wide range of reader-oriented theories distinguished by their definitions of reader, text, and context, and by various understandings of how these factors interrelate (Tompkins 1980). Further clarification is therefore necessary.

Text and Reader

The reader-oriented critic's central problem is to define the relationship of reader to text. Does authority for the production of meaning lie with the text, with the audience, or with both?[2] Answers to this pivotal question have spanned the hermeneutical spectrum from a modified formalism that acknowledges, but largely neutralizes, the audience (by holding that "the reader is in the text") to a sort of constructivism that effectively muffles the voice of the text (the text is "in the reader" or interpretive community). Both extremes defuse the issue by dissolving one of the poles (reader or text) into the other. According to one, the text generates not only the story, but also its ideal reader; so actual readers play no substantive role. According to the other, reading groups such as the biblical studies guild predetermine all that is perceived and valued by individual readers, regardless of the text in question. In either case, dialogue between reader and text is effectively halted since one or another of the "dialogue partners" has been silenced.

Near the center of this theoretical spectrum, but falling on the formalist (or text-grounded) side, is the theory of Wolfgang Iser (1972, 1974, 1978). Our model owes much to Iser's definition of the text and the reading process. Building on Roman Ingarden's massive study of the phenomenology of literature (1973), Iser asserts that the critic must consider not only the text "but also and in equal measure, the actions involved in responding to that text" (1972:279). Thus Iser moves significantly beyond most formalists in his understanding of the text: it is not a "solid object" whose meaning is self-evidencing, but rather, is more like a skeletal framework or gestaltic pattern, a schema riddled with "gaps and indeterminacies." The text does speak, but it simply does not—and cannot—tell all. The audience is therefore obliged to fill in the gaps and connect the discrete data provided by the text.

An example of this sort of textual gapping is evident in the episode of the ministering (or sinful) woman (Luke 7:36-50).

> Now one of the Pharisees asked him [Jesus] to dine with him. And he entered the Pharisee's house and took his place at table. And behold, a woman of the city, who was a sinner, when she learned that he was at table in the Pharisee's house, brought an alabaster flask of perfume, and standing behind him at his feet, weeping, she began to wet his feet with her tears, and kept wiping them with the hair of her head, and kissing his feet, and anointing them with the perfume.
>
> Now when the Pharisee who had invited him saw it, he said to himself, "If this man were a prophet, he would know who and what sort of woman is touching him, that she is a sinner." And Jesus responded by saying to him, "Simon, I have something to say to you." And he replied, "Say it, teacher."
>
> "A certain moneylender had two debtors: one owed five

hundred denarii, and the other fifty. When they were unable to repay, he graciously forgave them both. Which of them therefore will love him more?"

Simon answered, "The one, I suppose, to whom he forgave more." And he said to him, "You have judged correctly." And turning toward the woman, he said to Simon, "Do you see this woman? I entered your house; you gave me no water for my feet, but she has wet my feet with her tears, and wiped them with her hair. You gave me no kiss, but from the time I came in, she has not ceased to kiss my feet. You did not anoint my head with oil, but she anointed my feet with perfume. Therefore I say to you that her sins, which are many, are forgiven, seeing that she loved much; but the one who is forgiven little, loves little."

And he said to her, "Your sins are forgiven."

And those who were at table with him began to say among themselves, "Who is this, who even forgives sins?"

And he said to the woman, "Your faith has saved you; go in peace."

Commentators have long recognized that this passage does not provide essential information about the sinful woman's motivation; more precisely, the circumstances, chronology, and agency of her forgiveness are not related by the text. Jesus' parable (vss. 41-42), his remarks to the Pharisee, and the syntax of his references to the woman's forgiveness, all imply that she was forgiven *prior* to her appearance in Simon's house; her ministrations to Jesus would thus seem to be a consequence rather than a cause of her pardon (Fitzmyer 1981:686-87; Kilgallen 1985: 675-79). But the woman's experience of forgiveness itself lies entirely outside of the dramatized action, and is never described or explained by the narrator. The reader is thus given no concrete evidence about her absolution or what it had to do with Jesus, despite the fact that we need some such knowledge in order to make sense of her conduct in the present episode (Marshall 1978:306-307).

This lacuna is neither an example of poor storytelling (the author forgot to include salient information), nor, as some redaction-critics would have it, an instance of inept editing (the redactor or one of his predecessors mangled an oral tradition or written source and so left out vital material).[3] Rather, it is a textual gap which the reader must fill. Although such gaps are endemic to narrative, we rarely notice them because we are so accustomed to encountering and processing them. A literary *work* (which Iser distinguishes from a mere *text*) is generated only when a text is read, that is, when these gaps are filled by the reader. And, because the literary *work* is the proper object of interpretation, the critic is obliged to account not only for the text, but also for the reader and what happens when the reader engages the text. The reader-response critic "reads" the reader reading the text; in other words, the interpreter is responsible for the entirety of the reading process, not just for the formal features of the text or for the cultural repertoire of the reader. When we discuss the reading process below, we shall return to the story of the sinful woman and explain how the audience fills the gap we identified.

In theory, Iser grants equal authority to reader and text in the production of a literary work. In practice, however, he looks to the text as the final arbiter of meaning.[4] Unlike Fish (1980) and other more radical reader-critics, Iser argues that the text itself is a stable entity. The works produced by readers reading a text will inevitably vary somewhat, but the text is a constant, an invariable factor in the interpretive equation. In other words, a reader does not construct the text, only the work. Theoretically, readers of a text may produce an inexhaustible variety of meaning, but the text provides a reliable criterion for adjudicating among readings and so for establishing a range of critically acceptable interpretations.[5]

Critic, Reader and Context(s)

Iser's definition of the text as stable but schematic is one of the more innovative and attractive aspects of his theory. His treatment of the reader and the reader's role, however, is not so satisfying. On this vital issue, Iser is ambiguous at best, and reductionistic at worst. In theory he accords readers a creative role in the production of meaning, but in practice he reverts to the common notion of "inscribed readers," that is, an audience created by and in the text and thoroughly controlled by it. This concept is widely accepted but severely flawed. Readers cannot be both object and subject; that is, they cannot simultaneously be a part of the text's rhetorical structure *and* respondents to it. A text does proffer reading *roles* to its readers, but these roles are rhetorical strategies of the text, and thus, by definition, are not readers.[6]

Critics on the formalist side of the reader-response spectrum have often failed (or refused) to recognize that the audiences to whom they appeal are not immutable, innate properties of the text, but rather, are *heuristic constructs* imaged by the interpreters themselves.[7] Moreover, the image of "the" reader is inevitably projected through a prism consisting of the critic's assumptions about the cultural profile (social status, value system, reading competence, general background knowledge, and so forth) of a *real* audience, even if that audience is nothing other than the critic's own academic community. The neat and convenient division so often made between an inscribed reader (pure, constant, text-bound) and real (culturally-conditioned) audiences is thus misleading.[8] To appeal to a reader is concomitantly to bring into the interpretive equation the many "messy" cultural factors that both constrain and enable reading. In other words, the cultural context matters; it must not be ignored by the critic interested in understanding how a text is read.

In recent years no one has done more than E. D. Hirsch, Jr. to focus both scholarly and public attention on the significance of cultural knowledge for reading comprehension. As Hirsch points out, educators have too often confused the mastery of techniques (e.g., recognizing letters and words, and parroting their sounds) with the ability to grasp the significance of what is being read. To read is one thing, to read *with understanding* is another. The reader must possess a certain level of "cultural literacy," if he or she is ever to read with comprehension. And, the culturally literate person will be familiar with

> . . . the network of information that all competent readers possess. It is the background information, stored in their minds, that enables them to take up a newspaper and read it with an adequate level of comprehension, getting the point, grasping the implications, relating what they read to the unstated context which alone gives meaning to what they read. (Hirsch 1987:2)

What Hirsch refers to as the "unstated context" or store of background information, we shall call the *extratextual repertoire*, or, more simply, the extratext.[9] The extratext is made up of all the skills and knowledge that readers of a particular culture are expected to possess in order to read competently: (1) language; (2) social norms and cultural scripts; (3) classical or canonical literature; (4) literary conventions (e.g., genres, type scenes, standard plots, stock characters) and reading rules (e.g., how to categorize, rank, and process various kinds of textual data); and (5) commonly-known historical and geographical facts.[10]

The extratextual repertoire is one source of information the reader can access when he or she encounters a textual gap. Though readers are inclined to look to the work itself for cues and data needed to process upcoming passages (we naturally expect the work as actualized to the point of reading to provide guidance in what follows), the work does not in fact always cooperate. In such cases, the audience must turn to the extratext to help fill the gap and make sense of the story.

The extratext is more than just a supplementary reservoir of information for filling textual gaps, however. It also provides a reader with codes and criteria for evaluating and processing the text itself. Depending on the culture and period within which it is perused, therefore, a single text can result in many different readings. A missionary in Irian Jaya (formerly New Guinea) during the mid-1960's, for example, was shocked at the response of Sawi headhunters listening to the gospel story for the first time. The translator's narration had failed to elicit much response from his hearers until he got to the account of the betrayal of Jesus. At that point, however, there were chuckles of delight and whistles of admiration, for the listeners recognized in Judas a master of cold-blooded treachery, a characteristic lauded in their folklore and cherished in their everyday dealings with other clans. To the Sawi headhunters, Judas was the hero, and Jesus the dupe of the story (Richardson 1974:177-84)! We may dismiss this quite easily as an extreme misreading, but it effectively illustrates the idea that extratextual repertoires exert a strong influence on reading or hearing texts, and especially on the way character, motivation, and behavior are perceived and evaluated.

The extratextual repertoire presupposed by Luke is no longer familiar to us, for it now lies across a vast gulf of culture and time. Very few moderns, for example, would categorize the account of the ministering (or sinful) woman as a symposium, a ubiquitous type scene in Hellenistic literature.[11] The first-century Greco-Roman audience would certainly have recognized it as a symposium, however, and would have evaluated its elements (settings, actions, dialogue, characters) in terms of that generic framework. This is no ordinary supper, and those who regard it as such fail to grasp some of its implications. Later in our discussion we shall return to this story and identify some of those implications.

To summarize, the reader is an indispensable though variable factor in the interpretive equation. An audience "actualizes" or "concretizes" (to use Ingarden's terminology) the literary work, the true object of inquiry, on the basis of a text. Unlike a text, however, readers are not constant and immutable. Rather, they are contingent on many extrinsic variables, including the experiences and ideologies of the critics who construe them, and the cultural milieux within which they are understood to exist. Luke-Acts, for example, has been actualized in many different ways, depending on the varying values and data that readers from diverse periods and cultures have brought to it. But if readers do indeed play a role in determining and defining the literary work under consideration, and if our interpretive analyses are to be responsible, rigorous, and open to argument, then *we must identify the reader to whom we refer*.

WHO IS "THE READER" OF LUKE-ACTS?

In Quest of the Historical Theophilus

The quest for the audience of Luke-Acts is far more daunting than critics heretofore have imagined. Historical critics' rather naive and ultimately inconclusive attempts to identify Theophilus (Luke 1:3; Acts 1:1), the addressee, are predicated on two highly questionable premises: (1) we can identify *the* overriding purpose of the story, and (2) from that can quite safely infer a specific intended audience. The futility of this approach is shown clearly by the welter of conflicting results it yields. Luke-Acts resists attempts by interpreters to limit its intention to one or several principal agendas (Gasque 1975:302-308). Furthermore, the logical connection between purpose and audience is tenuous at best; even if one could identify *the* purpose of Luke-Acts, it might well be applicable to a number of real audiences in the Greco-Roman world of the late first century (Darr 1987: 74). If one determines, for example, that Luke's principal purpose was to present a positive picture of the interaction between Roman officials and believers, the question remains whether this positive characterization was intended to convince the Empire that Christianity deserved favorable treatment (Easton 1955:33), or to persuade the church that the Empire was ordained by God (Walaskay 1983). And what are we to make of Luke's oft-noted emphasis on Jewish matters? Was it designed to defend or commend the new faith to non-believing Jews, or to reassure Gentile or Jewish Christians about their roots, or again, to convince the Romans that Christianity was a Jewish sect and so deserved the protection and privileges afforded Judaism as a *religio licita*?

Even less credible are the ubiquitous attempts by historical critics to locate and reconstruct Luke's "community" or *Sitz im Leben* through simplistic allegorization (sometimes given a mantle of respectability by being called sociology). Does Luke include a large number of references to widows? His audience/community must include many older women without husbands. Do Pharisees take on a special role in this story as compared to the other gospels? Luke must be concerned about hard-line Jews in his community, or about his community's Jewish members being persecuted by Pharisees from outside, or about relations between a largely Gentile group and rabbinic Judaism. Is there a strong focus on Saul/Paul and Antioch in Acts? The readers surely are Syrian Christians of Pauline persuasion.[12] Jesus speaks of a "little flock" in Luke 12:32 and Paul uses flock imagery in his farewell address at Ephesus. Does this not mean that the story is meant for a small congregation of vulnerable Christians, beset by difficulties from within and without (so Esler 1987:25-26)? It is hardly surprising that such specific reconstructions of the Lukan audience have repeatedly failed to hold up under rigid scrutiny, for the data we possess (basically the text itself) simply cannot bear the weight of such narrow and intricate hypotheses (Cadbury 1927:302; Gasque 1975:302-308; Richard 1983:10; O'Toole 1984:13).

The Reader as Heuristic Construct

Literary critics, on the other hand, have largely ignored or oversimplified the task of identifying readers. Even interpreters who claim to be audience-oriented tend to (1) overlook or dismiss the significance of the text's original cultural environment (see McKnight 1988:150), (2) identify implicitly or explicitly critics with readers, and/or (3) locate the reader within the story (that is, as a permanently inscribed, perpetually implied aspect of the text). Although the latter two are not without insight, all these options are deficient. *The reader cannot be found by looking only to the critic, the text or the extratext, for readers are in fact the products of a complex interaction among all three factors.*

Our search for "the reader" of Luke-Acts must begin with a good long look in the mirror, for, to a greater or lesser extent, we tend to create readers in our own image. Critics cannot escape the circularities of interpretation by positing a neutral, "zero degree," objective, transcendent reader, or by appealing to some pristine original audience. To some degree, *the* reader is always *my* reader, a projection of my own experience of reading the text. And, of course, my particular cultural horizon—shaped by factors like gender, class, social setting, education, age, vocation, and ideological orientation—colors that reading.[13]

The imaging of readers is always conditioned by the critic's individual experience and cultural environment. It would be wrong to conclude from this fact, however, that we must simply identify the modern interpreter as *the* reader of Luke-Acts. Indeed, if our treatment of Lukan characters and characterization is to be truly *text-specific*, then the audience to which we refer should fit the cultural profile of the readers for whom the account was written. That is, we must reconstruct—to the fullest extent possible—the extratextual repertoire, literary skills and basic orientation of the original audience. In doing so, our ultimate purpose is hermeneutical, not historical: we are less concerned with discovering the identities of intended addressees than with ascertaining the type and degree of "cultural literacy" the author seems to have assumed for his audience. In other words, the question is not "Who is the reader *per se*?" but rather, "What did a reader have to bring to a text in order to actualize it competently?" Though the questions are clearly related (for example, how we construe the extratext might well have implications for identifying specific addressees), the differences in emphasis are significant, and so how we coordinate them is important.[14]

The difficulties of the reconstructive task are manifold and intimidating. We have already noted that critics can never escape fully the conditioning of their own place and time, or indeed, of the exigencies of the interpretive task, which is hardly the same as reading. The most we can hope for, then, is to image a *hybrid* reader, part ancient, part modern, part reader, part critic. And, our discussion of attempts by biblical scholars to ascertain the precise addressees of Luke-Acts has shown that the text alone is not a reliable tool for pinpointing intended readers. Because it is not precise, however, does not mean it is entirely useless in the quest. Indeed, it implies much about the *general* cultural knowledge and literary skills requisite for its audience.

The final, and perhaps most intractable problem for those who try to reconstruct the reader of Luke-Acts is the paucity of literary records from the time of writing. There are very many gaps in our knowledge of Hellenistic culture(s). Nevertheless, important data from this ancient time are available and should be tapped.

Profiling the Reader of Luke-Acts

Before we sketch out our image of the reader, we shall review pertinent portions of the argument thus far. Readers are heuristic constructs, imaged by critics to re-enact how texts are or were concretized into literary works. In building a mental image of the reader, critics invariably imbue it with certain of their personal and cultural characteristics. Nevertheless, a critic *can* construe (albeit somewhat imperfectly) a reader from a different place and time by drawing inferences from the text itself and by listening carefully to what remains of the literary culture of that period. Gaps in the image of the audience are filled (consciously or not) with information from the critic's own environment.[15] Here, we choose to reconstruct a text-specific reader, that is, one possessing the cultural and literary competencies that the author could assume on the part of his audience.

Who then is the (my) reader? As a culturally literate member of the late first-century Mediterranean world, the reader is well aware of, indeed lives by, the cultural scripts and norms of that world (see e.g., Malina 1989; Gowler 1989b; and Moxnes 1988). She or he knows basic historical, political, geographical, and ethnic facts about the Roman Empire, and about how that empire functions both militarily and politically. The reader also possesses a kind of stereotyped knowledge of major cities and peoples of the time. Athens is the city of philosophers, Jerusalem is (or was) capital of the Jews until its recent rebellion and downfall. This type of general, public, conventional knowledge is assumed.

Perhaps more interesting and to the point for our purposes, the reader is at home in popular Greco-Roman literature. When we place Luke-Acts against the background of current writing, it is immediately obvious that it was not written for the *literati* but for the lower to middle classes who were accustomed to such fare as romances (also called novels, and sometimes likened to modern soap operas because of their melodramatic tone), *exempla* (guides to morality based on the exemplary lives of sages), aretalogies (tales of the heroic deeds and miracles of so-called divine men), memoirs of revered philosophers, and biographies of military and political leaders.[16] Luke-Acts was popular literature, designed for those who were used to provocative—but hardly sophisticated or polished—narratives like Chariton's *Chaereas and Callirhoe*, a lengthy tale of separated lovers whose adventure-filled quest to reunite takes them around the Mediterranean.[17] Luke has written the most literate of New Testament narratives, but it must still be classified as *popular* literature (so Aune 1987:77; Pervo 1987:1-11; and Tolbert 1989:59-79).

What most clearly distinguishes Luke's reader from the vast majority of Greco-Roman readers in the late first century, is an intimate knowledge of the Jewish scriptures in Greek (Esler 1987:25). Luke-Acts is saturated with the language, imagery, settings, and flavor of the Septuagint (LXX). It is hard to find a part of Luke's narrative that has not been affected by this intertextual linkage. Direct quotation, imitation of writing style, borrowing of character types (the "barren woman" of the LXX is a paradigm for Elizabeth, for example) and settings, and numerous allusions (from the obvious and direct to the highly nuanced) are used to establish an unmistakable relationship between the two writings. In order to read Luke-Acts with any depth whatsoever, therefore, the reader must be steeped in the LXX. And, because non-Jews were not familiar with the Jewish scriptures, we can safely infer that Luke-Acts is intended for a highly hellenized audience within the broad stream of Jewish tradition (Jews, whether Christian or non-Christian, "god-fearers," and Gentile Christians).[18]

Many other attributes of the reader cannot be reconstructed by comparing the text with the extratext, and so are more highly speculative. We may assume that the reader is an adult who is able to read, not just to listen as someone else reads aloud.[19] For the sake of clarity, we work with a first-time reader, that is, one who has not read Luke-Acts and formulated opinions about it previously. Furthermore, our reader does not know Mark, Paul's letters or so-called Q. Although Mark may very well have come before Luke, we cannot be certain of that fact; and even if it did, we cannot assume knowledge of Mark on the part of the reader. It is simply inappropriate to image the reader as redaction-critic—lexicons, concordances, and gospel parallels at hand—constantly trying to discern whether what he or she reads is editorial gloss, or from one or another source. That is not reading. While the reader may know some basic facts about Jesus and his movement ("the things of which you have been informed'' [Luke 1:4 RSV]) we cannot with certainty specify an exclusively Christian audience (contra Esler 1987:24-26).[20] While we may well find it advantageous to consider the audience open-minded and receptive rather than suspicious and antagonistic, it will hardly be helpful to construe it as already fully cognizant about and convinced by the "truth" (*asphaleia*, Luke 1:4) of Luke's narrative. If the audience were but a mirror image of the author's experience, knowledge, and values, then he would have had little reason to write the highly rhetorical text we have before us.

WHAT DOES THE READER DO?

As we have already intimated, reading is a complex activity entailing the dynamic interaction of reader, text, and extratext. While reading, one performs a variety of cognitive acts within a temporal (sequential) framework. This mental process is neither self-generated nor unfettered; it is actuated and constrained by textual patterns (i.e., the rhetorical patterns of the text) and by literary and social conventions (i.e., the extratext).[21]

The cognitive "moves" the reader makes are many and varied. Iser catalogs some of these as follows:

> We look forward, we look back, we decide, we change our decisions, we form expectations, we are shocked by their non-fulfilment, we question, we muse, we accept, we reject; this is the dynamic process of recreation. (1972:293)

Stanley Fish describes reading as:

> . . . the making and revising of assumptions, the rendering and regretting of judgments, the coming to and abandoning of conclusions, the giving and withdrawing of approval, the specifying of causes, the asking of questions, the supplying of answers, the solving of puzzles. (1972:126-7)

For our purposes, the cognitive activities of reading may be broadly grouped under the following headings: (1) anticipation and retrospection; (2) consistency-building; (3) identification; and (4) defamiliarization.

Looking Ahead, Looking Back

Anticipation and retrospection are continuous, complementary activities. Moving through the text, a reader begins to formulate expectations and opinions which then become the basis upon which subsequent data is processed. In turn, one reassesses previously-formed expectations and opinions in the light of new information and insights.

> Every sentence contains a preview of the next and forms a kind of viewfinder for what is to come; and this in turn changes the 'preview' and so becomes a 'viewfinder' for what has been read. (Iser 1972:284)

Ideas about characters, events, settings, ideology, etc. are continually being reaffirmed, negated, revised, and supplemented. And, precisely because these mental constructions are sequential, cumulative, and subject to change, it is essential that the critic be cognizant of the degree to which they have been formulated at any particular point in the reading process. How readers evaluate a character at one juncture, for example, may very well not be how they feel about that character at some other point.

In the dialectic of reading, each word, sentence, or other textual unit both illuminates and is illumined by what precedes it.[22] And, of course, as the reading progresses, the activities of anticipation and retrospection become increasingly complex as information accumulates.

Making It Whole

Anticipation and retrospection cover only a part of reading, however. Oscillating between forward and backward views, readers are also attempting "to fit everything together in a consistent pattern" (Iser 1972:288; 1978:118-29). As opinions develop and expectations shift with the progression of reading, the audience continually tries to build a consistent and coherent "narrative world." By correlating discrete elements of the text (incidents, perspectives, actions, narration, character traits and settings), and adding extratextual information when necessary, the audience is able to image patterns (what Iser calls *Gestalten*) which cover textual gaps, help to resolve tensions, and clarify ambiguities.

The point is that readers fully *expect* texts to provide them with sufficient data and guidance (including cues to the intended extratextual codes and information) to construe a narrative world that hangs together and makes sense. Current debates between post-modernists and formalists on the issue of "holism" in narrative need to be informed by this insight from reader critics.[23] If we are to talk about holism, it must be a conditional holism, and we must refer to the literary work rather than to the text. That is, there is no such thing as a holistic text (holy maybe, and holey, definitely, but holistic, no), for all texts have gaps, tensions, inconsistencies, and ambiguities. And, although some of these will never be completely resolved, the reader can and does process the majority of them. At least in the case of Luke-Acts, the audience is able to actualize a coherent and highly consistent work on the basis of the textual and extratextual information available. And, once again, *we are concerned primarily with the work and the ways in which it is generated*, not simply with the text.

Investment and Identification

As readers construe a narrative world, they unconsciously or consciously oscillate between thorough involvement in it and more detached observation of it (Iser 1972:288; 1978:118-29). For our purposes, the most interesting feature of this oscillation is the variability of "distance" between the reader, the narrator, and the characters.

> In any reading experience, there is an implied dialogue among author, narrator, and other characters and the reader. Each of the four can range, in relation to each of the others, from identification to complete opposition, on any axis of value, moral, intellectual, aesthetic, and even physical. (Booth 1983:155; see also Iser 1972:296-97)

As we shall see, it is important to determine the extent and causes of reader identification with, or repudiation of, both the narrator and characters in Luke-Acts.

Defamiliarization

Our discussion of the reading process has focused largely on the kinds of cognitive activities carried out by the reader. What of the other two factors in the equation—the text and extratext? These factors both enable and constrain the reader's mental moves. First, the *text* provides a series of stimuli which elicit and guide audience responses. In other words, it is a rhetorical framework, designed strategically to foster a sequence of mental images and cognitive acts by the reader. The text also controls point of view, a vital element in the shaping of values.

Much has already been said about the final factor, the *extratext*, and its place in the reading process. It bears repeating, however, that readers must bring to a text a shared set of conventions (a "language") that enables effective communication to occur. The reader

> comes to the text with a complex literary competence, what Culler describes as a set of shared reading conventions. The author employs these conventions, linguistic and literary, to 'control' the reader's response; the reader uses these conventions to make the sequential interpretations required by the discourse. (Mailloux 1982:91)

Readers are manipulated by the novel placement, modification, and negation of conventions. A text would communicate little (and be quite boring) if it were simply a reiteration of the familiar. In order to evoke reader response, the text must set the familiar in an unfamiliar context, a process Iser terms "defamiliarization" (1972:288). But, the original context of these conventions must "remain sufficiently implicit to act as a background to offset their new significance" (1978:69). Defamiliarization forces the reader to evaluate norms, values, and traditions in a new light.

READING THE STORY OF THE SINFUL WOMAN

In order to read the account of the ministering (or sinful) woman with any depth, a reader must perform many of the cognitive activities described above.[24] We have already noted that readers were expected to recognize this dramatic episode as a

Hellenistic symposium, a ubiquitous type scene within Greco-Roman literature. In this stereotypical narrative frame, a prominent person invites a renowned sage and various other philosophical types to dine. At the gathering, a conveniently loaded incident (sometimes called a *fait divers*) occurs, sparking a philosophical debate among those invited. The sage proves his superior wisdom by getting the better of the debate. In this case, Simon the Pharisee is host, Jesus is the sage, other Pharisees serve as guests and potential debaters, and the anointing of Jesus' feet by the sinful woman is the *fait divers*.

This conventional structure helps to focus the reader on the sinful woman's actions and Jesus' explanation of them, for surely they will be the topic of the expected debate. At this very point, however, there occurs a gap in narrative logic that has befuddled historical-critical commentators. As we noted above, the point of Jesus' parable (the one who is forgiven much, loves much), and the logic of his dialogue with both Simon and the woman presuppose that she received forgiveness *prior* to entering the house. In other words, she expresses herself in these dramatic ways because she has been forgiven, not in order to be forgiven. The reader, however, knows nothing about the woman prior to this episode, except what Jesus and others say about her, that she was a sinner and was forgiven. But the reader needs more than this in order to make sense of her behavior toward Jesus in this scene. Why does she feel compelled to come *to him*, and what do her actions really mean? Somehow she has connected Jesus with her experience of forgiveness, but how?

Cues for filling this gap in character motivation lie in the preceding episode, the account of messengers coming to Jesus from the imprisoned John the Baptist. There, in Jesus' discourse about John's status and role (Luke 7:24-35), a sharp dichotomy is drawn between Pharisees and lawyers on the one hand, and tax collectors and sinners (*hamartoloi*) on the other. What distinguishes the two groups, according to the omniscient narrator, is that the sinners had been "baptized with the baptism of John," but the Pharisees had "rejected the purpose [*boulen*] of God for themselves, by not having been baptized by him [John]" (Luke 7:29-30). What then is this "baptism of John?" Once again, the reader understands only through retrospection. The Baptist had preached a "baptism of repentance for the forgiveness of sins" (Luke 3:3). His goal was to prepare the "hearts" of the people to "*see* the salvation of God" when it arrived (3:4-6). Those who repent of sin (which the Lukan John defines largely in terms of social/economic injustice) are forgiven and thereby are granted the capability of perceiving the salvation of God as represented in Jesus. The ones who do not repent remain spiritually blind to the divine revelation in their midst. Thus the paradox—which Luke often uses to ironic effect—that those who should recognize Jesus as the Christ do not, while those who should not (the acknowledged sinners) do.

With this dichotomy in mind, the reader processes the story of the sinful woman along the following lines. Simon, a leader of the Pharisees, is representative of that group with its spiritual problems. The sinful woman stands for the sinners who experienced the baptism of repentance for the forgiveness of sins (Kilgallen 1985:675-79). In other words, these two characters help readers to concretize the contrast between Pharisees and sinners that has been developing and will continue to evolve throughout the story. More immediately, however, the reader's retrospection allows him or her to understand the woman's actions toward Jesus. Since she has already been forgiven, she is able to recognize Jesus as the "one who comes." Her strange behavior is motivated not only by appreciation for absolution from sin, but also by a knowledge of who Jesus is, an insight the Pharisees lack. Why does she anoint Jesus (7:38b)? Because she recognizes that he is the Christ (the *anointed one*). The woman, then, is a paradigm of the sinners who have been forgiven and therefore are willing and able to respond to Jesus in an appropriate manner. By this point, the reader has been conditioned to identify with the ministering woman, and has been distanced from the Pharisees and their point of view.

The gap between reader and Pharisees is widened even further by Luke's manipulation of the extratext in this episode. Contrary to the opinion of many gospel scholars, the fact that

Jesus dines with Pharisees here and elsewhere in Luke (see 11:37-54 and 14:1-24) in no way elevates the Pharisees in the eyes of the audience. Quite the contrary is true, at least for readers who are familiar with the symposium type scene. Luke *modifies* (or defamiliarizes) this convention in such a way that the Pharisees are denied even the secondary status of the sage's "worthy opponents." Neither Simon nor the other Pharisees who dine with Jesus are allowed to dialogue with him or to rebut the serious charges that he brings against them. The obvious implication is that they are unable to do so. Thus, the reader has nothing to place on the positive side of the Pharisees' ledger. Here and elsewhere in Luke symposia are used only as stages for Jesus to criticize severely his Pharisaic hosts and fellow guests; in no way do they paint the Pharisees as either colleagues or benefactors of Jesus. Indeed, as utilized in this story, their effect is quite the opposite.

We have sketched but a few of the many cognitive processes a reader utilizes in order to make sense of the story of the sinful woman. Retrospection, gap-filling, identification, and an ability to access the proper extratextual data are all brought to bear in reading this dramatic episode.

CONCLUSION

We began this chapter by noting two significant, but usually overlooked, facts: that readers "build" literary characters, and that critics "build" readers. In fact, readers build the entire narrative on the basis of the text and the extratext; and critics construct more than just readers. Indeed, an interpreter selects, balances, orders, and construes many of the complex elements that shape interpretation. Little reflection is needed to realize that critics are not passive conduits for meaning. On the contrary, they strive to convince others of particular understandings of texts. Critics adopt the audacious role of pointing others toward an "optimal" reading. In reality, what the critic writes is no less rhetorical than the text itself. Critics are not simply well-informed general readers (though they like to cast themselves as such) but creative re-readers whose many selections specify and delimit what is to be perceived and how "best" it is to be understood by others. Wayne Booth likens this process of selection to choosing among a variety of optical lenses:

> . . . our choices of a given inquiry work like our choices of optical instruments, each camera or microscope or telescope uncovering what other instruments conceal and obscuring what other instruments bring into focus. (1983:405)

Expanding upon Booth's simile, we might say that the critic grinds and assembles a series of lenses through which others are to read; and then the critic directs the sequence in which these lenses are to be utilized. By reconstructing a particular socio-historical context, identifying specific literary influences, and emphasizing certain textual data (while ignoring others), critics attempt to persuade others to accept their readings.

Using imagery somewhat similar to Booth's, George Steiner compares critical choices to "prescriptive perspectives" and notes that these should be made explicit.

> The motion of criticism is one of 'stepping back from' in exactly the sense in which one steps back from a painting on a wall in order to perceive it better. But the good critic makes his motion conscious to himself and to his public. He details his recessional steps so as to make the resultant distance, the elucidative measure, the prescriptive perspective—distance entails 'angle' of vision—explicit, responsible, and, therefore open to argument. (1979:423)

The complex "optical instrument" that we have developed in this chapter is designed to re-enact how Luke-Acts was first read. Our interpretive field of view is thus limited to a specific time and place, and by the reality of the text. Furthermore, our model requires immersion in the work as it develops; that is, a reading lens is by definition one that is always moving, readjusting, and refocussing, since it "travels along *inside* that which it has to apprehend" (Iser 1978:109). Unlike a fixed, external perspective from which one attempts to scan the entirety of Luke-Acts as some kind of static, aesthetic object, our interpretive angle of vision is contingent on the dynamics of reading, the continuing dialogue between text and reader.[25]

2

BUILDING LUKAN CHARACTERS

A survey of literary theory once prompted critic Charles C. Walcutt (1966:5) to lament that characterization is treated much like the weather in Mark Twain's famous quip—everyone talks about it but *nobody does anything about it*. Most critics would agree that character is fundamental to narrative, and all interpreters are obliged to deal with it in one way or another; but theorists have tended to shy away from it. This reluctance to grapple with character and characterization as theoretical problems is hardly surprising, for "character is much more difficult to talk about than most other literary concepts" (Wilson 1978/79:730). Indeed, as Frank Kermode puts it, character is a "source of opacity, of complex, various and never definitive interpretation" (1979:75). Despite these difficulties (or perhaps *because* of them), however, it is important to "do something about" the theoretical issues involved in characterization, rather than just "talking about" characters.

The purpose of this chapter is to delineate our approach to characters and characterization in Luke-Acts. Based on the model developed in Chapter 1, which focuses on the dynamics of reading (the creative, progressive interaction among audience, text, and extratext), our approach to characterization is (1) holistic and contextual, (2) sequential and cumulative, (3) attentive to both the literary and social forces that conditioned reading in Greco-Roman times, and (4) observant of the text's rhetoric.

CHARACTERS IN THE NARRATIVE WORLD OF LUKE-ACTS: HOLISM AND CONTEXT

As we saw in the previous chapter, holism is a much maligned and much misunderstood concept in biblical studies. We should not claim that *the text itself* is analogous to a solid object—whole, seamless, integrated. Rather, holism should refer to the literary work that the reader construes on the basis of the schematic text. By accepting this important distinction, we need not retreat into redaction-criticism with its division of Luke-Acts into a host of separate stories, each to be analyzed in isolation from the rest. Neither must we succumb to the tendency, endemic in formalism, of ascribing to the text properties it does not possess. To speak of Luke-Acts as holistic is actually to speak of a reader's building of consistency among discrete textual data. And even the literary work that a reader produces on the basis of the text can never be whole, smooth, and completely integrated. It will always evidence some gaps, inconsistencies, indeterminacies, and ambiguities. The reader is able, nevertheless, to construe a coherent, adequately integrated world on the basis of Luke's text and the appropriate extratext.

The world that the reader of Luke-Acts images is, of course, the proper context within which to interpret its inhabitants, the characters. Too often, characters have been analyzed in isolation rather than within what Harvey (1965:31) calls the "complicated structure of artificially formed contexts" in the literary work. This "complicated structure" includes a framework of causally-linked incidents (the plot) as well as geographical and cultural settings. Most significant for understanding characters, however, is the intricate and extensive matrix of relationships among the *dramatis personae* themselves (Harvey 1965:52). Each one of these character-shaping contexts merits further discussion.

Character and Plot

Many theorists subordinate character to plot. This ranking of literary elements can be traced back to Aristotle's famous dictum that "the plot is the first principle and as it were the soul of tragedy: character comes second."[1] Henry James, perhaps the most outspoken critic of this dictum, sought to turn it around: in the creative process, character precedes plot.[2] There is a growing consensus, however, that this argument about priority is baseless and, in any case, hermeneutically insignificant (Kermode 1979: 77). Character and plot are interdependent, and both are essentials of narrative. Audiences "actualize" plot in terms of character and character in terms of plot. Where the interpretive emphasis falls depends largely on the varying interests of critics, readers, and authors (Chatman 1978:113; Johnson 1977:24).

We hardly need to argue that Luke-Acts is emplotted. It reports a series of causally-linked incidents that develop from beginning to middle to end. In other words, it has a particular "contour" tracing the development and resolution of a conflict or conflicts (Petersen 1978:86-91; Parsons 1987:71-77). By modern standards, of course, Luke's plot is not complicated. Relationships among characters in this ancient story seem much more significant than the relation of characters to plot.

> In Luke-Acts, there are really no sub-plots; the secondary characters do not lead lives of their own, or have their own stories, but are important solely as they are drawn into contact with the central characters. Whatever the small and enlivening touches of individuality given them by the author, it is in their response to the main characters, and as representatives of particular modes of response that their importance for the story is found. (Johnson 1977:24)

Still, awareness of plot structure is necessary if one is to grasp the nuanced development and modulation of Lukan characters, especially primary characters like Jesus, John, Paul, and certain disciples/apostles. Indeed, Lukan characters are sometimes so exclusively identified with a specific plot function that they may be said to embody or signify that function (in Luke's passion narrative, for example, Judas = Betrayal, Peter = Denial).[3]

Character and Setting

Character is always conditioned by the cultural and geographical environments in which it appears. Settings furnish valuable clues about how the reader should assess the significance of characters and evaluate their relationships one to another. Often, geography provides convenient markers for plot movement and thus can aid in understanding how a particular character relates to the plot. The dramatic action in the third gospel follows a geographical schema leading from Galilee through Judea, and finally to Jerusalem; in Acts it travels from Jerusalem to Rome in ever-widening circles. Locations like Bethlehem, Galilee, Jerusalem, the environs of the Jordan river, Samaria, Athens, and Rome, as well as topographical features like mountains, plains, deserts, and seas carried certain extratextual connotations and thus provided theologically charged settings within which to evaluate characters (Conzelmann 1960:18-94).

Perhaps the best-known example of how geographical settings condition and define characters in Luke-Acts is the strange case of John the Baptist and his area of ministry. As we shall see in more detail below, the reader of Luke's gospel is manipulated by rhetorical devices to subordinate John to Jesus in the hierarchy of God's messengers. One such rhetorical device is the *sygkrisis* (comparing and contrasting) of the infancy narrative. Another is the geographical (and temporal) isolation of John's ministry (in the area of the Jordan; Luke 3:1-20) from that of Jesus (Galilee, Judea and Jerusalem).[4] Although John is alive when Jesus begins his ministry, he does not, in Luke's Gospel, directly participate in that ministry or even have a part in its inauguration, for he is conveniently absent when Jesus is baptized (Luke 3:19-21).

Also of significance for characterization in Luke-Acts is an abundant assortment of cultural settings. The idealized and pious Jewish peasantry which forms the backdrop of the birth narratives (see, e.g., Luke 1:5-23) is a far cry from Athens' Areopagus, that sophisticated philosophy forum in which Paul addresses Epicureans and Stoics, among others (Acts 17:16-34). These cultural settings raise specific expectations concerning speech and behavior, and so provide reference points for the reader building a character. By proving adept in many different environments, for example, Paul becomes one of the most well-rounded characters (if not *the* most well-developed) in the entire narrative. Readers see him in so many cultural contexts that they are able to construe a rather complex image of him.

Character and Characters

The fundamental matrix within which we construct a character is the web of interrelationships that develops among all of the figures in the story world. In other words, characters are delineated largely in terms of each other, just as we are defined by our relationships in real life.

> By far the most important of contexts is the web of human relationships in which any single character must be enmeshed. So much of what we are can only be defined in terms of our relations with other people; indeed . . . we can say with the philosophers that other people must exist if only to show us what we ourselves are not . . . What we are offered is an exercise in contrast and comparison, a variation on the old theme of unity in variety, of similitude in dissimilitude, which is one of the major formal pleasures of art. But the pleasure is more than merely formal; we are also aware of a real analogy between our responses as readers of fiction and the process whereby in actual life we establish a person's reality by considering his many relationships, by viewing him through many perspectives. (Harvey 1965:52-53)

The apposition (including opposition) of characters is thus rhetorical: characters function "to reveal *other* characters—to make, by their own choices and acts, rhetorical judgments on the choices and acts of others" (Springer 1978:191; see 189-90; and Booth 1984:103). To an extraordinary degree, intermediate agents in Luke-Acts are assessed on the basis of their interaction with the protagonists, especially Jesus. And the effect is reciprocal: protagonists are delineated and evaluated largely by the variety of responses they elicit from secondary and tertiary characters. What Culpepper says concerning Jesus in John's gospel can, with minor modification, be applied to the protagonists of Luke-Acts:

> [The other characters] are in effect the prism which breaks up the pure light of Jesus' remote epiphany into colors the reader can see. In John's narrative world the individuality of all the

> characters except Jesus is determined by their encounter with Jesus. The characters represent a continuum of responses to Jesus which exemplify misunderstandings the reader may share and responses one might make to the depiction of Jesus in the gospel. The characters are, therefore, particular kinds of choosers. (1983:104)

Thus a dialectic is set up: intermediate characters help the reader to construct the many images projected upon Jesus (Davidic messiah, prophet, teacher, etc.). They, in turn, are evaluated in light of their responses to him and the other Lukan protagonists. This process will become clearer in our discussion of rhetorical patterns in Luke-Acts.

NARRATIVE SEQUENCE AND THE ACCUMULATION OF CHARACTER

A pragmatic approach to characterization requires that we be especially sensitive to the narrative's sequence. The goal is not to arrive at a static conception of a character (for example, the author's mental image of that persona), but rather, to follow the reader's *successive* construction and assessment of that character while reading the text.[5] Like all narrative elements, *character is cumulative*. Thus the means and timing of its accumulation must be taken into account by the interpreter. As Springer has rightly argued,

> character is not given to us like a gift in the hand, or like a picture on the wall, but . . . it does in fact accumulate. This must make perfect sense since the story, unlike the picture on the wall, moves across time—we must turn the page in order to find out what else there is to know about the character, what new actions and choices there may be to expand or modify our knowledge, what decisions we are to make about whether the character is fixed or in change, individual or antithetical to another character, minor or main. (1978:179)

Because character is cumulative, it is essential that we be cognizant at all times of the degree to which a character or a character group has been constructed at each point along the text continuum. Too often, interpreters of Lukan character have failed to take sequence and accumulation seriously. A common tendency is to pull together discrete data from all parts of Luke's narrative with little, if any, regard for its linear accretion. As a result of this oversight, Lukan characters have often been distorted. An example of such distortion is found in the way the Pharisees have been handled by recent interpreters of Luke-Acts. We shall return to this problem and treat it in much detail later (see Chapter 4). At this point it must suffice to observe that many studies of this sort have been based on a *reverse* reading, and thus have led to highly questionable conclusions about how this Jewish group is depicted in Luke's narrative. Beginning near the end (with Paul's defense speeches at his trials in Acts 22-26), moving back to the Jerusalem conference (Acts 15), to the Gamaliel episode (Acts 5), and finally to the gospel, these studies purportedly demonstrate that Luke paints an ambiguous—negative, but also somewhat irenic or sympathetic—portrait of the Pharisees. Readers processing the information *in its intended order*, however, will hardly develop a favorable (or even ambiguous) impression of this group because of the Acts accounts; much to the contrary, the strongly unfavorable impressions gained in the gospel cast a cynical and ironic shadow over the Gamaliel story and all other references to the Pharisees in Luke's second volume.

Character Indicators

Although some of the raw materials needed for the audience's "character-building exercises" (Kermode's term, 1979:77-78) are supplied by the extratext, most are available in the text itself. A plethora of intratextual indicators guide the reader's building of characters. Alter summarizes the many ways in which narratives like Luke-Acts indicate character.

> Now, in reliable third-person narrations . . . there is a scale of means, in ascending order of explicitness and certainty, for conveying information about the motives, the attitudes, the moral nature of characters. Character can be revealed through the report of actions; through appearance, gestures, posture, costume; through one character's comments on another; through direct speech by the character; through inward speech, either summarized or quoted as interior mono-

> logue; or through statements by the narrator about the attitudes and intentions of the personages, which may come either as flat assertions or motivated explanations.
>
> The lower end of this scale—character revealed through actions or appearance—leaves us substantially in the realm of inference. The middle categories, involving direct speech either by a character himself or by others about him, lead us from inference to the weighing of claims. Although a character's own statements might seem a straightforward enough revelation of who he is and what he makes of things, in fact the biblical writers are quite as aware as any James or Proust that speech may reflect the occasion more than the speaker, may be more a drawn shutter than an open window. With the report of inward speech, we enter the realm of relative certainty about character: there is certainty, in any case, about the character's conscious intentions, though we may still feel free to question the motive behind the intention. Finally at the top of the ascending scale, we have the reliable narrator's explicit statement of what the characters feel, intend, desire; here we are accorded certainty, though biblical narrative . . . may choose for its own good purposes either to explain the ascription of attitude or to state it baldly and thus leave its cause as an enigma for us to ponder. (1981:116-17)

The indicators of character can be placed in two categories: those that *show* and those that *tell* (about) character (see Abrams 1981:20). Characterization in Luke-Acts tends more toward showing than telling. The various narrative settings discussed above, for example, show characters by providing the backdrops against which figures take on an idiosyncratic shape. Other ways the text shows character are by revealing a figure's (1) choices, (2) behavior, and (3) thoughts (internal monologue or direct speech).[6]

Strictly speaking, all character indicators are *told* in that the entire story is narrated. However, under "telling" we place only direct narrative descriptions and evaluations of characters. Although seldom recognized as rhetorical, these descriptions play a crucial role in positioning readers vis-à-vis *dramatis personae*. Even seemingly innocuous references to a character raise specific expectations (and subdue others) concerning that figure (Docherty 1983:8-10). Names and personal information like emotional make-up, titles, family ties, and physical attributes are very significant in this regard. The appearance of a name in the text creates what Docherty (1983:47) calls a "*blanc sémantique*," a gap that "prompts us to read on and 'fill' with . . . significance the empty space in the name as it occurs in the fictional world."[7]

All of these character indicators—showing and telling—have an effect, moving the reader to develop certain expectations, and conditioning his or her responses to upcoming encounters with the character. Based on the magnitude and diversity of their roles and the degree to which they are delineated, characters fall along a continuum from simple to complex. The simplest—or "flattest"—figures have a single function (they embody a response to Jesus). The reader is given little or no personal information (like name, appearance, family, status, etc.) about them, and they appear but once and for a short period only. Characters are considered to be more complex—or "rounder"—as these factors increase.[8]

Roughly speaking, the characters of Luke-Acts may be divided into three groups: background or tertiary figures, like the crowds (*ochloi*) or the people (*laoi*); intermediate or secondary personae, such as the Pharisees and tax collectors; and protagonists, or primary characters. This taxonomy of characters basically follows that of Harvey (1965:56-58), and provides us with a convenient way of grouping the various actors in Luke's drama. It would be wise to keep in mind, however, that all such categories are fluid and so should not be rigidly applied. What we actually find in Luke-Acts is a rather broad continuum of characters. Although theorists are fascinated by taxonomy ("Is this figure an agent, a type, a full-blown character, or something else?"), such categorizations have often proven to be of minor interpretive value, particularly when the text in question exhibits an uncomplicated plot structure and a rather plainly-ordered set of characters.[9]

Persons or Words? The Ontology of Literary Character

Our insistence that characters be understood in terms of the complex of literary contexts in which they are found, and in terms of narrative sequence, determines our position on a major issue in modern characterization theory. Should characters be treated like autonomous individuals or as strictly literary phenomena? Are the figures we come to know in a narrative world persons or words? Do they transcend the text or are they entirely constrained by it?[10]

The confusion on this issue arises precisely because we come to "know" characters in literature in much the same way that we get to know others in real life. In both cases, we forge an image of the person based on the unique, more or less organized, set of *traits* that he or she exhibits. Our knowledge of these traits and how they are related allows us to anticipate how that person will react in a particular situation or environment. Traits are deemed to transcend settings and inhere in the person, whether an actual individual or a literary character.

Such similarities often make it difficult to distinguish the real from the story world, for the "illusion of individuality" attends characters, especially the "round" ones.[11] The reader is thus inclined to speculate about what the character did before appearing in a particular episode and what he or she will do when that scene ends.[12] Speculation and anticipation of this kind are normal aspects of the reading process; they help readers fill the gaps and build connections within the text. But there are certain limits beyond which such speculation is no longer of interest for the critic. Extended rumination on a character's "life" outside the story may well be the imaginative foundation on which further narratives are authored—the growth of the synoptic tradition was fueled in this manner (Kermode 1978:98-99)—but it surely falls outside the critic's bailiwick. Although our ways of knowing real people invariably inform constructions of literary character, the narrative context itself remains the primary limiting and shaping framework. As Forster put it, characters are "bound in a hundred ways to their literary context" (1927:65). When the critic extracts or isolates a figure from its proper context, the rest of the narrative world is left in a mess, and both character and story are distorted. Even those characters based on historical personages must, therefore, be construed and assessed according to the constraints of the specific narrative within which they appear (Scholes 1968:17; Springer 1978:21; Thompson 1978:3-4; Fleck 1984: 21-41; and Hochman 1985:7-8, 59-85).

A reader's knowledge of literary character is different in a number of ways from our knowledge of other (real) people in daily life. First, the encounter between audience and character is not truly interactive. That is, the reader images a character, but is not actually confronted by the character. The immediate emotional and practical consequences which we must take into account in our relations with others are wholly absent from the reader/character relationship. Furthermore, the myriad "senses" we have of other human beings through personal contact (like body language, facial expressions, tone of voice, touch, and so forth) are missing from a literary encounter. In short, the reader's relationship to a character is a totally verbal experience, somewhat detached and intellectual (see Walcutt 1966:7). Second, literature provides us with the god-like ability to peer into the secret lives (thoughts, motives, emotions) of others, lives that would be barred to us in our day-to-day existence. As Harvey states it, "life allows only intrinsic knowledge of self, contextual knowledge of others [but] fiction allows both intrinsic and contextual knowledge of others" (1965:32; also Forster 1927:64). Third, we have no counterpart in daily life for the omniscient narrator's assessment of the nature and intentions of others. Our knowledge of other people can never be so definite, direct, or immediate, for it is always based upon inference from our discrete, limited contacts with them.

In summary, we "tread a delicate line between the view that readers must apprehend a character in their own terms and the view that readers must honor the terms laid down by a text" (Hochman 1985:7-8). Characters are not just words (the sum of all verbs in the text, as some structuralists claim) or textual functions, but rather, affective and realistic personal images generated by text and reader. We think about characters as persons, and this aspect of characterization should not be ignored. But characters are not people, and thus the critic must always bear in mind the relevant distinctions between knowing a person in daily life and imaging a character within a literary work.

EXTRATEXT AND CHARACTERIZATION

While performing their character-building exercises, readers continually supplement them "by inferring from the repertoire of indices characteristics not immediately signaled in the text, but familiar from other texts and from life" (Kermode 1979:78). That extratextual factors must be taken into account in the evaluation of character and characterization in Luke-Acts has been argued at length (see Chapter 1). Little more comment is necessary at this point. Suffice it to say that awareness of Hellenistic convention (character types and typical situations) and intertextual linkage between the Lukan corpus and the Septuagint is necessary for full interpretation of Lukan characters. Literary characterization was highly conventionalized in the Western tradition at least through the time of Chaucer. That is, narrative characters—even those in historical works—were largely illustrative, symbolic, and typed, rather than representational, mimetic, and heterodox as they tend to be in modern novels.[13] Thus, it is imperative that we reconstruct the framework of literary and social conventions that constrained the ancient reader's understanding of characters like those we encounter in Luke-Acts.

One issue of extratextuality that we shall not pursue at any length is that of the overall genre of Luke-Acts. It is true that some character types are "genre specific," and therefore it behooves one to have a firm grasp of a work's generic antecedents. Despite a recent upsurge of scholarly interest in the subject, however, a definitive answer to the question about gospel genre (often posed as an either/or issue with only one option possible) has not been forthcoming.[14] In the headlong rush to show that the gospels are not *sui generis*, critics seem to have lost sight of the fact that they might well be *genus mixtum*.[15] Like all literary conventions, genres are extratextual phenomena, and thus are very difficult to identify with certainty. They are rarely codified, vary widely in terms of their degrees of formulation, and often exhibit a strong tendency toward hybridization. The very number and diversity of solutions proposed for the problem of gospel genre in general and of Luke-Acts' genre in particular seem to warrant the notion that what we are dealing with here are quite thorough mixtures of many popular literary strains within first-century Greco-Roman culture. We will certainly be able to understand some aspects of Luke-Acts by comparison with similar aspects in various ancient genres, but it is highly unlikely that we will ever be able to classify it *as a whole* under a single, rigidly-formulated literary category.[16]

THE RHETORIC OF CHARACTER IN LUKE-ACTS

By definition, a pragmatic approach entails analysis of ways in which characters and characterization affect an audience. That is, it requires critics to be especially observant of how figures contribute to a narrative's rhetoric. How is the audience, as the builder of Lukan characters, encouraged to adopt a certain system of values and a particular point of view?

Since the early 1950's Lukan scholarship has focused largely on the temporal schema of Luke-Acts as a key to understanding its intentionality (Ernst 1977:7). Redactional analysis revealed that Luke revised Mark's "early expectation" eschatology in order to account for the delay of the parousia and to explain the roots of an ongoing, rapidly institutionalizing Christian movement. Because he wished to produce a *foundational document* for the church, Luke reshaped the story in terms of an overarching, tripartite history of salvation (the era of the law and prophets, the glorious epoch when Jesus was on earth, and the church age; see Conzelmann 1960). Many of the idiosyncratic themes and motifs in Luke's story could be attributed in one way or another to this larger agenda.

Scholarly attention to Luke's understanding of time (whether for or against Conzelmann's dominant thesis) produced a number of valid insights concerning his narrative's structure. However, the redaction-critical identification of a unique schema of salvation history, or of other related themes—the centrality of the temple and Jerusalem, the inclusion of the Gentiles, the Spirit, prayer, possessions, and so forth—does not, in and of itself, constitute a demonstration of the text's *rhetoric*. These may well be salient themes of Luke-Acts. Although they tell us much about the *what* of the text, however, they do not tell us *how*, in reading the story, we are led to embrace them. In other words, little has been done to explain the rhetorical strategies for persuading the audience to accept and assimilate these and other facets of Luke's world-view.[17]

Wayne Booth (1974; 1979; 1983) has done much to raise awareness of the ubiquity of rhetoric in literature. Indeed, little that we encounter in a text cannot be viewed in some way as exerting a persuasive force on the reader. This is no less true of Luke-Acts than of other narratives. Context and sequence, for example, have rhetorical effects. In treating specific Lukan passages, we shall consider carefully the myriad rhetorical forces that impinge upon the reader. At this point, however, we shall limit our discussion to three major rhetorical strategies related to characterization: (1) the establishment of two mutually-reinforcing, authoritative, and utterly reliable perspectives or "points of view;" (2) the employment of intermediate characters as paradigms of perception; and (3) the comparing/contrasting (*sygkrisis*) of protagonists to determine their statuses and elucidate their roles in the divine plan.

Establishing Narrative Authority

When reading Luke-Acts one takes up many different points of view, from the narrator's panoramic perspective to various angles of vision held by the different characters. Largely by evaluating and juxtaposing these discrete viewpoints, the reader ascertains and is oriented toward the work's "horizon" of norms and values. Luke-Acts, unlike much modern fiction, utilizes a rather definite hierarchy of viewpoints. As a result, the audience is seldom at a loss in assessing events and personages in the story. Anxiety and confusion are not the reader's lot, for the narrative employs two utterly reliable, authoritative, and mutually-reinforcing frames of reference that condition everything (including other points of view) in the story.

The most significant, all-encompassing frame of reference is that of the narrator. Like other biblical narrators, the narrator of Luke-Acts is omniscient, omnipresent, retrospective, and fully reliable.[18] But, unlike other biblical narrators, "he" changes voice from first to third person and back again.[19] His general perspective is that of a highly specialized observer looking back on a series of events in the past, not that of a character who is experiencing events first-hand. He provides readers with reliable commentary on persons, events, settings, and objects in the story, and mediates the crucial "inside" views of characters' thoughts, emotions, and intentions.

> All of these kinds of commentary serve the purpose of heightening the intensity with which the reader experiences particular moments in a book. Though they may do other things as well, they are primarily justified by some service they perform in molding the reader's judgment on one scale of values or another. (Booth 1983:197)

In these ways the reliable narrator is able to regulate the "distance" between reader and character. That is, the reader's evaluation of and identification with (or sympathy for) various characters is largely controlled by the narrator.

As in much of the scripture, the narrator's point of view in Luke is god-like. Indeed, it is complemented and authenticated by a carefully and tightly constructed "*divine*" frame of reference. In essence, this frame constitutes the point of view of a persona who, although not dramatized in the narrative, actually initiates and largely controls the action! God remains offstage, and so the divine perspective, like that of the narrator, is "external" to the story proper. The initial indication that Luke's narrative is governed by an external, sacred point of view is the reference in the prologue to "the things that have been fulfilled among us" (Luke 1:1). Because fulfillment implies prediction and/or promise, this phrase points the reader outside the perimeter of the story and toward a far broader salvation-historical horizon (it implies that relevant things have happened *before* and *since* the events related in the story), and links the two. Luke's story is but a part of a much larger, ongoing story in which God plays the major role.

But how, then, is the reader made aware of God's actions and will? How does one determine what God—this invisible, mysterious super-agent—has done? The answer, of course, is that readers are provided with carefully-authenticated oracles which explicate how the divine impinges on personages, events, and natural forces. It has long been noted that the author was very careful to establish precise lines of authority among characters, and to confirm every major new phase in the progression of Christianity. Thus Peter is the first to convert a Gentile, and Paul the first to reach Rome. This same concern is also manifested in the ways *divine* authority is conferred upon persons, events, and speech. In this narrative, the divine point of view is invariably expressed or authenticated through the auspices of the Holy Spirit.[20] Each protagonist is confirmed as such by an overt action of the Holy Spirit. Even the Lukan Jesus is validated in this manner. He is born of the Spirit (Luke 1:35), and he bears the Spirit. The text hammers the latter point home quickly. Robert Tannehill (1972:68) has noted that "apart from the genealogy, each of the major sections of material between the baptism of Jesus and the announcement [at the Nazareth synagogue] in 4:18 is introduced by a reference to Jesus as the bearer of the Spirit."

Moreover, every speech that purports to represent the divinity (especially prophetic or predictive words) must bear the Spirit's stamp of approval, or else it remains subject to suspicion. Those sayings that are authorized by the Spirit are always borne out in the narrative (i.e., they are "fulfilled"). Even the sayings of relatively minor figures such as Zechariah and Simeon (Luke 1:67-79; 2:25-35) take on great significance when the narrator informs us that they are inspired by the *pneuma tou theou*.

The scriptures are a primary oracle through which the divine impinges upon the characters and events of Luke-Acts. For example, Jesus is shaped and evaluated to a great extent with reference to the scriptures. When the Lukan Jesus explains himself to unseeing disciples on the way to Emmaus, he does so in terms of scripture: "And beginning with Moses and all the prophets, he interpreted to them in all the scriptures the things concerning himself." It is clear that the reader—who purportedly "sees" better than these disciples—is supposed to construe the image of Jesus against the backdrop of the sacred writings. In Luke's hierarchy of authority, however, even the promises, predictions, and prefigurations found in scripture are placed under the aegis of the Spirit. That is, a pneumatic (and christological) hermeneutic is used to control how the writings are applied to the present narrative. The scriptures alone are not sufficient to legitimate anything; they too must be "accredited" in each case by the Spirit, or by a figure who has the Spirit's sanction.[21]

Sometimes these sources of accreditation or legitimation can pile up and become syntactically unwieldy. Note, for example, how many authorities are invoked by the early Christians in Jerusalem as they begin their prayer for boldness (*parresia*):

> Sovereign Lord, who made the heaven and the earth and the sea and everything in them, who by the mouth of our father David, thy servant, said by the Holy Spirit . . . . (Acts 4:24b-25a; followed by quotation from Psalm 2:1-2)

Unscrambling this omelet of authority, we find the following hierarchy (in descending order): the creator God, the Holy Spirit, David, scripture.

Readers of Luke-Acts soon recognize that the divine impinges on this narrative world in certain carefully designated ways. The sources of divine accreditation and approbation are delimited and specified meticulously. Much like the narrator's perspective, the divine frame of reference provides the audience with a consistent and highly authoritative guide for constructing and/or evaluating characters and their roles in the action.

The Rhetoric of Recognition and Response

Fundamental to this study is the observation that, through a variety of rhetorical strategies, Luke-Acts maneuvers its readers into alignment with the "witnesses" (*autoptai* or *martyres*) who constitute the insiders of the story. That is, the Lukan text is designed to persuade its readers to become believing witnesses of and to "the things which have been fulfilled among us" (Luke 1:1). From beginning to end, the text urges one to *see*, *hear*, and *respond* to these things in an appropriate manner (i.e., in accord with the narrative's value-system). Readers are bombarded with an array of rhetorical weaponry intended to convince them that these events are of ultimate significance, and, concomitantly, that there are correct and incorrect ways of perceiving them.

Direct commentary by the Spirit-authenticated protagonist is one such persuasive ploy.

> And turning to the disciples privately he said, "Blessed are the eyes which *see* the things that you *see*. For I say to you that many prophets and kings wished to *see* the things you are *seeing* but did not *see*, and to *hear* the things you are *hearing*, but did not *hear*." (Luke 10:23b-24)

This is all, of course, for the benefit of the reader, who, along with the disciples, has been "seeing and hearing" (or reading) the wonderful things to which the Lukan Jesus refers. The effects of such a statement are (1) to heighten the reader's appreciation for what he or she is reading, and (2) to make the reader reflect on *how* they are reading. In this, and many other ways, an analogy is drawn between the reader's reading and the characters' hearing and seeing.

The ubiquity of this rhetoric of perception is not difficult to demonstrate.[22] First, Luke *begins* on a note of perception and witness. This is especially significant in that openings usually establish major expectations for the reader.[23] The prologue (Luke 1:1-4) has generally been plumbed for what it reveals about historicity, purpose, and genre, while its persuasive functions are rarely noted. This ornate opening serves as a powerful rhetorical entree to the entire work. It not only focuses attention on "the things that have been fulfilled," but introduces three paradigms of recognition and response to what has occurred (which is really what is about to "occur" in the narrative). In other words, the prologue is already setting the reader up to perceive and respond to the upcoming events and personages in a certain way.

One model of perception mentioned in the prologue is a group: "those who were eyewitnesses from the beginning" (*hoi ap' arches autoptai*), and who, by implication, faithfully transmitted what they had seen and heard. The second paradigm is the narrator who "traced everything carefully from the beginning." Reference to beginnings is hardly coincidental here, for the reader is also *beginning* the reading process. An analogy is being set up between what the reader is about to do (observe and assess) and what both the eyewitnesses and the narrator have already done. The audience is encouraged to align with these two authorities, who constitute the insiders of the story (note the references to this group in the phrases "among us" [1:1] and "to us"[1:2]). What divides those on the inside from those on the outside is not just *what* is perceived, but *how* one perceives and responds to it. This notion of correct perception will serve throughout the story as a criterion dividing insiders from outsiders.

Theophilus will represent the ideal (*kratistos*) reader, that potential/incipient believer ("friend of God"), whose very name implies that he is well-disposed toward, receptive of and, indeed, eager to witness and understand (*epignos*) the divine agenda as it is revealed in the upcoming narrative. Pseudo-Cicero, an ancient expert on rhetoric, was well aware of the technique of setting up an ideal reading role in the prologue so as to predispose readers to a literary piece. He recognized that the purpose of the direct opening (where hearers are directly addressed), is "to enable us to have hearers who are attentive, receptive, and well-disposed" (*Rhetorica ad Herrenium* I, iv, 6; quoted in Ginsberg 1983:23). In all these ways, then, the prologue begins to maneuver or position readers to perceive and respond to what they will "see and hear" in the narrative.

Second, in the *final* episode of Luke-Acts, the same emphasis on perception and response as criteria of inclusion appears. When Paul reaches Rome, he gathers "the leading men of the Jews" and attempts to convince them of Jesus' identity "from both the law of Moses and from the prophets" (Acts 28:23). Some who listen to him truly hear (perceive) his message and believe; others do not. When he sees that some have failed to comprehend his words, Paul quotes Isaiah 6:9-10 to them:

> "Go to this people and say,
> 'You will keep on hearing,
> But you will not understand;
> And you will keep on seeing,
> But you will not perceive';
> For the heart of this people has become dull,
> And they have closed their eyes;
> Lest they should see with their eyes,
> And hear with their ears,

> And understand with their heart and turn again,
> And I should heal them." (Acts 28:26-27)[24]

This authoritative word, sealed by the Holy Spirit (28:25b), summarizes the perceptional criteria that distinguish between the outsiders and insiders of the story—criteria that are completely familiar to the reader by this point. The Lukan Paul concludes on a bitter note: God's salvation has been sent to the Gentiles, for "they will listen" (28:28). The story thus begins and ends with a strong emphasis on correct perception.[25]

This rhetoric of perception is, however, most often and most clearly manifested in the interaction of the secondary characters with the protagonists. The narrative focuses attention on whether or not these secondary characters *recognize and respond* correctly to the divine will being manifested through the protagonists. The text repeatedly *foregrounds* descriptions of the ways in which the intermediate and background figures do or do not perceive (watch, observe, look, see, listen, hear), cognitively appropriate (know, understand, apprehend), and commit themselves to (repent, witness to, believe) what confronts them in Jesus and other agents of the divine.

Much of Luke's rhetoric of perception employs the verbs "to see" (*horao*) and "to hear" (*akouo*). It is not difficult to *see* why these verbs are utilized. In Greek as in English, these words have double meanings. They can refer to merely sensory perception or to full (noetic) comprehension. When we ask of an errant child, "Do you hear me?" we do not mean primarily, "Are the sounds of my voice causing your eardrums to vibrate?" but rather, "Do you truly understand what I am saying, and its implications, and that I expect you to respond in a certain manner?" The verb to see is also used in these dual senses, meaning both to sight objects and to comprehend something fully (You see?). This duality of meaning proves to be an important tool for establishing irony. Often, the blind "see" better than the sighted, and those who observe most actually "see" least.

In reading about characters witnessing the salvific persons, messages, and events, the reader witnesses them as well. Because the narrative foregrounds recognition and response as values, the reader is forced to reflect on his or her own seeing and hearing of all these things. In the interplay between the perspectives of the reader and the secondary characters, the reader is encouraged to reject some ways of seeing and hearing, and accept and emulate others. A "hierarchy of perspectives" develops, with characters representing various modes and levels of recognition and response. These are graded (largely by the narrator and other authoritative voices) on the basis of their ability to perceive and embrace the divine will as manifested in the persons, messages, and activities of the protagonists.

The ideal character observes the divine, fully recognizes it, comprehends its significance, embraces it immediately and without reservation, and testifies about it to others. The prophet Simeon embodies these ideals early in the story (Luke 2:25-35). He is not only approved by the Spirit, but also described by the narrator as righteous and devout (*dikaios kai eulabes* [or, *eusebes*]). When he sees Jesus, he immediately recognizes the babe's significance and proclaims it: "My eyes have seen thy salvation!" At the far end of the spectrum are the Pharisees who, as we shall see, carefully observe many of Jesus' works and hear many of his words, but fail utterly to recognize what they see and hear. Failing to recognize what they observe, they cannot possibly respond appropriately.

A wide range of paradigmatic figures fall between these two extremes. The rich young ruler sees, hears, and comprehends, but is unwilling to respond positively. The synagogue-goers of Jesus' home town witness to Jesus and respond favorably to *part* of what he says, but finally reject him because he wishes to include the Gentiles in the Kingdom. In the first part of the story, even the disciples, although they do begin to recognize and respond to the Lord, fail fully to comprehend him. This points up an interesting distinction among the secondary characters in Luke-Acts. Some are in continuing roles that allow for the development of the ability to recognize and respond; others continue to appear in the story, but remain static in their incomprehension (e.g., the Pharisees); and still others show up but once and respond (e.g., Zacchaeus) or fail to respond (e.g., the rich young ruler) correctly.

What we find in Luke's story, then, is what one critic calls a counterbalancing of perspectives. This arrangement, which often appears in devotional, didactic, and propagandistic narrative, is simple and straightforward, entailing a "very definite hierarchy of perspectives" whose "quality and defects . . . . are clearly graded" (Iser 1978:100). In these arrangements, the protagonists always represent the principal perspective. Through them the "fundamental catalog of values" unfolds. In the Lukan story the determinative factor in whether a character recognizes and/or responds correctly is the status, or quality, of that character's "heart." According to Simeon's oracle (Luke 2:34-35), the child Jesus is "set for the fall and rise of many in Israel, and for a sign that is spoken against . . . that the thoughts (*dialogismoi*) out of many hearts may be revealed."[26] Those who "rise" (that is, are valued) in this story-world are those who, "because they *hear* the word with a *noble and good heart*, hold it fast and bring forth fruit with steadfastness" (Luke 8:15). Characters who have hearts that are not fully right fail to grasp the message (truly hear, see, and internalize it) and so their value "falls."[27] The ability to perceive correctly, which is a prior necessity for correct response, is thus tied directly to one's value system and inner orientation. Humility, repentance, generosity, and so forth allow for spiritual insight; pride, an unrepentant spirit, greed, and injustice cause spiritual blindness.

We have been able to sketch but the contours of this complex and pervasive rhetoric of recognition and response. Below, in our treatments of the Pharisees and Herod the Tetrarch, we shall have opportunities to return to it and flesh out more fully several of its aspects.

Not Quite Parallel Lives (*Sygkrisis*)

Greco-Roman readers would have recognized almost immediately that the juxtaposition of John's and Jesus' birth stories (Luke 1 and 2) reflected the prevalent rhetorical convention of *sygkrisis* (comparison/contrast). Often, biographers paralleled the lives or exploits of famous persons so that the audience would compare and contrast—and ultimately rank—them in terms of their significance and continuing influence.[28] Familiar with this extratextual code, the reader of Luke-Acts would automatically begin to contrast the two protagonists of Luke 1-2, looking for ways in which one holds the upper hand over the other. In other words, readers were aware that they were to deduce which of these two was greater, and why. The result, of course, is a subordination of John the Baptist and his disciples to Jesus and his followers. In the next chapter, we shall analyze this rhetorical pattern further, and explain how it affects the characterization of John and other figures beyond the infancy narratives.

Character Building/Building Character

We have outlined but a few of the strategies of persuasion in Luke-Acts. Fuller and more specific treatments appear in following chapters. Despite its preliminary nature, however, our overview of the "rhetoric of Lukan character" amply evidences the *dialogical quality* of characterization. The process of constructing character is neither neutral nor unidirectional. Even as we fashion *dramatis personae*, we are being positioned and maneuvered—indeed, shaped—by the rhetoric of the text. While building Luke's characters, the audience experiences a certain character building of its own! And, of course, the reader-critic must monitor and explain the reader's evolution as the literary work unfolds.

3

RECAPITATING JOHN THE BAPTIST: HOLISM, RHETORIC, AND CHARACTERIZATION

THE (LITERARY) DECAPITATION OF JOHN BY MODERN LUKAN SCHOLARSHIP

Fragmenting Luke-Acts into sources, forms, tradition, and redaction has resulted (predictably) in the "dismemberment" of many of its literary characters. Nowhere is this syndrome more apparent than in the case of John the Baptist. Indeed, one cannot help but observe that historical critical treatments of John have often committed the hermeneutical equivalent of Herod's egregious act: they have "decapitated" the character of John in Luke-Acts by bracketing off the infancy narratives (Luke 1-2), a section of the text containing preliminary, programmatic information that the reader must have to construct the character of the Baptist in the remainder of the story.[1] Although some Lukan scholars (e.g., Oliver 1964; Minear 1980:120-30) have spoken against this widespread tendency to ignore the import of Luke 1-2 for understanding John, little of a constructive nature has appeared to explain precisely how John is characterized in the work as a whole. Largely for want of salient methodology, critics have failed to explain what results when one "recapitates" the Baptist by taking into account Luke's infancy narratives. How *does* John appear when the narrative is understood as a sequential, linear whole that is constructed by a reader who weaves together text and extratext? Our purpose here is to answer this question by offering a minimalist sketch of how the audience of Luke-Acts builds John's character.[2]

Our thesis is tripartite: (1) contrary to Conzelmann and his followers, the reader can and does build an image of John that is consistent throughout the story; (2) what governs and gives coherence to John's characterization is the rhetoric of *sygkrisis* (comparison and contrast) between John and Jesus set up in Luke 1-2; and (3) John epitomizes the prophetic tradition that (from the Lukan point of view) predicts the coming of the Messiah and prepares the hearts of the people *to recognize and respond to him correctly* when he arrives. The relationship between Jesus and John the Baptist is thus a prism through which we are to view the complex (continuous but discontinuous) relationship between the church and its Jewish matrix. Through this narrative lens, the two appear to be inextricably, permanently linked and yet delineated, ranked, and ordered with care.

"WHAT THEN WILL THIS CHILD BECOME?" JOHN THE BAPTIST IN LUKE 1-2

A plethora of personal information about Jesus and John hits the reader of Luke 1-2. We learn of their families and the places where they reside, their lineage, and the wonderful circumstances of their births, dedications, namings and upbringings. This cache of familial and personal data not only "rounds out" the figures of John and Jesus, but also clues readers that these two will play pivotal roles in the upcoming story (since the strictures of narrative economy preclude using so much space and time on lesser figures). But beyond these rather simple observations, how are we to process all this information, especially with regard to John?

A difficulty that confronts the reader of these chapters, of course, is that John himself appears only obliquely in them (as an infant and, fleetingly, as a *paidion* growing up in the desert; 1:80). He is not yet a dramatized, volitional agent who speaks, or acts, or makes choices that *show* his character. All information on John in this section is indirect, mediated by the narrator or by other characters. In addition, what the reader learns here is all anticipatory, proleptic. It becomes quite obvious that we are not to focus on John as child, but to garner information that aids us in understanding what John *will be* when grown (i.e., "the day he is manifested to Israel"; 1:80). A question raised by John's neighbors shortly after he is circumcised and named *focalizes* the issue of how John is to be construed: "What then will this child become?" (1:66b) These tertiary characters serve as performative paradigms for the reader, modeling the tasks of retrospection (by "pondering" what they have seen and heard) and anticipation (by articulating the question that readers are to ask concerning what will occur in the upcoming narrative).[3] Of course, the audience has received much more information about these awesome occurrences than have the story's characters. The reader's task is clear: assemble all this information concerning John with an eye to how he will function later.

Given this task, how does the reader process the information about John in Luke 1-2? As the reader reaches the end of the birth narratives and joins John's neighbors (and Mary, another of these "performative figures") in pondering the fantastic events which have transpired, he or she organizes and evaluates information on the Baptist *in terms of his relationships to other characters and groups in the narrative*. Character is largely shaped by contexts; and, as we saw in Chapter 2, the primary context for constructing character is the web of relationships developed among characters. Thus, although John is not a well-dramatized figure at this point in the narrative, the audience has already begun to shape certain expectations about him based on how various characters and groups in Luke's story world relate to his birth: the divine (God, the Holy Spirit, Gabriel, the god-like narrator); Elijah; his family and people; and—most importantly—Jesus.

The Baptist and the Divine: Establishing John's Authority

John's status and authority as a protagonist in the story are established primarily with reference to God (as represented by an angel and the Holy Spirit) and the omniscient narrator (who often assumes the audacious role of speaking for the divine). Early on, Gabriel prophesies to the awestruck Zacharias that John will "be great in the sight of the Lord" (1:15). In addition, the angelic messenger maintains that John will be filled with the Holy Spirit even before being born. As we noted in the preceding chapter, the Spirit is the authorizing entity *par excellence* in the narrative; one does not speak or act with full authority in this story world without the Spirit's approbation. John is the only human character other than Jesus to receive the Spirit *before birth*. All this implies that the divine sanction will be given to *all* activity and speech by these two protagonists, a fact that sets them apart from every other figure in the narrative (other figures are used by the Spirit as oracles *at points*, but they also speak or act without the Spirit's guidance [e.g., Zacharias]). The angel's prophecy is borne out in dramatic fashion: John leaps *in utero* at his mother's encounter with Mary, who is pregnant with Jesus, the one conceived of the Spirit (1:44; see Fitzmyer 1981:363; George 1970:151).

The drama and intrigue that permeate John's miraculous birth and naming serve to identify him as a special agent in the divine plan. Much has been written recently on how John's conception and birth parallel those of many important figures in the Septuagint, and so we need not repeat those arguments here. Suffice it to say that, because of these intertextual links, the reader is ready to rank John among the most significant of messengers in the history of salvation. Similarly, the fact that John is named by God is an unmistakable indicator of his future greatness.[4] The narrator's final note about John is that he grew *strong in spirit* and was in the deserts until the day of his revelation to Israel. This is an anticipatory remark, a hook for the reader to look for John later, but it also covers the time of his childhood: nothing happens during his young adulthood to undercut or mitigate John's privileged relationship to the divine.

John and Elijah

The reader learns much more from divine oracles than the simple fact that John will be great. Gabriel, in his announcement to Zacharias, predicts that John will go *enopion autou* ("before him") to prepare and reform Israel for the Lord (1:16-17). Indeed, he will proceed "in the spirit and power of Elijah." The quotation that follows ("to turn the hearts of the fathers back to the children") is a clear indicator that the intertextual link to be forged here is not with the Elijah narratives of the Deuteronomistic History, but rather with Malachi's prediction that Elijah would return before "the great and glorious day of the Lord" (see LXX Malachi 3:1, 22-23). Although this linkage is unmistakable, the sense of the passage is muddied somewhat by the modifying phrase "in the spirit and power of." Is John to be strictly *identified* with Elijah (i.e., as Elijah *redivivus*), or is one simply to understand that John will be *like* Elijah in certain of his functions? Should readers identify, or only draw analogies between, these two prophetic reformers?[5] At this point in the reading process, the reader does not have enough information to decide on this issue; however, the intertextual allusion is sufficiently clear to encourage readers to look for further Elijianic motifs or traits.

The second oracle concerning John, that voiced by his father, also speaks to the issue of John's future role. Zacharias says to his son (but really to the reader, since John is just a baby):

> "And you, child, will be called 'prophet of the Most High;' For you will go before the Lord to prepare his ways; to give his people knowledge of salvation in the forgiveness of their sins." (1:76-77)

Here, John again is identified as the prophet of the Lord. His specific function is defined as preparing the people of Israel by calling on them to repent of their sins. Especially noteworthy is the emphasis on *knowledge*: the people will be able to know (recognize) salvation only upon forgiveness of their sins. John's role, then, is preparing hearts to "see and hear" correctly when God acts decisively, when light comes to dispel the darkness (1:79). Once again, Malachi's prophecy about one who will precede the Lord is echoed. This time, however, no direct reference to Elijah is made. Only Malachi 3:1 is quoted, not 3:22-23 with its explicit identification of the messenger as Elijah. The emphasis of both oracles, then, falls on the *function* of

John as forerunner, preparer and reformer, rather than on his identification with Elijah *per se*.

John and His Family and People

Readers and hearers of ancient narratives are expected to put much stock in a character's lineage and culture—the familial and ethnic roots from which he or she grew. Descriptions of one's family or tribe are intended to inform us about a person's likely influences, tendencies, and agenda. The portrait of John's family in Luke 1-2 is suggestive in this regard. Zacharias and Elizabeth are like an idyllic tapestry woven from colorful strands of Jewish tradition. The narrator deems them righteous before God and blameless with respect to the law, for they "walk in all the commandments and ordinances of the Lord" (1:6). They are elderly and barren (1:7), a set of circumstances that causes the audience to compare them with some of Israel's venerable patriarchal and matriarchal figures (e.g., Abraham and Sarah). They live in Davidic ancestral territory (Judea), and both come from priestly families. The cult is well-represented here, for Zacharias is portrayed as an active priest still practicing in the temple (1:8-23). Along with Simeon and Anna (2:25-38), John's family fairly exudes the traits of what has been called temple-piety, a kind of idealized, highly romanticized, view of Jewish religious life (see Brown 1977:267-68 n. 13; 351; 488; Fitzmyer 1981:316). From all of this, the reader learns that John is both the product and the representative of a kind of Judaism that combines essential features of the tradition in a pietistic mode. This is the kind of Judaism that will be prepared to perceive and respond correctly to the new revelations of God.

There are strong indicators in Luke 1-2, however, that these pious folk may be the exception in Israel, rather than the rule. Zacharias, Elizabeth, Simeon, and Anna may be prepared to perceive the salvation of the Lord, but many others are not. Indeed, John's role is necessary precisely because "many of the sons of Israel" are needful of turning back to God (1:16) and having their trespasses forgiven (1:77). Jesus, Simeon tells the reader, is "set for the fall and rising of many in Israel, and for a sign that is spoken against . . . that the thoughts [*dialogismoi*] out of many hearts may be revealed" (2:34-35). Already the audience is beginning to distinguish between the ideal kind of Judaism represented by John's family, Simeon, and Anna, and Israel in general. John is a product of (Luke's) ideal Judaism, and his responsibility is to bring the rest of Israel into line with that ideal so that divine revelation will be recognized.

John and Jesus

As we have observed several times, the rhetoric of *sygkrisis* (comparison and contrast) strongly influences the building of John's character. A reader familiar with this rhetorical pattern would recognize it at work in Luke 1-2 and proceed to compare and contrast the data on John and Jesus. Precise juxtaposition of parallel episodes surrounding the births of these characters sets up and triggers this comparative task and provides the venues for its execution.[6] Major points of comparison follow:

(1) The two annunciations (Luke 1:8-23 and 1:26-38). Gabriel predicts that John will be great (1:15), an ascetic, the reformer and preparer of Israel for the Lord (1:16-17). Gabriel also avers that Jesus will be great, but adds that he will occupy the throne of David (1:32). Furthermore, Jesus will be called the son of the Most High (*huios hypsistou*). Elizabeth will conceive her son in a natural (albeit miraculous) manner, but Mary will conceive of the Holy Spirit (1:35). John will *receive* the Holy Spirit while still in the womb, but Jesus actually *will be engendered* by the Spirit;

(2) The births and circumcisions (Luke 1:57-66 and 2:1-21). Except for the special circumstances around his naming, the birth and circumcision of John are uneventful. The nativity of Jesus is accompanied by much spectacle, however, and is infused with great meaning. An angelic oracle informs certain shepherds (and the reader as well) that the newborn will be "a savior, Christ, Lord" (2:11).

(3) The prophetic oracles (1:67-79 and 2:22-38). Zacharias, prophesying under the influence of the Holy Spirit, predicts that John will be called *prophetes hypsistou* and will prepare the Lord's ways by reforming his people and giving them knowledge to see the light of God's salvation when it arrives (1:76-79).

Jesus' mission has a notably larger scope. Seeing the Christ child at the temple, the prophet Simeon is filled with the Spirit and raises his voice in prayer and praise to God:

> ". . . my eyes have seen your salvation,
> Which you have prepared in the presence of *all peoples*,
> A light of revelation to the Gentiles,
> And the glory of your people Israel." (2:30-32)

John's specific task will be to prepare *Israel* for the arrival of the Lord; in Jesus' person and ministry the salvation of the Lord will be manifested both in Israel and throughout the world. Jesus *is* the Lord and has already been accorded that title on two occasions (1:43 and 2:11).

(4) The childhood summaries (Luke 1:80 and 2:40, 52). Young John, living in the wilderness, grows "strong in spirit," while Jesus (so the narrator tells us twice) becomes "full of wisdom" and the "grace of God is upon him." The attribution of wisdom to a protagonist (especially at an early age) was very important, for *sophia* was the primary virtue distinguishing a holy sage from others in the biographical literature of the period. The second most valued trait was asceticism, the very life-style that John is depicted as adopting (Cox 1983:21-25).

Even this cursory overview of parallels reveals their effect on the reader's characterization of John and Jesus. Although both are to be "great" (divinely ordained protagonists in the new era of salvation history), they are distinguished and ranked in terms of their natures, roles, and the scope of their tasks. As the "prophet of the Most High," John will be responsible for *preparing Israel* to recognize the Lord's salvation (*soterion*) when it arrives. As "son of the Most High," Jesus will manifest and mediate the divine salvation not only to Israel (as Davidic Messiah), but also to *all peoples* (as a savior, a title usually reserved for emperors). The reader cannot avoid recognizing a qualitative difference between these figures.

The rhetoric of Luke 1-2, however, goes beyond differentiating between John and Jesus. The intersection of the birth stories is the symbolic meeting of the two protagonists *in utero*. Because it breaks the pattern of parallel scenes, the tale of Mary's trip to see Elizabeth (1:39-56) commands attention. It provides the setting for the only fully dramatized encounter between Jesus and John in the Lukan corpus (as we shall note below, the baptism scene is highly enigmatic). When Elizabeth's son "leaps" at the sound of Mary's voice, the import is clear: through contact (even such indirect contact) with Jesus, John has been imbued with the Spirit "while yet in the womb." The authentication, and indeed, the authorization of John is dependent upon Jesus; the prophet is subordinate to the Lord.

In conclusion, the reader of Luke 1-2 develops a nuanced and rather full prognosis of the natures, rankings, relationship, and roles of John and Jesus in the upcoming narrative. Most important among the many textual indicators for defining this prognosis are reliable commentary by the narrator, divine oracles, intertextual echoes from the Septuagint, and the juxtaposition of scenes about the two protagonists. The function of reliable commentary by both narrator and divine figures is plain: the audience is simply told how to evaluate characters and events, as well as what to expect as the story continues. The complex of intertextual linkages has several functions. First, it thoroughly knits together this story with the earlier story of God's interaction with Israel as found in the Septuagint. It also provides initial categories for guiding the reader's construction of characters, thus supplying vital factors in eliciting expectations about John and the persons with whom he will interact. Furthermore, this thorough immersion in allusions to the Septuagint *sensitizes* the reader to look for other linkages of the same sort in the rest of the narrative.

In a similar manner, a certain momentum carries the rhetoric of *sygkrisis* forward throughout the reading process. Once the activity of comparing and contrasting primary characters is set in motion, it remains in effect (even after the paralleling of scenes ends). The reader carries not only the static results (raw data) of this activity into the remainder of the story, but also the very process of comparing and contrasting itself. Thus, the reader will continue to compare John and Jesus in as many categories as the text makes available—their messages, their disciples, their fates, and their relationships to other characters like Pharisees and political rulers. This continuing *sygkrisis* is one dynamic that traditional Lukan scholarship has overlooked in its assessment of the Baptist.

By constructing John in relation to other characters in the birth narratives, the reader develops a well-formed and complex pre-understanding of his upcoming role in the body of the story. John is to be a fully sanctioned agent of the divine purpose (*boule*), for he bears the Spirit of God. He will be a great *prophet* in the tradition of Elijah. It is not clear whether he really is Elijah, or whether he is merely like Elijah, but in any event, he will be an extremely important figure, for he prepares the Lord's way. It is quite clear to the reader that John's activities will involve readying the "hearts" of the people to recognize the salvation of God (= light) when it arrives. But what form will that preparation take? Repentance has been mentioned, but beyond that the specific means John will use to ready his people has not been revealed. What is already plain is that the scope of John's mission is limited to Israel. The way his own family is depicted is certainly meant to buttress this aspect of his image. They are, from the Lukan point of view, the quintessential Jewish family—pious, observant, devout, temple-oriented, and expectant. John's task will be to urge all of his people toward this idyllic profile. His relation to Jesus is already clearly laid out for the audience. John is the preparer for divine salvation; Jesus *is* that salvation. These two are carefully coordinated but different agents in God's plan for the world's redemption. John is the lesser of the two, and yet his message is absolutely necessary if the people are to recognize Jesus for what he is. Many questions remain, of course. What will be John's message to Israel? How will they react to it? Will John himself specifically identify Jesus for the people? Indeed, will the preparer meet and interact with the one whose way he prepares?

JOHN'S MINISTRY AND IMPRISONMENT (3:1-22)

The text's announcement of John's "manifestation to Israel" is dramatic indeed:

> In the fifteenth year of the reign of Tiberius Caesar, Pontius Pilate being governor of Judea, Herod being Tetrarch of Galilee, and his brother Philip tetrarch of the region of Ituraea and Trachonitis, and Lysanias tetrarch of Abilene, in the high priesthood of Annas and Caiaphas, the word of God came to John the son of Zacharias in the desert. (3:1-2)

Quite obviously, something bold, new, and of universal import is beginning. This is not simply a burst of erudition on the part of the author (so Loisy 1924:134), nor is it just the historian's attempt to set the story in a specific historical and geo-political setting. Its significance is revealed primarily in its final clause: "the word of God [*rhema theou*] came to John son of Zacharias in the desert." The reader recognizes this as a formula commonly used in the Septuagint to introduce prophetic episodes (see especially Jer 1:1a). A clear intertextual link has been forged, and it helps the reader to process all of these data. John is cast securely in the role of Hebrew prophet (as was predicted in 1:76), and the political and religious rulers listed in 3:1-2a are now understood as his opposite numbers (and perhaps as his opponents; see Darr 1987:201-209). John has yet to utter a word, make a choice, or take action. Though the reader knows much about him, John has remained in the wings. Now he stands at center stage, ready to deliver a most important word to Israel.

The text provides the reader with but a brief sketch of what John preached and did. Given what the reader knows from both the birth narratives and the Septuagint, however, that outline suffices to fill out John's character. An introductory verse depicts him as an itinerant prophet who moved about in the region of the Jordan "preaching a baptism of repentance for the forgiveness of sins" (3:3). The significance of this activity is elucidated by a scriptural quotation (3:4-5), a nearly exact rendering of Isa 40:3-5 (LXX):

> The voice of one crying in the wilderness:
> Prepare the way of the Lord,
> Make his paths straight.
> Every valley shall be filled,
> And every mountain and hill shall be brought low,

> And the crooked shall be made straight,
> And the rough ways shall be made smooth;
> And *all flesh shall see the salvation of God.*

Unlike all previous quotations of scripture, this one is not recited by a character, but is delivered by the narrator himself. Thus only the reader—not other characters in the story—receives this authoritative interpretation of John's role. In identifying John's task as preparing the way of the Lord, this passage confirms the predictions of Luke 1:17 and 76 (which, in turn, were based on intertextual allusions to Mal 3:1, 22-23). What is common to all these passages is the motif of preparing the way. The topographical imagery of the Isaiah passage is clearly figurative or symbolic, i.e., meant to refer to the religious configurations of the people's hearts rather than to real mountains. Preparation does not involve leveling hills, but redirecting the spiritual or ethical orientation of the Lord's people.

Here alone among the gospels, the Isaiah quote is extended by one verse: "And all flesh shall *see the salvation of God.*" Most commentators have noted that this additional clause sounds Luke's common theme of universalism. A largely overlooked effect of these words, however, is that they remind the reader of Simeon's prayer of praise to God upon seeing baby Jesus: "my eyes have seen your salvation which you have prepared in the presence of all peoples" (2:30-31). The repentance which John's preaching seeks to elicit among the people of Israel is not an end in itself, but a necessary pre-condition for perceiving God's salvation when it/he confronts them. Thus Jesus and his disciples will go on preaching repentance and the forgiveness of sins even as they proclaim good news about the kingdom of God. John's message is part and parcel of their own, and there is no discontinuity between John and Jesus in this regard.

Three vignettes of John's interaction with his audiences follow the Isaiah quotation. These scenes are posed as typical rather than specific, as shown by repeated usage of the imperfect tense. In Luke's gospel, John's preaching is depicted as essentially hortatory. Like the prophets of old, he delivers a threat of divine judgment, proffers a challenge to repent, and then exhorts the people to "bring forth the fruit" of their repentance. This fruit is defined as concern for the welfare of others, especially those who are less fortunate. The main stumbling block to genuine repentance and the fruit-bearing that results from it is abuse of privilege and power. Disregard for the welfare of others is often rooted in religious elitism ("We are descendants of Abraham"; vss. 7-11), or a bureaucratic system in which tax collectors are urged to defraud a vulnerable populace (vss. 12-13), or a military system that allows soldiers to extort civilians (vs. 14). Like the ancient prophets, Luke's Baptist defines righteousness in terms of social justice rather than in terms of religious affiliation, wealth, or social status.[7]

A fourth scene involving John's ministry (vss. 15-17) is quite distinct from the preceding three. Aroused by John's preaching and baptism, the people "debate within their hearts about John, as to whether he might be the Christ" (3:15). Once again, this inner conflict is for the reader's benefit. It raises anew one of the primary issues posed—and at least initially resolved—in the infancy narratives, that is, the proper distinction between John and Jesus. All questions about John possibly being a messianic figure on a par with Jesus are here put to rest, for the Baptist himself states: "As for me, I baptize you with water; but he who is mightier than I is coming, and I am not fit to untie the thong of his sandals; he himself will baptize you with the Holy Spirit and with fire" (vs. 16).

This limited and rather general depiction of John's ministry is singularly anti-climactic after the spectacular introductions accorded both John and Jesus in Luke 1-2. Anticipation raised for John's "manifestation to Israel" is hardly rewarded with a striking scenario. Indeed, the entire account is remarkable for what it does *not* relate. Whereas the infancy stories highlighted John's *persona* (naming, family, life-style), here his importance as an individual is almost totally subjugated to his preaching and its effects (Conzelmann 1960:24). The audience is given only a short commissioning scene and a few personal details. Elijianic motifs from Mark—camel's hair, honey, locusts—are nowhere to be found in this account and therefore cannot help the reader to construct John as the returning Elijah.[8] Furthermore, the audience learns nothing of his asceticism, or anything concrete about the baptism he practices.

Most importantly, perhaps, Luke's John never defines himself as the immediate forerunner or herald of either the eschaton (e.g., he does not proclaim the coming of God's *basileia*) or the Messiah. Contrary to what we read in John 1:23, 29-38, Luke's Baptist neither identifies the Christ nor points to himself as a sign of the arrival of divine salvation. In Luke, John is not the medium of a new revelation, but a reformer preaching a condensed version of the ancient prophetic call to social justice and repentance. He does not do miracles or "signs," and he does not teach the people to look for such. His entire function is reorienting the people's spiritual vision so that they can recognize and respond to the "salvation of God" when it appears. The text does not deny John a forerunner role, but it forces the reader to circumscribe that role quite drastically. In Luke's story world, the forerunner is a preparer of hearts, not a self-conscious signaler of the Lord's coming. Though the *reader* understands John as a kind of forerunner, he or she also realizes that John and the people who comprise his audience (in the story) are not yet cognizant of the imminence of God's salvation as mediated by Jesus.

Herod's Imprisonment of John

John's exit from center stage is consistent with his calling as prophet. Summing up John's ministry as hortatory preacher, the narrator signals that this particular account is at an end (3:18).[9] Herod puts John in jail because—in good prophetic fashion—John has castigated his ruler for sundry evil practices. His denunciation of Herod is in line with the depiction of his preaching in the preceding section: he condemned all evil perpetrated by those in positions of power. Although the story is quite opaque (What happened with Herodias? What were all of Herod's other evils?), the reader fills the story's gaps in a general way—the Tetrarch has transgressed the ethical boundaries of John's preaching. Here Herod plays the evil king to John's prophet, a pattern well-established in the Deuteronomistic History.[10] What is surprising, however, is the absence of a confrontation scene. The narrator tells us it happened, but fails to dramatize it. John is thus deprived of a stage on which to demonstrate his zeal, uphold the law, or deliver an oracle. Jesus, not John, will be given a scene of confrontation with Herod (Luke 23:6-12). The idealizing effect of such episodes is dampened in John's case because the narrator *refers* to it opaquely, rather than *describing* it in all its dramatic detail.

Jesus' Baptism (Luke 3:21-22)

Only after reading of John's imprisonment does the reader learn about Jesus' baptism (3:21-2). John is not mentioned at all in this short pericope, and the baptism scene is so muted that it appears almost inconsequential: "Now when all the people were baptized, and when Jesus also had been baptized, and was praying . . ." (vs. 21). Here the Spirit descends on Jesus after the baptism *while he is praying*. (Walter Wink [1968:83 n.1] has even suggested that *baptisthentos* be understood in the middle voice, thus denoting that Jesus was not baptized by anyone else, but rather, that he baptized himself!) In any event there is no one-on-one interaction between Jesus and John. The reader probably envisions large crowds of people being baptized *en masse*; Jesus is among them, but he is not singled out as special by John or by any other human being. The lack of interaction between the two protagonists at this critical juncture creates an unmistakable tension for readers who have been waiting for John and Jesus to meet. That tension will carry over into the rest of the narrative. At the same time, the opaqueness of the account helps readers avoid a possible conflict—how could the greater of the two protagonists be baptized by the lesser? How could John inaugurate Jesus' ministry or play a part in his reaffirmation by the Spirit?[11]

The placement of John's imprisonment by Herod is strategic. It caps off the account of the Baptist's mission to Israel and constitutes the final parallel between his career and those of the ancient prophets. It also serves to remove John from center stage before Jesus' ministry begins, and to avoid depicting the Baptist as in any way superior (or equal) to Jesus. The Herod passage is crucial, therefore, to guiding characterization of John in relation to Jesus—a process that will not conclude until Acts 19. Already the reader is beginning to construe an image of John as reformer but not inaugurator, a forerunner but not a herald, a preparer but not a witness, a prophet but not a proclaimer of the advent of God's kingdom.[12]

JESUS AND THE DISCIPLES OF JOHN (LUKE 5:33-35 AND 7:18-50)

The reader has formulated a complex image of John, and yet a number of gaps, tensions, and questions remain. There has been no definitive, satisfying scene in which Jesus and John recognize and interact with one another. Everything in the birth narratives pointed forward to a coordinated—although differentiated—effort by these two protagonists, and yet their relationship must be pieced together without explicit guidance, without their presence as fully dramatized characters, and without an actual encounter between them. The synopsis of John's mission and Jesus' baptism in Luke 3 leaves readers without a sense of closure on this issue, for the two charismatic heroes glide past one another with nary an exchange of words or sign of mutual recognition. What has been the effect of John's ministry? How does it relate to what Jesus is about to do? What is John's understanding of Jesus, and what does Jesus think of the Baptist? Since John is now in prison, how will readers resolve these important questions?

Certain information in the report of Jesus' Galilean mission helps the reader to resolve some—but not all—of these tensions. In Luke 5:33 one learns for the first time that John has his own disciples. We can only speculate that they are a special group, selected from among the multitudes that came to be baptized by John. They are representative of their master and so function as a narrative extension of his character. Here they are likened to "the disciples of the Pharisees" and contrasted with the disciples of Jesus. The latter "feast and drink" while the former "fast and pray." Jesus explains (through imagery) that his disciples recognize that now is a time to celebrate, for the bridegroom (= Messiah) is present (5:34). The implication, of course, is that these other disciples and their masters have not yet perceived his true identity. The disjunction between John and Jesus is thus clearly reiterated. Readers do not understand these words to be critical of the Baptist, however. Unlike the Pharisees, he and his disciples have not yet had a chance to hear and see Jesus.

Luke 7 is pivotal to the characterization of John, for here one finally reads of an overt attempt at contact between John and Jesus. Word of Jesus' supernatural deeds is spreading through the countryside (7:17), and John's disciples relay the report back to their master (7:18). The Baptist dispatches two disciples who ask of Jesus, "Are you 'the one who is coming,' or shall we look for another?" The question is significant: John does not consider himself to be the Messiah, but he does not yet realize who Jesus is. Too, it is the *correct question to ask* given the report he has heard. John's ignorance of Jesus fully accords with what has happened in the story thus far. Since a recognition scene has not occurred and John was not privy (so far as we were told) to the Spirit's descent upon Jesus, the Baptist cannot be faulted for his lack of knowledge about Jesus. Furthermore, though he does not directly witness what Jesus says and does, John knows precisely the appropriate question to ask of one who preaches and performs such miracles. In other words, he is a paradigm of the "right" kind of Judaism—one that is expectant and open-minded, prepared to recognize and embrace this new agent of God's plan. The Pharisees and their disciples serve as convenient foils to John and his disciples, for they observe Jesus' ministry but fail to recognize him or even to ask the appropriate (identity) question (see Chapter 4).

Jesus gives John's disciples a demonstration of his power to heal and exorcise (7:21), and then sends them on their way with a command to tell their teacher what they have witnessed: the blind receive their sight, the lame walk, lepers are cleansed, the deaf hear, and the poor have good news preached to them (7:22). To the individual whose heart is prepared to recognize the Messiah, this is sufficient information indeed. But readers never learn whether John, ostensibly still in prison, receives this good news, much less how he responds to it. Once again, the audience experiences a lack of completion, a gap, and anticipates filling it with new information that may become available in the narrative. Those who prepare Israel's hearts (John the Baptist and his disciples) have yet to *demonstrate* their acceptance of "the one who is coming."

The scene shifts quickly. Jesus begins to address the crowds about John (7:24), and the reader finally learns what he thinks of him. According to Jesus, the Baptist is a prophet, yes, but more than a prophet. John is the *final* messenger, the one who, according to scripture (Mal 3:1), comes just before the advent of the Lord.[13] The reader can only surmise that Jesus believes John to be his forerunner, his precursor, the one who has prepared for his coming. And Jesus goes further, stating that John is the greatest "among those born of women" (7:28). This astounding accolade is immediately followed, however, by a qualifier: "but the least in the kingdom of God is greater than he." Before the reader can think through the implications of the first saying (Is John greater than Jesus?), the second clause renders such speculation meaningless.

Jesus' mission—to manifest the kingdom of God—is obviously of a higher order than John's. Yet the two are intimately and perpetually linked, as the narrator's commentary on Jesus' saying makes clear. The tax collectors, sinners (vs. 34), and others who had received John's baptism unto repentance "justified God" upon hearing Jesus' saying concerning John; but the Pharisees and lawyers rejected the purpose (*boule*) of God for themselves by not undergoing John's baptism (7:29-30). If one's heart has not been properly prepared through repentance and the bearing of spiritual fruit, then one cannot recognize God's salvation when it arrives. The following episode, that of the ministering woman, is meant to illustrate this lesson. Simon the Pharisee fails to perceive that Jesus is the promised one, but the sinful woman recognizes him immediately.[14] The reader surmises that this woman is one of the sinners who has experienced John's baptism of repentance for the forgiveness of sins. The remainder of the narrative is strewn with similar illustrative episodes wherein tax collectors and other marginalized people in Israel respond correctly to the Lord while Pharisees, scribes, lawyers, and priests do not. Without the work of John, who would recognize Jesus?

HEROD, JOHN, AND JESUS (LUKE 9 AND 23)

Herod the Tetrarch is the only secondary character with whom both John and Jesus interact. The reader thus looks to this ruler as a locus of *sygkrisis* between the two protagonists. That is, Herod serves to sharpen further the distinctions and commonalities that characterize them. John is off the scene when the Tetrarch begins to hear disturbing rumors about another, somewhat similar, person within his realm (Luke 9:7). Some are even claiming that this new charismatic is actually John come back from the dead! This inside view of Herod's anxious thoughts shocks readers, for it is the first they have heard of John's death. In Luke's story, readers learn little about the circumstances of John's demise. Herod's perturbed ruminations result in a short soliloquy which dismisses the notion that Jesus is John *redivivus*: "John I beheaded; who then is this about whom I hear such things?" (9:9) This is a carefully-worded focalizing question placed at a strategic point in the narrative.[15] It not only dissociates John from Jesus, but also crystallizes the issue at stake as Jesus prepares for his journey to Jerusalem: the true nature of Jesus' identity and ministry.

The issue resurfaces almost immediately in the question that Jesus poses to his disciples: "Who do the people say that I am?" (9:18b) Once again, the first option put forward is the Baptist. Peter, of course, squelches any notion that this might be true by confessing, "[You are] the Christ of God" (9:20). These are all examples of the text reinforcing the distinction that readers have already learned to make, that John and Jesus are distinct in God's plan.

Jesus endures further encounters with his ruler, and these trigger the process of comparison and contrast between John and Jesus. The similarities between the two are obvious, for both courageously confront the wicked Tetrarch. But the superiority of Jesus even on this score is firmly maintained. The audience *hears* about John condemning Herod, whereas the *autarkeia* (self-control) and *parresia* (boldness) of Jesus vis-à-vis the Tetrarch are fully dramatized (see 13:31-35 and 23:6-12). John is denied the conventional stage—the ruler's court—upon which to manifest his powers and voice his message. The idealizing forum is reserved for Jesus. Although Jesus does not speak (23:9), he is found innocent. John speaks (so we are told) and is beheaded. The Baptist plays a conventional role in a tragic "charismatic versus ruler" episode, but with Jesus the conventions are broken. Indeed, Jesus' demeanor before Herod puts him above the familiar scenario. This is no ordinary prophet or sage matching wit and will with an angry despot, but someone whose identity and destiny place him far beyond such mundane categories. There is no need to display wisdom, powers and courage. For Jesus, authentication and idealization will come not because he has conquered the fear of death, but because he defeats death itself.[16]

RETROSPECTIVES ON THE BAPTIST

Following the notice of his beheading (Luke 9:9) John is no longer a dramatized character in the narrative. He lives on, however, in the persons of his disciples and in frequent reminiscences by the followers of Jesus. These retrospectives are invariably positive, affirming John's ministry and its implications for both Jesus and the church. When, for example, one of the disciples asks Jesus to "teach us to pray, as John taught his disciples," Jesus obliges with the (Lukan version of the) Lord's prayer (11:1-4). Though it has been largely overlooked by critics, there is a paralleling of the two movements evidenced here that has strong implications for the reader's understanding of Paul's strange experiences with the "disciples" in Ephesus (see below).

Most of the retrospectives on John, however, serve to "fine tune" the reader's understanding of the Baptist's strategic role in the unfolding divine plan. Such recalibration is needed precisely because John represents the vital but extremely tricky dialectic of continuity and discontinuity between the eras in salvation history. John is like a sign that marks both the end of the old and the beginning of the new; but he is also the means by which old and new are integrally related. Readers require much guidance to understand such a complex role, and the retrospective commentary of various authoritative figures helps in this regard.

Perhaps the most controversial passage in all of Luke is the pronouncement by Jesus that "the law and the prophets were until [*mechri*] John; since then the good news of the kingdom of God is preached . . ." (16:16). Many critics have understood this as a simple either/or statement. Either the phase of law and prophets extended *through* John, so that he belongs only to that stage, or the law and prophets ran *up to* John, meaning that John belongs to the new age of the preaching of the kingdom. But the statement is ambiguous, not definitive, and has borne far too much weight in modern interpretive controversies (Minear 1980:122). The reader understands the verse in terms of what has come before, the characterization of John to this point. John does *not* preach the kingdom of God; and in this regard he is different from what came after him. But his baptism for repentance and his Spirit-inspired distillation of the law and the prophets were the distinctive catalyst that allowed the preaching of the kingdom to take root. In this sense he belongs to the new era. In short, the reader views John's locus as "both/and" in Jesus' retrospective on salvation-history.[17]

Jesus next refers to John during a confrontation with the chief priests and scribes in Jerusalem (Luke 20:4-6). He frustrates his antagonists by posing a theological question which they cannot answer without implicating themselves. He asks, "Was the baptism of John from heaven or from men?" Two lessons may be learned from this encounter: (1) Jesus' opponents do not believe that John's baptism was divinely sanctioned, but (2) the people (including Jesus) do. These lessons reinforce the idea that John's mission was something new, even revolutionary ("the people will stone us!"; vs 6), not simply a rehash of timeless ethical truths. The baptism of John *divides Israel* into those who can recognize God's kingdom when it appears (e.g., tax collectors and sinners) and those who cannot (Pharisees, priests, rich people, and scribes). For Luke's Jesus, then, John's ministry marks the beginning of a distinct new phase in the divine scheme, even as it epitomizes an earlier, still relevant, phase.

In Acts, authoritative believers reinforce the complex, two-sided view of John's role that readers of the Gospel have developed. When the apostles contemplate choosing Judas' replacement, their criterion is that the candidate be one who "accompanied us during all the time that the Lord Jesus went in and out among us, *beginning from the baptism of John* until the day when he was taken up from us" (Acts 1:21-22). Jesus' mission is deemed to begin with John's activity. And yet, in remarks made at Cornelius' house, Peter emphasizes the distinctiveness of Jesus' revelation.

> "You know the word [*logon*] which he [God] sent to Israel, preaching good news of peace through Jesus Christ . . ., the word [*rhema*] which was preached throughout all of Judea, beginning from Galilee *after* [*meta*] *the baptism preached by John* . . . ." (Acts 10:36-37)

From the Christian perspective in Acts, John was both the harbinger of Jesus' revelation and the last agent of the previous era of divine disclosure.

As it becomes increasingly clear that a majority of the Jews do not accept the message about Jesus, the pivotal role played by John in the Christian (re)construction of history is foregrounded once again. In his speech to the synagogue in Antioch of Pisidia, Paul highlights John's preparatory function in Israel.

> "Of this man's [David's] posterity God has brought to Israel a savior, Jesus, as he promised. Before his coming John preached a baptism of repentance to all the people of Israel. And as John was finishing his course, he said, 'What do you suppose that I am? I am not he. No, but after me one is coming, the sandals of whose feet I am not worthy to untie.' " (13:23-25)

According to Paul, some in Israel *do not recognize* (*agnoesantes*) Jesus, despite having the prophets read to them every Sabbath (13:27). The reader understands this as another explanation of Jesus' rejection by many Jews. It is based on a lack of recognition, which in turn is based on a refusal to hearken to the prophets, the epitome of whom was John. That is, John was the prophetic prism through which Israel was to perceive the Messiah. Those who rejected the proper lens also forfeited their chance to see and embrace God's salvation.

The link between John and what has followed is unmistakable. But the reader of Acts is also encouraged to distinguish John's ministry from that of the church, especially in terms of baptismal practice. Both Jesus and Peter maintain that "John baptized with water, but you [post-ascension believers] shall be baptized with the Holy Spirit" (Acts 1:5; 11:16). There can be no confusing of John's ministry with that of the church.

PAUL, APOLLOS, AND THE DISCIPLES OF JOHN IN EPHESUS (ACTS 18:24–19:7)

One unsettling matter concerning John continues to haunt readers well into Acts. Although some in Israel accept the baptism of John and so are able to recognize and respond correctly to God's revelation in Jesus, neither the Baptist nor his disciples are shown to follow suit. Will those who prepare Israel's hearts be allowed no satisfying scene in which they accept "the one who is to come?" There is a disquieting lack of closure to this story line, but things finally come together near the end of Paul's ministry in a section that focuses on the continuing problem of Jewish rejection of the gospel (see 18:5-6, 12). Although Paul's preaching in Asia and Greece has persuaded a small number of Jews, the majority reject it forcefully. One group of Jews, however, embraces the gospel message without hesitation. Apollos, an eloquent man well-versed in the scriptures, had been instructed in the "way of the Lord," and "taught accurately the things about Jesus" (Acts 18:24-25b). But, the reader is told, he is lacking in one way: he knows only the baptism of John! (18:25c) How can one teach accurately about Jesus, but be cognizant only of John's baptism? Are these not contradictory affirmations? At first reading they appear to be nothing less than inconsistent statements, so the reader is presented with a problem: how to "build consistency" in the face of this apparent tension.[18]

Given this somewhat confusing information, the reader surmises that Apollos is either one of the Baptist's disciples or another Israelite who has experienced John's baptism. That is, he is one of those Jews who is fully prepared for the Lord's advent. He may even have heard reports that gave him an inkling that Jesus was the Coming One. These are not outlandish speculations for the reader since the text has repeatedly presented John's message as part and parcel of Jesus' message. One could conceivably preach at least *part* of the message about Jesus, know *some* of "the Way of God," without possessing all of the salient information. Only after Priscilla and Aquila instruct him (18:26b) is Apollos said to "show by the scriptures that the Christ was Jesus" (18:28b).

The reader's speculations about Apollos are confirmed in the following episode, wherein Paul discovers twelve mysterious "disciples" at Ephesus:

> He said to them, "Did you receive the Holy Spirit when you became believers?" They replied, "No, we have not even heard that there is a Holy Spirit." Then he said, "Into what then were you baptized?" They answered, "Into John's baptism." Paul said, "John baptized with the baptism of repentance, telling the people to believe in the one who was coming after him, that is, in Jesus." On hearing this, they were baptized in the name of the Lord Jesus. When Paul laid his hands on them, the Holy Spirit came upon them, and they spoke in tongues and prophesied. (19:1-6)

Here at last is the closure that the reader has been seeking to the John the Baptist story. John's disciples are prepared indeed, for they immediately accept the good news about Jesus and are initiated into the community of the Holy Spirit. In essence, they skip directly from the era of "the law and the prophets" to that of the Spirit-filled church.

The rhetoric of these passages is unmistakable. In the midst of reading about the overwhelming rejection of the gospel by Jews in Asia and Greece, the reader is given a contrasting report of a group of properly-prepared Jews, that is, of Baptist Jews, who grasp the true significance of the gospel message and embrace it.

CONCLUSIONS

The reader of Luke-Acts constructs a consistent, compelling, and complex image of John the Baptist. From the birth narratives to the episodes involving Paul in Ephesus, John serves as a model of Israelite preparedness for the advent of the Lord. He is the litmus test of Jewish readiness. Those in Israel who accept his "baptism of repentance" and prophetic understanding of justice, and who look expectantly for the Lord, are able to recognize and respond correctly to Jesus and his message. Those who do not will not "see and hear" the salvation of God when it/he encounters them. John is thus an integral part of Luke's overall rhetoric of perception, a rhetoric designed to shape the reader's view and to settle some historical questions (e.g., Why did some Jews accept Jesus while many rejected him?). As we shall see in Chapter 4, Luke's Pharisees stand at the other pole of this paradigmatic spectrum: they observe much but perceive nothing, for they have not received John's baptism of repentance, and thus their hearts are not properly prepared.

As preparer of the way of the Lord, John is the second most important character in the narrative. He is fully sanctioned by both the Holy Spirit and the narrator. Furthermore, he acts as a transition figure in that he sums up the age of the law and the prophets, but also initiates the new age of the revelation of God's salvation. Nevertheless, he is carefully played off against Jesus, and in each case he is shown to be the lesser of the two. They stand to one another as a prepared Israel stands to the Spirit-filled church, that is, as those Jews ready to *become* the church. John's cultural roots in a pious, idyllic Judaism make him the perfect one to call Israel back to its (supposed) former purity. Linking John with Elijah—at least tangentially—helps to define his role as precursor of the Lord. So much weight is placed on the Baptist as preparer and forerunner, in fact, that the reader becomes very invested in him and wishes to see him and his disciples recognize Jesus. They are not shown to do so, at least not immediately, and the tension this creates helps to maintain reader interest in the matter until it is resolved much later, when Paul encounters the disciples of John in Ephesus.

4

OBSERVERS OBSERVED: THE PHARISEES AND THE RHETORIC OF PERCEPTION

INTRODUCTION[1]

Recent literary-critical research on Luke-Acts has yielded a certain consensus about the story's central conflict: the tension that drives the entire work is the repudiation of God's salvation (*to soterion tou theou*; see Luke 2:30-32; 3:6; Acts 28:28) by the majority of Jews. Time and again in this story, the chosen people refuse the divine redemption presaged in scripture, authenticated by the Holy Spirit, prepared for by John the Baptist, manifested in Jesus of Nazareth, and witnessed to by the apostles. In Norman Petersen's oft-repeated words, "*the rejection of God's agents by God's people in connection with God's sanctuaries (synagogues and temple) is the plot device by which the movement of the narrative as a whole is motivated*" (1978:83; Petersen's emphases).[2]

Increased appreciation of the importance of this conflictive theme, along with recent concern about anti-Semitic tendencies in Christian scripture, have sparked great interest in the portrayal of

Jews—and especially of Jewish leadership groups—in the Lukan writings. Most notable among recent publications on the issue are monographs by Brawley (1987) and Sanders (1987), and a collection of essays edited by Tyson (1988). Despite this flurry of critical activity, however, it cannot be said that our understanding of at least one of these Jewish groups—the Pharisees—has been notably enhanced. With few exceptions, recent studies of the Pharisees in Luke-Acts have done little more than reiterate and nuance the old notion that (1) Luke's Pharisees are a heterogeneous amalgamation of negative *and* positive traits (with the former appearing mostly in the Gospel, the latter in Acts), but that (2) we should weight the positive characterizations more heavily because they indicate editorial "upgrading" from the way the Pharisees are handled in Luke's sources.[3] Luke has a "soft spot in his heart" for this particular leadership group, or so the common wisdom holds. Below we shall examine this view and the arguments behind it in greater detail. At this juncture it suffices to observe that it is flawed because of the redaction critical assumptions undergirding it. As we have argued (in the Introduction), historical critical methods fragment the text, and thus prove unsuitable for analyzing larger narrative phenomena like character. The tendency to atomize Luke-Acts has largely blinded critics to the story's *linearity*, and so to the sequential (reading) dynamics that mold the Pharisees into a group character. This failure to address adequately the accumulation of character is shared by some recent literary analyses of Luke's Pharisees (e.g., Gowler 1989a; 1991).[4]

When a reader-response theory of characterization is applied to Luke-Acts, a very different image of the Pharisees appears. We shall argue that, when analyzed from the reading perspective, the Pharisees appear to be more completely and consistently *distanced* (negative) and more complex in terms of their narrative functions than biblical critics have heretofore realized. In this story the Pharisees are consistently-drawn as a group character which serves as a *paradigm of imperceptiveness*. Laden with irony, they continuously observe (*paratereo*) Jesus and other agents of God and yet utterly fail to recognize the significance of either the persons and events they see or the messages they hear. The Pharisees embody the pervasive Lukan theme of "seeing but not seeing/hearing but not hearing," the scriptural source of which is found at Isaiah 6:9. This theme (and the variations on it) is designed to ensure that the reader, who observes them observing, not just "see and hear" as they do, but truly "perceive and understand" (= read/listen receptively). We have already spelled out the basic elements of this rhetorical strategy (in Chapter 2). Below we shall explicate its function in more detail, especially with regard to its use in reinforcing the value-system of Luke-Acts. First, however, we must probe somewhat more deeply into Lukan scholarship's conventional approach to the Pharisees, for only then can we demonstrate how our understanding of them differs—and why.

THE PHARISEES AS BAD GUYS/GOOD GUYS: A CRITIQUE

Near the beginning of the movement to apply literary methods to New Testament narrative, Luke T. Johnson (1977:116-17, 197-98) sagaciously cautioned that the widespread notion of a (somewhat) favorable treatment of the Pharisees in Luke-Acts had by no means been proven and should not be assumed. Although he had not mounted a complete study of the subject, Johnson's literary analyses of key passages (especially the Gamaliel scene) convinced him that there were major problems with the conventional wisdom on the Pharisees in Luke's story. Hardly any recent critics, however, have felt it necessary to heed Johnson's warning. Most have simply incorporated the common understanding of Luke's Pharisees into their work. For example, in both his dissertation (1978:13) and a recent book (1987:84), Brawley firmly asserts that the Pharisees are highly respected by Luke and his community. They are conciliatory figures standing on "the fringe of Christianity" and spanning the gulf that divides Jewish and Gentile Christians from the non-Christian Jews of that day. Even Sanders (1985:141-61), whose study of Jews in Luke and Acts has elicited strong reactions due to its highly negative conclusions, regards the Pharisees as the bright spot in a rather bleak overall picture. He quotes with approval Baur's remark that Luke "almost . . . make[s] the

Pharisees into Christians" (146). The breadth of this sentiment among critics of Luke-Acts can scarcely be overstated.[5]

The argumentation in most of the recent studies of Pharisees in Luke-Acts is strikingly similar, and is perhaps exemplified in an oft-quoted article by Ziesler (1978-79). In fact, this summary argument runs like a computer virus through subsequent treatments of the Jewish leadership group. The conventional reasoning is the following: *One begins at the end of the story and works backwards toward the beginning.* At Acts 26:5, in the course of his apologia before Agrippa, Paul of Tarsus claims to have lived as a Pharisee (*ezesa pharisaios*). At an earlier trial, before the Sanhedrin, he even claims that he *is* a Pharisee, and that he is being tried for his belief in the resurrection of the dead. At this the Pharisees on the Council take his side against the Sadducees and thus block his possible conviction and condemnation (23:1-10). Earlier still, Paul defends himself to the people of Jerusalem by reminding them that he was educated in that city at the feet of Gamaliel (22:3), the prominent Pharisaic leader. And according to Luke's report of the so-called Jerusalem conference, the believing community there actually had Pharisees within its ranks (15:5). Gamaliel, a great Pharisaic leader, urges the Sanhedrin (5:34-42) not to hassle the early Christian movement: if it is not *ek theou*, he says, it will come to naught; if it is divinely-ordained then we cannot, indeed must not, fight against it. In all of these cases, therefore, the Pharisees (and/or Pharisaism) are depicted, if not positively, at least in a neutral light; and at points they even seem to advance the Christians' cause. All of this, furthermore, is quite distinct from Luke's pejorative depiction of other Jewish authorities.

Approaching the Gospel after developing this rather positive image of the Pharisees from Acts, one begins to perceive laudable traits of this group in the first half of the narrative also. For example, they are strikingly absent from the passion narrative in Luke, thus avoiding any direct stigma for the death of Jesus. And although they plot against Jesus, they do not conspire *to destroy* him (as in Mark). At one strategic point in Jesus' journey toward Jerusalem (13:31), some Pharisees even warn him that Herod is out to kill him. And finally, Luke alone among the evangelists reports that, on three separate occasions, Pharisees invited Jesus to be a dinner guest in their homes. So, although Luke retains some of the anti-Pharisaic polemic of his sources (e.g., the "woes" against Pharisees), his ultimate goal is actually to upgrade the Pharisees by editing those sources and by adding incidents that reflect well on the group.

Plausible though it may appear, the argument just sketched is fatally flawed. The most obvious weakness is its almost ludicrous disregard for the sequence or linearity of the story. As we have already argued (see Chapter 2), character accumulates according to a specific sequence within the narrative continuum. To alter that order of succession is thus to change the story and, *mutatis mutandi*, its characters. References to the Pharisees in Acts take on a very different complexion when read in their proper sequence, that is, after the reader develops an image of this sect from reading the Gospel of Luke.

The methodological problems in the standard treatment of the Pharisees run even deeper than the failure to recognize sequence, however. By definition, redaction criticism posits Luke-Acts as a bifurcated mix of two very different kinds of material: tradition and redaction. This assumption about the nature of the text leads inevitably to the valuing of some references over others, not for literary reasons (e.g., direct commentary by the omniscient voice of the narrator), but simply because some are deemed more "Lukan" than others. This is one reason references to Pharisees in Acts are weighted more heavily than are those in the Gospel of Luke (Acts must be more directly in tune with the editor's agenda because it is [or seems to be] less dependent on sources). Paul's claim to be a Pharisee in Acts 23, for example, is much nearer to the redactor's actual sentiment about the Pharisees than is Jesus' lengthy condemnation of them in Luke 11 (largely from Q).[6]

It should hardly surprise us, then, that at least two images of the Pharisees appear when Lukan critics don redaction critical lenses: (1) the redactor's own, and (2) others in sources that he failed to modify fully due to "the force of tradition." In this way, the story world is shattered, its shards each refracting the light differently. Consistency and continuity of characterization are lost, along with the broader narrative structures which guide the reader's construction and evaluation of character. Rhetorical patterns largely disappear. And irony, which rests on the complex development of relationships among characters and, especially, on the varying levels of knowledge among them, dissipates.

Driving the entire redaction critical enterprise, of course, is not the desire to understand characters in the story as it now stands, but rather, the quest to rediscover the editor's (and the "Lukan community's") opinion of a *real* group or groups within a narrowly defined social environment.[7] The pitfalls of this kind of procedure are well-documented, and strong warnings against the abuse of historical criticism have been voiced (see Johnson 1979) within the last two decades. And yet, Luke-Acts is still viewed as basically a window on a specific phase of the church's evolution. Distinctions between real world and story world are thus ignored; and critics pass with ease from one realm to the other, often by means of simplistic allegorization.[8] So Pharisees in this story must actually represent respected non-Christian Jewish leaders in contact with Luke's community (Brawley), or problematic Christian Jews (Sanders), or worthy non-Christian Jews (Sanders).

That these speculations are based on historical *a prioris* is evident. Brawley (1987:92), for example, brings a specific preunderstanding of Luke's social environment to his analysis: "Luke writes in an environment where the Pharisees hold a rather respectable position for both Luke and his readers. And this accounts for the positive way the Pharisees function in Luke-Acts." Even more to the point: the author "takes over the Pharisees in a historical, cultural, and religious context in which they demand admiration and assigns them a commensurate role" (105). Sanders (1985:161-62) argues along similar lines: the "unfriendly Pharisees" of Luke's story are actually "the traditionally Jewish Christians whom Luke does not like," while the "friendly Pharisees" of the story are the Jewish "linkage between Christianity and the ancestral Israelite religion." We need not dwell on the deficiencies of such allegorization. In essence, critics have rewritten the story according to an idealized and highly conjectural script about how the real author and his "community" related to Jews and Judaism at the time of writing. These hypothetical scenarios have largely determined how the textual evidence is arranged and assessed, and thus the present organization of the narrative is simply ignored.

Our short critique (even deconstruction) of the conventional wisdom concerning the Pharisees in Luke-Acts, and particularly of the methodology underlying it, is negative but quite instructive. Sometimes we need to clear the underbrush of deeply-rooted ideas before we can begin to plant something new in its place. We shall look at the Pharisees in the Lukan corpus as the reader did, that is, *by beginning at the beginning and moving toward the end.* This process will be unencumbered by the narrow and highly speculative reconstructions of "Luke's community" (and its relationships to various types of Jews and/or Judaism) that have fettered previous studies of the Pharisees. Before we begin, however, we shall review some of our observations about the rhetoric of characterization in Luke's narrative.

VALUE-FORMATION AND THE RHETORIC OF PERCEPTION

As we have already argued, Luke-Acts focuses its reader's attention on issues of recognition and response. The secondary characters are largely cast as various kinds of lookers and listeners who observe the divine will manifested in Jesus and the other protagonists of the story. And, of course, when reading about the secondary figures witnessing salvific persons, messages, and incidents, the reader witnesses them as well. The audience is thus sensitized to its own "seeing and hearing." In the ongoing interplay between the perspectives of the reader and intermediate characters, the reader is persuaded to reject some ways of seeing and hearing and to adopt others. A hierarchy of perspectives thus develops, with secondary characters representing various modes of recognition and response. They are graded (mostly by the narrator and other authoritative figures) on the basis of their ability to perceive and embrace God's salvation as revealed in Jesus and the other divinely-ordained messengers. This arrangement of carefully graded perspectives, in turn, is the means by which the narrative unfolds a "fundamental catalog of values" (Iser's term). In Luke-Acts, what determines whether a character will recognize and respond correctly is the quality of that figure's "heart," their moral orientation or proclivities. At its root, therefore, Luke's rhetoric of perception is designed to shape the character of the reader, to persuade the reader to adopt certain values in order to be an ideal witness of and to God's salvific initiative.

As the reader constructs the Pharisees, it soon becomes clear that they fail to perceive because their hearts are not right. In fact, many of the story's values find convenient contrasts in the spiritual shortcomings of the Pharisees. Once again, the audience is being urged (through narrative discourse) to shun these faulty attitudes, inclinations, and the flawed perspective they engender. When reduced and set into a formal sequence, the dialogue between text and audience about the Pharisees goes something like this:

> *Text*: The Pharisees see and hear the divine revelation in Jesus and others; indeed they observe it quite carefully.
> *Reader*: Do they respond appropriately?
> *Text*: No.
> *Reader*: Why not?
> *Text*: Because they consistently fail to recognize it.
> *Reader*: Why?
> *Text*: Because their hearts are not right.
> *Reader*: In what sense(s)?
> *Text*: They are unrepentant, prideful, lovers of money, complainers, unjust, scoffers, and so forth.

To summarize, the Pharisees become *caricatures of a morality to be avoided*, for it blinds and deafens one to God. If one is to read with insight, he or she must avoid the mindset (or heartset) displayed by Luke's Pharisees.

"NOT WITH OBSERVATION": THE PHARISEES AS PARADIGMS OF IMPERCEPTIVENESS

What follows is a sequential survey of how the reader builds the image of the Pharisees in Luke-Acts. Given the limitations of space, our treatment cannot be comprehensive. The purpose will be to illuminate the most significant factors influencing each stage of this group character's construction.

Enter the Pharisees: The Dynamics of Group Characterization (Luke 5:17-26)

The introduction of the Pharisees to Jesus and to the reader is auspicious indeed. They appear early in Jesus' ministry at one of his teaching and healing sessions (Luke 5:17-26). The narrator informs the reader that "there were Pharisees and teachers of the law sitting there, *who had come from every village of Galilee and Judea and Jerusalem*." Every community in the entire geographical arena of Jesus' ministry has at least one representative from the Pharisees present when Jesus both forgives a paralytic's sins and heals him![9]

This sweeping claim about the numbers of Pharisees at Jesus' healing of the paralytic should not be taken as simply "another case of Lukan hyperbole," as one commentator asserted on the way to dismissing its importance. Rather, it has implications for how the Pharisees are to be constructed as the reading progresses. In short, it reinforces the audience's natural proclivity to build a group character synecdochically. By introducing (at the beginning of their storyline) a representative group of Pharisees (from all over Palestine), and by presenting them as responding to Jesus *in concert*, the narrative encourages readers to continue to construe them consistently, homogeneously, collectively. Group traits will be imputed to every individual Pharisee. And, reciprocally, what a particular Pharisee is, does, and knows will be attributed to the entire group. When Jesus next encounters Pharisees, for instance, the reader will assume—unless informed otherwise—that they know about Jesus' forgiving/healing of the paralytic, even if the text does not specify that these particular Pharisees had been at that earlier incident. Consistency-building is a natural aspect of the reading process; here, at the introduction of the Pharisees, that tendency is encouraged by the narrator.

These initial reader-response insights already undermine the widespread notion that Luke portrays two very different groups of Pharisees. As evidence for that common notion, some scholars have pointed out that at points where Mark has "*the* Pharisees," Luke substitutes "*some* Pharisees" or "*a* Pharisee." The implication of these editorial additions is (supposedly) that Luke intends to distinguish thereby some (bad) Pharisees from the rest, and so to distance their pejorative traits from the group as a whole.[10] If one takes into account the dynamics of reading, however, this way of arguing loses its force. The reader's inclination to build the group consistently, as well as the reinforcement of that drive in this introductory passage, militate against readers making facile distinctions among Pharisees in Luke's story. The text would have to be much more explicit and emphatic in its differentiations for the audience to distinguish among the Pharisees in this manner.

At Luke 5:17 the Pharisees are linked with the "teachers of law" (*nomodidaskaloi*); and the juxtaposition of *them* as teachers and Jesus' teaching (*didaskon*) sets up the potential for contrast and comparison between the two. How will these teachers relate to *the* teacher (the one who already, as a child, taught the teachers in the temple)? This question in the reader's mind anticipates an upcoming debate between Jesus and the Pharisees.[11]

The initial reaction of the Pharisees to Jesus is not to believe but rather to "dialogue in their hearts" since he has forgiven a man's sins (5:21). They do not hesitate to classify his actions as a dire blasphemy. This negative response is emphasized through repetition: first, the narrator reports it, then he tells us that Jesus perceived their *dialogismous* (5:22), and finally, they are accused of doing it by Jesus (5:22). The reader will not miss the import of all this. According to Simeon's oracle in Luke 2:34-35, Jesus is set "for the fall and rise of many in Israel, and for a sign that is spoken against . . . that the thoughts (*dialogismoi*) out of many hearts may be revealed" (on the significance of this oracle see Tannehill 1986:40-44). Already the Pharisees are being tagged as some of those in Israel who do not understand Jesus and begin to oppose him in their hearts.

A glimmer of hope remains that the Pharisees will respond to the divine revelation correctly. Jesus maintains that his healing of the paralytic is carried out "in order that you may know that the Son of Man has authority on earth to forgive sins" (vs. 24). All those who observe the miracle (including Pharisees) are astounded and fearful and begin to glorify God, exclaiming, "Today we have seen strange things (*paradoxa*)" (vs. 26). Glorifying God is surely a positive reaction to Jesus' miracle, and many critics have seized on this as an early indicator that the Pharisees will be portrayed in a somewhat positive light throughout Luke-Acts. But the careful reader or hearer questions the nature of the response, because the narrative fails to inform us as to whether Jesus' audience truly understood the significance of the miracle as Jesus himself has explained it (i.e., as establishing his authority to forgive sins). Have these observers truly *perceived*, or have they merely seen? The audience will try to answer this question as the story continues.

Tax Collectors and Pharisees (Luke 5:27-32)

The Pharisees have been introduced, and the reader has begun to form a mental image of them. In the following episode, a group that will function as their opposite number or foil is introduced. Jesus asks Levi the tax collector to follow him. Levi's response is positive and immediate. He not only follows Jesus but prepares a large banquet for him. Other tax gatherers join in the feast as well. Then the Pharisees complain to Jesus' disciples about Jesus eating with "tax collectors and sinners."

Three aspects of this passage merit further attention. First, this is but the beginning of a long series of scenes in which the Pharisees are unfavorably contrasted with sinners/tax collectors. This juxtaposition reaches its climax in Luke 18 and 19, with the parable about the tax collector and the Pharisee praying together and the story of Zacchaeus, the chief tax collector (*architelones*) who so wishes to see Jesus. The reader processes this contrast in terms of the *reversal theme* established early on in the narrative: those of low estate will rise, and the proud and mighty will fall (1:51-3; 2:34). Once again, the purpose of all this is to contrast ways of responding to Jesus. The Pharisees, whom one expects to recognize and respond to Jesus correctly (because they know the law and the tradition), do not; the sinners and tax collectors, who should not be able to recognize or respond correctly, do. These two groups do not actually advance the plot of the story (Why are the Pharisees at Levi's house anyway?), but serve as opposing (and ironically reversed) paradigms of perception.

Second, the word describing the Pharisees' reaction to Jesus eating with sinners is *egoggyzon*. This striking word is a nuanced allusion to the murmuring of the people of Israel against God and Moses during the exodus and wilderness wanderings.

> And the Lord spoke to Moses and Aaron, saying, "How long [must I endure] this evil congregation? I have heard what they murmur (*goggyzousin*) against me, [even] the murmurings (*gogguysin*) of the sons of Israel, which they murmured (*egoggysan*) concerning you. Say to them, 'As I live,' says the Lord, 'just what you complained about, so shall I do to you. Your carcasses will fall in this wilderness; and all of you . . . from twenty years old and upward, all who murmured (*egoggysan*) against me shall not enter into the land . . . .' " (Numbers 14:26-30a LXX)

Already in the second episode involving the Pharisees, then, a parallel is drawn between the recalcitrant ancestral Israelites who habitually murmured against their Lord and their leaders (and thus were condemned to die outside of the promised land), and the Pharisees, who murmur against Jesus and thus become outsiders who fail to enter the "kingdom."[12]

Third, in Jesus' defense of his actions, he states that, "I have not come to call the righteous, but sinners to repentance" (5:32). This explanation perplexes the reader. Why does Jesus not simply condemn their self-righteous attitude? Jesus' answer seems to imply that the Pharisees should be grouped with the righteous, but the reader has already begun to construct them in a different way. The reader's puzzlement about these issues (What constitutes true righteousness? Who is righteous?) will be resolved, but not immediately.

Feasting and Fasting (Luke 5:33-39).

The Pharisees continue to badger Jesus, criticizing the fact that his disciples *feast* while their disciples and those of John the Baptist *fast and pray*. Jesus defends his disciples' actions, saying, in essence, that they are celebrating him and the new age he brings. The distinctions between the groups of disciples, then, are based on whether they belong to the old order or the new. For the reader, the apposition of John's disciples with the Pharisaic disciples is especially important. As we have seen, by this point the reader has constructed John quite fully; as the "prophet of the most high," he is the epitome of what is good and necessary and enduring from the previous epoch, but he is not a participant in the new era of the kingdom (see Chapter 3). The various groups mentioned here represent three different possibilities for the reader: (1) to misappropriate the tradition (the disciples of the Pharisees); (2) to adhere to the tradition correctly but fail to grasp the new because the opportunity to do so has not arisen (John's disciples); (3) to recognize and respond to Jesus in the proper way (Jesus' disciples/the sinners).

At this point in the story, then, several significant groups of secondary characters have emerged and begun to interact: Jesus' disciples, the Pharisees (and their disciples), the tax collectors and sinners, and the disciples of John. These group characters, along with the protagonists, comprise a developing web of human relationships within which the image of each group or individual will be constructed. The Pharisees have already begun to play the role of those who emphasize outward appearances and the letter of the law to the neglect of other values and spiritual insight.

The Grainfield Incident (Luke 6:1-5)

The reader has anticipated a confrontation between Jesus and the Pharisees over matters of religious law. It finally erupts when Jesus' disciples pick and eat grain on the Sabbath. The narrative shifts the focus quickly from legal argumentation to Jesus' identity and authority: "The Son of Man is lord of the Sabbath." To this the Pharisees give no response whatsoever, and their silence leaves a gap which the reader must try to fill with upcoming narrative data.

The Man With the Withered Hand (Luke 6:6-11)

This passage helps the audience to consolidate and reinforce several developing aspects of the Pharisees' image. It forcefully answers the question of whether or not the Pharisees accept

Jesus' claim of authority over the Sabbath (and thus over religious laws in general). The narrator tells us that the scribes and Pharisees stood by prepared to accuse Jesus of violating the Sabbath (6:7), and responded with fury (*anoias*; 6:11) when he did so by healing a man with a withered hand. They have clearly failed to recognize Jesus as Lord of the Sabbath, for they seek to submit him to it.

At verse 7, the scribes and Pharisees are said to "observe him [Jesus] closely." The verb *paratereo* (to scrutinize, to observe carefully) is quite unusual; and, as we shall see, it comes to be strongly associated with the Pharisees in this narrative. Already their actions have established the Pharisees in the reader's mind as the great observers of the story; since their first appearance they have been vigilant and curious, scrutinizing and critiquing all that Jesus and his disciples do and say. Now the narrator has tagged them with an idiosyncratic word denoting this penchant for observing.

The irony, of course, is that the observers fail to see. The problem has to do with their hearts. Once again, the reader finds that Jesus knew their *dialogismous* (6:8), or inner thoughts. This is clearly meant to summon a recollection of Simeon's oracle which predicted opposition to Jesus in Israel (see above). By this time in the reading process, the Pharisees are very firmly cast as the opponents of Jesus, and this characterization of them is strongly reinforced at the end of the scene by the narrator's ominous note that "they discussed what they might do with him."

The rhetorical function of the references to "dialoguing in the heart" is to deter suspicious or cynical reading. Characters sometimes perform cognitive actions that are meant to be emulated by the reader (Rabinowitz 1987:55); they may be *performative*, not just informative. When Mary (with whom readers identify strongly) "treasures" and "ponders all these things in her heart" (Luke 2:19 and 51), the reader is to respond similarly, that is, to value, remember, and reflect on the significance of what has transpired. But this rhetorical technique can also be used with characters or groups who have been *distanced* from the reader. When, for example, the Pharisees "dialogue in their hearts," the audience is being encouraged *not* to criticize, question (hostilely), or resist believing what they "see and hear" about Jesus.

This is a natural point for major retrospection. In two short chapters a barrage of data about the Pharisees has hit the reader. How has all this data been evaluated, sorted, and shaped into an image? The Pharisees are (or, consider themselves) authorities on Israel's law. But they disagree with Jesus' interpretation of the law, and (implicitly as well as explicitly) reject his claim to superior interpretive authority. Furthermore, although they are persistent and careful observers, they utterly fail to see in Jesus' person, proclamation, and activities the inauguration of "the acceptable year of the Lord" (Luke 4:19). In fact, they oppose him in their hearts (by dialoguing) and express their opposition by murmuring, an activity that links them with those in the exodus generation who grumbled. They are holdovers of the old, seemingly incapable of perceiving or participating in the new. Several lines still stand open: Are they righteous in some sense, as one of Jesus' remarks seemed to imply? Do they reject Jesus' authority to forgive sins? Indeed, do they, or will they, acknowledge Jesus as Son of Man?

"Are You the One Who Comes?" (Luke 7:24-35)

The next reference to the Pharisees consists of a pejorative comment by the narrator. From prison John has sent some disciples to ask Jesus if he is "the one who comes." The ignorance behind this question is fully consonant with the characterization of the Baptist thus far. He epitomizes the prophetic era; his message is necessary to prepare the hearts of the people to see and hear and believe the coming one. In this narrative, however, John does not specifically identify Jesus as Messiah. And, as we have shown (in Chapter 3), their ministries do not overlap. Rather than answering John's query directly, Jesus simply asks the messengers to report what they have *seen and heard*: the blind receive sight, the lame walk, the dead are raised, and the poor have the gospel preached to them. That is enough evidence for anyone whose heart has been prepared. The reader never learns of John's reaction to the news, but assumes a positive response.

Jesus then delivers a discourse on John's person and career. He was the designated forerunner who prepared the way. He was the greatest individual among those born of women. And yet, "he who is least in the kingdom of God is greater than he" (7:28). These words galvanize the crowd. The reliable narrator's interpretation of the crowd's response(s) is highly significant for the reader's construction of the Pharisees.

> And when they heard this, all the people and the tax collectors—having been baptized with the baptism of John—justified God. But the Pharisees and lawyers—not having been baptized by him (John)—rejected the purpose (*boulen*) of God for themselves. (7:29-30)

The Pharisees now clearly stand outside the will of God. But what does the baptism of John have to do with it? The reader will answer this question through retrospection, by remembering John's activities and message. He preached "a baptism of repentance for the forgiveness of sins" (3:3). His task was to ready the hearts of the people so that they would be able to "see the salvation of God" (3:6) when it appeared. The gist of John's message was that the fruit of repentance is true concern for the welfare of others, especially the less fortunate (see our discussion of this message in Chapter 3 above). The primary stumbling block to repentance is the abuse of privilege and power, that is, social injustice. Whether religious prejudice and elitism ("We are descendants of Abraham"; 3:7-11), economic inequities (3:12-13), and/or socio-political tyranny lie behind these abuses, they must all be done away with before genuine repentance can take place. Like the prophets, John defines true righteousness in terms of social justice rather than in terms of religious affiliation, social status, or wealth. That all these vignettes illustrating John's teaching involve money or possessions is hardly coincidental, for throughout the narrative, characters' attitudes toward possessions determine their ability to recognize and respond to "the salvation of God."

The reader assumes that there is a logical connection between the Pharisees' rejection of God's will (*boulen*) and their failure (or refusal) to undergo John's baptism. That is, the reader will now attribute the anti-values of John's message to the Pharisees: they are unrepentant, and their lack of repentance has to do with religious elitism (which they have already exhibited in relation to the tax collectors) and arrogance, injustice vis-à-vis the economically or socially disadvantaged, and an unhealthy focus on material possessions and money. Each of these pejorative traits will, in fact, be attributed more directly to the Pharisees as the story unfolds.

Once again, the character groups interacting with Jesus here represent the three fundamental types of responders which we have identified. The disciples of John (and John himself) are those who have repented, whose hearts are prepared for the salvation of God, but who have not yet had the opportunity to see or hear it.[13] The tax collectors and sinners represent those who have repented and have seen and responded appropriately to God's will. The Pharisees and lawyers are those who, because they lack certain spiritual or moral qualities, have not repented and therefore fail to see and respond correctly when confronted with God's will as manifested in Jesus.

The Pharisee and the Sinful Woman Revisited (Luke 7:36-50)

In Chapter 1 we analyzed aspects of this episode in order to illustrate gap-filling and certain functions of the extratext. At that point we concentrated largely on the characterization of the woman and her relationship with Jesus. Here we shall examine more fully the portrayal of the Pharisees in this familiar episode. As we have already argued at length, the audience draws on materials from the preceding incident (Jesus' speech about John) to process the present, gap-ridden, scene. In Simon the Pharisee the reader sees a representative of all the Pharisees who (the narrator told us) rejected God's will for themselves by not experiencing John's baptism (7:30). The sinful woman stands for their opposites, the sinners who did undergo the baptism of repentance (7:29).

So the reader is already primed to process this narrative in terms of contrast between (unrepentant) Pharisees and (repentant) sinners. The reversal of status and fortunes foreshadowed in the infancy narratives is occurring. Viewed from this perspective, the rest of the incident is highly ironic. When Jesus' Pharisaic host witnesses the woman's ministrations to Jesus, he says to himself, "If this man were a prophet, he would know who and what sort of woman this is who is touching him, for she is a sinner." Jesus interrupts Simon's "dialogue in the heart" (actually an internal monologue) to turn the tables on him. The fact that Jesus knows what Simon is thinking shows that Jesus is indeed a prophet; and what Jesus says implicates the Pharisee rather than the woman as the *hamartolos*. Jesus *does* indeed recognize a sinner in his presence, but it is *not* the woman.

Jesus proceeds to draw out the contrast between the woman and the Pharisee:

> Simon gave Jesus no water for his feet/
> the woman used her very tears to wash them.
> Simon gave Jesus no kiss of greeting/
> the woman repeatedly kissed his feet.
> Simon did not anoint his head with oil/
> the woman anointed his feet with costly ointment.

The woman's highly positive response is possible because she has repented and has the concomitant ability to perceive the true identity and significance of Jesus. Simon's grudging treatment of Jesus indicates a spiritual blindness caused by religious bigotry (see, e.g., his evaluation of the woman) and a lack of repentance. Jesus' remark, "He who is forgiven little, loves little," could be taken two ways: either Simon does not need (much) forgiveness, or he has been forgiven little because he has not repented. The reader inclines toward the latter meaning; Simon, given his self-righteousness, could well be understood as opting for the former. With the aid of irony-laden episodes like this, the reader begins to resolve the issue raised earlier as to who is really righteous and who but appears (or claims) to be righteous.

Jesus' criticism of Simon and praise for the woman concretize the contrast between Pharisees and sinners that has been evolving. The reader is thus encouraged to continue contrasting these groups throughout the narrative. In what remains of this episode, the breakdown (or defamiliarization, as we saw in

Chapter 1) of the symposium convention severely undercuts those treatments which see in Jesus' meals with Pharisees a positive depiction of the group. The host in most symposia engages in a dialogue with the honored sage; Simon, however, does not engage in such a dialogue and is allowed no chance to rebut Jesus' serious charges against him. The strong implication is that he cannot rebut them. (The rhetorical ploy of silencing Jesus' opponents appears elsewhere as well.) The reader is thus given nothing to place on the positive side of the ledger for the Pharisees. Here, as well as in Luke 11:37-54 and 14:1-24, the symposia serve only as stages for Jesus to criticize severely his Pharisaic hosts and fellow guests. They in no way portray the Pharisees as the benefactors, colleagues, or even worthy debating opponents of Jesus.[14]

"Like Unmarked Graves": Jesus' Denunciation of the Pharisees (Luke 11:37-54)

This second symposium with Pharisees becomes an occasion for Jesus to barrage the Pharisees and lawyers with a list of damning accusations concerning the state of their "hearts." Once again, a Pharisee plays the host, and Jesus plays the invited sage. This time, the *fait divers* is Jesus' failure ceremoniously to wash his hands before reclining to eat. The Pharisee is astonished by this omission. Jesus then severely castigates the Pharisees *in general* for being preoccupied with external cleanliness while neglecting internal purity.

Because Jesus (the fully reliable protagonist) utters them, and because it has already been intimated that the Pharisees are more concerned with external than internal purity (see Luke 5:27-32; 7:36-50), these related but more specific charges (woes) are quickly added by the reader to the increasingly negative image of this leadership group. They are full of extortion (*harpages*) and wickedness (*ponerias*; vs. 39). They are foolish (*aphrones*; vs. 40), for they place a higher value on religious exercise (like almsgiving) than on heartfelt morality. They tithe the smallest of herbs, yet neglect fundamental moral values like justice and the love of God (*agape tou theou*; vs. 42). Furthermore, what they truly crave is not real righteousness but the religious limelight (the best seats in the synagogues and honorific salutations in the marketplace; vs. 43). Like unmarked graves, they sport a spotless surface masking filth inside (vs. 44).

The only response to Jesus' harangue is an irony-laden whine by one of the lawyers: "Teacher, in saying this you reproach us also." This self-indictment simply reinforces the links between Pharisees and lawyers that have been forged since the two groups first appeared. The reader therefore assumes that Jesus' ensuing criticisms of the lawyers also reflect poorly on the Pharisees—guilt by association, so to speak. The essential charge delivered here is that they hinder, rather than assist, others' attempts to please God. Jesus also maintains that they approve of the killing of prophets by their ancestors, a thinly veiled allusion to their opposition to Jesus' own prophetic message of justice and love of God as opposed to legal casuistry. The latter charge leads nicely into the narrator's ominous note: the scribes and Pharisees begin to *press* Jesus in hopes of forcing him to say something that will get him in trouble (11:53-54).

Because the characterization here is rather straightforward, a few additional interpretive notes will suffice. First, there is a great deal of irony in the Pharisaic host's (implied) criticism of Jesus for not washing (vs. 38). The reader cannot help but observe that the one who criticizes Jesus' failure to "baptize" himself (*ebaptisthe*; vs. 38) before the supper has not himself been baptized with the baptism that really counts, that unto repentance (7:30)! Second, the rhetoric of contrast between what is outside and what is inside epitomizes the problem with the Pharisees in Luke-Acts. Their unhealthy preoccupation with "how things look" is exactly the cause of their inability to *see* things for what they actually are. Third, it does not take a social scientist to recognize that there is much in Jesus' condemnation of the Pharisees that has to do not with moral abstractions, but rather with concrete economic and social ills. According to Luke's Jesus, the Pharisees and the lawyers take advantage of others. They extort (or steal), neglect justice, and set aside the love of God. Such abuse of possessions, power, and position virtually defines the narrative's perspective on evil.[15] And fourth, Jesus indicts *all* the Pharisees, not just some. Once again, the reader is strongly encouraged to build this group as a single character.

The Hypocrisy of the Pharisees (Luke 12:1-3)

When Jesus warns his disciples to "beware the leaven of the Pharisees, which is hypocrisy," the audience processes his words on the basis of Jesus' lengthy denunciation in the previous scene. In light of that critique, the Pharisees' hypocrisy consists of a certain external piety which masks internal wickedness. That this is what Jesus means by his enigmatic epithet is further supported by the following verses (2-3), which refer to the inevitability of "hidden things" being revealed. Simeon's oracle about "thoughts out of many hearts being revealed" (Luke 2:35) is applicable once again.

The Pharisees, Jesus, and Herod (Luke 13:31-35)

This significant passage lies at the center of Luke's famous travel narrative. The essential thing Jesus teaches his disciples (and the reader) during this journey to Jerusalem is that he must suffer and die as part of the divine plan. At Luke 13:31-32, some Pharisees approach Jesus and advise him, "Go away from here, for Herod wishes to kill you." The warning is ironic, for the reader knows that Jesus is well aware (and accepting) of where, when and why he will die. The Pharisees' report is useless, therefore, and betrays a misunderstanding of Jesus and his mission. As Tannehill (1986:153) has seen, Jesus' response plays on this irony. Yes, he must go on, but not to avoid being killed; rather, he must depart *in order to be killed*! The time, place and means of his death are part of a divine plan. Thus, his fate cannot be determined by the whims of a petty tyrant like Herod (13:32-33).[16]

Of course, one could still see the warning as positive, even if given in ignorance. The text does not specifically identify the Pharisees' motivation in warning Jesus, or give any indication of whether their report about Herod is factual. These important gaps must be filled by the reader using less direct data. Based on the characterization of Herod and the Pharisees up to this point, the reader is quite confident that: (1) the report about Herod's wish to kill Jesus is accurate (they are probably not *lying*, for Herod has proven quite capable of killing the Lord's prophets), but (2) the Pharisees' motives for delivering it are not commendable. Why are they warning Jesus, when it is clear that they oppose him and have begun to plot against him as well (11:53-54)? Are they using Herod's threat in hopes of suppressing Jesus' prophetic voice, or of hurrying his departure from their territory, or of frightening his followers? What does not seem likely (though it remains a possibility) is that the Pharisees acted out of benevolence; there has been no preparation for such a trait in the characterization of the Pharisees to this point.[17]

This passage has long been a linchpin of the widely-accepted argument that the Pharisees are "upgraded" in Luke-Acts. Viewed from a reader-oriented perspective, however, it can hardly be categorized as solid evidence for such an argument.

Sabbath Banquet at the House of a Leading Pharisee (Luke 14:1-24)

In this passage, the reader once again engages the symposium convention, but this time the meal is hosted by a "*leader* of the Pharisees" and occurs on the Sabbath (a loaded situation, to say the least). The focalizing event is Jesus' healing of a victim of dropsy. Once again, the narrator draws attention to the fact that the Pharisees are "observing carefully" (*parateroumenoi*; 14:1). And, as before, they are unable to reply to Jesus' defense of his actions. In all its appearances in Luke, therefore, the symposium is truncated so that Jesus' fellow-diners are given no voice. The rhetorical effect of modifying the conventional scene in this way is to elevate the status of Jesus and to lower that of his fellow diners, the Pharisees. Jesus is not simply the revered sage among lesser philosophers; rather, he is an absolute authority. Any and all counter-arguments from Pharisees are not worthy of expression and so are not voiced.

The reader processes the next three incidents in this rather lengthy episode in terms of Mary's oracle of reversal:

He has done mighty deeds with his arm;
He has scattered *the proud*
    in the thoughts of their heart.
He has brought down rulers from their thrones,
And has *exalted the humble.*
He has *filled the hungry* with good things;
And *sent away the rich empty-handed.* (Luke 1:51-53)

In Luke 14:7-11, Jesus chides the invited guests for picking out places of honor at the table. Although not informed about who these other guests are, the reader identifies them as the lawyers and Pharisees to whom Jesus spoke in verse 3. According to Jesus, their pride and preoccupation with status will be their downfall, because "everyone who exalts himself will be humbled, and he who humbles himself will be exalted" (14:11).

Then Jesus proceeds to excoriate his host, the leader of the Pharisees, concerning his guest-list and the motivation behind it (14:12-14). The strong implication is that the Pharisee has invited friends, relatives, and wealthy neighbors in hopes of reciprocation. If he were to invite the blind, crippled, lame, and poor, there would be no doubt about his intentions, for such people could not possibly repay him. Once again, readers see strong evidence that the Pharisees' "heart problems" have to do largely with unhealthy attitudes toward social status and wealth. Indeed, Jesus' criticisms here presage a much fuller, more direct attack on such attitudes among the Pharisees.

In the final incident of the episode, a guest makes a remark revealing his failure to recognize in Jesus the presence of God's kingdom, God's rule: "Blessed is everyone who *shall* eat bread in the kingdom of God" (14:15). Jesus responds with the parable of the great supper, in which those who were initially invited turn down the invitation, and the poor, crippled, lame, and blind are brought in. The master commands that the house be filled, so that "none of those who were [originally] invited" might participate (14:23-24). The message is clear: the banquet is taking place *now* rather than in the future. The invitation has been given, but has been ignored by those who were expected to take part. Now others—the marginalized, oppressed and poor—are participating. In light of Jesus' reprimand of his host for failing to invite these kinds of persons, and in light of Mary's oracle predicting just such an inversion of rich and poor, the reader cannot help but apply this lesson of reversal to Jesus' fellow diners, the lawyers and Pharisees. This Pharisaic supper is the opposite of the messianic banquet, and invitations to the latter are already offered in the words and deeds of Jesus. Only the sinners seem to be accepting.

This is the final scene in which Jesus eats with Pharisees. At this point it is important to make one more observation about the common argument that Jesus' dining with Pharisees shows them in a favorable light. At 13:23, when Jesus is asked if only a few will be saved, he replies affirmatively. Few will be permitted to enter the door. The Lord will turn many away, despite their pleas for recognition:

> "*We ate and drank in your presence*, and you taught in our streets." And he will say, "I tell you, I do not know where you are from; depart from me, all you evil-doers." (13:26-27)

Social interaction with Jesus does not insure inclusion in the kingdom. Those who do not recognize the Lord in the present—despite having dined with him—will not be recognized by the Lord in the future when they realize their mistake and *do* wish to join the messianic banquet. The irony of Jesus sitting at banquet with persons who ignore the invitation to *the* (eschatological) banquet is powerful indeed. In light of this potent rhetoric of irony, it is hard to imagine a reader admiring the Pharisees simply because they "eat and drink" with Jesus.[18]

The Sheep, the Coin, and the Son (Luke 15:1-32)

This well-known chapter consists of a brief introduction and three parables about losing and regaining precious things. In the introduction (15:1-2) the narrator identifies two familiar groups of people listening to Jesus: (1) tax collectors and sinners, and (2) Pharisees and scribes. Upset because Jesus receives and dines with sinners, the latter group murmurs (*diegoggyzon*). Once again, this intertextual allusion brings to mind the negative imagery of those stiff-necked Hebrews who grumbled about

Moses and Yahweh in the wilderness (see above). Jesus' parables are responses to this murmuring and the attitudes behind it. By implication, then, Jesus' words speak to the situation at hand; his simple figurative stories will—in the reader's mind—refer to himself, the sinners and tax gatherers, and the Pharisees and scribes. And because the latter are identified as Jesus' primary audience (Jesus tells the parables because of their complaints), the reader will ponder how they might process these pointed stories. The reader is listening to Pharisees listen to stories about themselves.

As noted, all three parables deal with the loss and eventual recovery of something—or someone—precious. Jesus' audience will allegorize the parables in terms of Jesus/God (the loser and also the finder or receiver), tax collectors and sinners (the thing or person lost), and Pharisees/scribes (what is *not* lost).[19]

The first two parables establish the ideal that God rejoices over the repentance of sinners. Jesus concludes his parable about lost sheep with ". . . there will be more joy in heaven over one sinner who repents than over ninety-nine *righteous* people needing *no repentance*." Jesus (= shepherd) has found the sinners (=sheep) and welcomed them back into the fold. But who are "the righteous who need no repentance?" Here the reader experiences a degree of cognitive dissonance. The Pharisees and scribes in the crowd will probably see themselves as belonging in this category, but reader construction of these leadership groups to this point in the tale does not support their being deemed righteous. Jesus himself even asserts that they failed to repent when they should have. At this point, the reader differentiates his or her perspective from that of the Pharisees and scribes. There are two factors relieving the reader's interpretive tension. First, Jesus has not asserted that the Pharisees are righteous. The parables he tells can be applied only indirectly, and he never explicitly links Pharisees with the ninety-nine sheep. Second, the reader has already been made aware of the distinctions between the Pharisees' *self*-righteousness and *real* righteousness. Luke's Jesus has played off the self-delusion of the Pharisees on this score before. But the issue lingers: why does Jesus tell these stories that seem to encourage

Pharisees to believe that they are indeed the "righteous ones?"

The final parable, that of the loving father, reiterates the pattern of loss and recovery developed in the first two. Here the Pharisees in Jesus' audience are identified with the obedient but unforgiving older son who resents his father's (= God's) exuberant reacceptance of the errant younger son (= sinners). As Donahue (1988:151-62) has seen, the sons have a distorted view of sonship; both misconstrue their relationship to their father, thereby alienating themselves from him and from each other. Both view themselves as *servants* or *slaves*, as those whose worth is dependent on their productivity. The father, however, regards them as *sons*. They are of intrinsic worth to him. He loves them unconditionally (without regard to their behavior) and equally. The younger son is willing to accept the father's construal of the relationship (father/son, not master/slave) and so reconciles with him. In the final scene, the father entreats his older son to do the same, but the parable ends before we learn of his response. The ultimate responsibility for familial reconciliation rests with the older brother. In this case, the allegory is not troublesome. The Pharisees observe many laws but are self-righteous, "neglect the love of God," fail to recognize the repentant tax collectors and sinners as siblings and, indeed, reject them. Under such conditions, a reconciliation in the family of God is impossible.

In retrospect, the reader recognizes that Jesus has used the Pharisees' self-righteousness to entrap them with the final scene of this last parable. That is, the reader perceives the Pharisees as having strongly (but wrongly) identified themselves with those "righteous ones who need no repentance" in the initial stories. In the third parable, therefore, they would readily identify with the older brother. With the role reversal at the end (younger son reconciled, but older son alienating himself from both father and brother), however, the Pharisees are forced to judge themselves.

The Pharisees as Lovers of Money (16:14-16)

In chapter 16, the reader's attention is focused on wealth and its relation to spiritual health. Jesus tells a few important parables to the effect that one cannot simultaneously serve "God and Mammon" (16:13b). The Pharisees' response and the narrator's descriptions of them are highly significant:

> Now the Pharisees, who were *lovers of money* (*philargyroi*), were listening to all these things, and they were ridiculing (*exemykterizon*) him. And he said to them, "You are those who justify (*dikaiountes*) yourselves before men, but God knows your hearts; for that which is valued highly among men is detestable (*bdelygma*) in the sight of God." (16:14-15)

We need not dwell on the effect of the narrator's claim that the Pharisees are "lovers of money." In Luke's story world, the love of money really is the root of all evil. It is a prime cause of spiritual blindness and failure to respond correctly to divine revelation.[20] The blunt criticism voiced here by the narrator is but the capstone of a long-developing dimension of the Pharisees' image. Various information has accumulated to the effect that the Pharisees have attitudinal deficiencies when it comes to money or material possessions. From Simon's failure to provide Jesus with the niceties due a guest, to Jesus' accusation that the Pharisees extort money and give alms for the wrong reasons, to the harangue about inviting only rich guests to dinner, the narrative has been preparing its readers for just such a judgment on this leadership group.

Three other bits of data from this passage also contribute to the increasingly negative image of the Pharisees. First, they are said to ridicule (*exemykterizon*) Jesus. Any facade of respect for Jesus that they might have displayed before (calling him teacher, for example) is here thrust aside. Second, Jesus accuses them of justifying themselves in the sight of men. Here the protagonist voices what the reader has been suspecting all along, namely that the righteousness of the Pharisees is not really righteousness at all. They may appear pure to humans, but God is aware that their hearts are impure (16:15). And third, the values of the Pharisees may be *exalted* by humans, but they are detestable to the divine. The Pharisees thus serve as another example of exalted ones being demoted in the great reversal that occurs with the advent of the kingdom of God.

The Kingdom of God Comes Not With Observation (Luke 17:20-21)

The next appearance of the Pharisees is highly ironic:

> When asked by the Pharisees when the kingdom of God would come, he [Jesus] answered, "The kingdom of God does not come with observation (*meta paratereseos*), nor will they exclaim, 'Look, here it is,' or 'There!' For, in fact, the kingdom of God is within your ken [*entos hymon*]." (17:20-21)

This passage has long been considered a Gordian knot for the Lukan interpreter. Part of the difficulty here has been caused by the usual form-critical practice of paying little attention to the narrative setting (this is the husk—the kernel is the saying).[21] The fact that the *Pharisees* ask the question, however, must not be disregarded by the critic, for this information provides the clues by which the reader unravels Jesus' enigmatic saying. The question itself is ironic on the surface, since the Pharisees have been observing the advent of the kingdom for some time now in the deeds and words of Jesus. In fact, Jesus has stated unequivocally, "If by the finger of God I cast out demons, then *the kingdom of God has come* (*ephthasen*) *upon you*" (11:20).[22]

In light of this and of the reader's image of the Pharisees up to this point, the first clause of Jesus' reply is simple and should be translated quite literally: "The kingdom of God comes not with observation." Because this is confusing when not understood in a broader context, many modern translators have rendered it, "The kingdom of God does not come *with signs to be observed*." Besides being redundant—signs are, by definition, to be observed—this translation shifts the focus of the saying from *the activity of observation* to (purported) objects of observation, objects never denoted by the text. Jesus' pronouncement is not a condemnation of signs or of the value of signs or even of looking for signs. The kingdom *does* come with signs; the problem is that many people cannot recognize them! The saying is not about signs, but about spiritual perception, the ability truly to perceive the sovereign activity of God in the world.

The word *paratereseos* ("observation") is especially significant in eliciting the irony of this encounter between Jesus and the Pharisees. This rather rare word (in its verbal form) has already been associated in the audience's mind with the Pharisees. They have proven to be the great scrutinizers of Jesus and everything connected with his ministry. There is thus no need—or warrant—for reading into the word *paratereseos* technical meanings such as "looking for signs of the eschaton during Passover." The correct frame of reference for understanding this saying is the narrative itself. Jesus, the narrator, and the reader all realize that the Pharisees have been observing Jesus, and he tells them candidly that the kingdom does not come (i.e., they will not perceive or experience it) via such observations. The Pharisees are living proof that one can observe carefully and yet fail to perceive, for they scrutinize but never recognize. The reader uses the ironic sense of the opening clause to unpack the meaning of the enigmatic final sentence also: "For behold, the kingdom of God is *entos hymon.*" The work so far does not support the understanding that the kingdom is immanent to the hearts of the Pharisees (or to the hearts of anyone for that matter). Most critics have thus chosen to translate *entos* as among. Though this is preferable to the former option—in preserving the ironic sense of the passage ("The kingdom is right here among you, but, despite looking very hard, you do not see it")—it remains quite difficult to establish a lexical precedent for such a translation of *entos* (Liddell-Scott even fails to include "among" in the semantic options for the term). The expected rendering of "among you" would be *en meso hymon* rather than *entos hymon.*

Given the characterization of the Pharisees so far, we ought to translate *entos* as "within" in this verse. One of the common usages of this word was to express location or position within a particular range, e.g., *within* twenty stadia, *within* the province, and so forth. In this case, the meaning of *entos hymon* would be "within your range." And, based on the narrative context, the reader understands this to be a range of perception. Or, to use an old Scottish term, "the kingdom of God is within your ken." This rendering is preferable to "the kingdom of God is among you" not only because it retains the more literal "within" for *entos*, but more importantly, because it maintains a semantic connection with the term *paratereseos* in verse 20 and indeed with the entire theme of spiritual perception as developed in the gospel to this point. In other words, it focuses the reader's attention not just on the presence of the kingdom, but also on the Pharisees' inability to recognize it.[23]

The Pharisee and the Tax Collector at Prayer (Luke 18:9-14)

This striking parable caps a number of developing dimensions of the Pharisees. Pharisees and tax collectors are now well-known categories for the audience, and they have been contrasted in the narrative repeatedly since chapter 5. At this point, the contrast is sharpened and voiced with authority by both the narrator and Jesus. The narrator readies the reader for the parable by observing that it was told "to certain ones who trusted in themselves that they were righteous and despised others." And, of course, the praying Pharisee of the parable exhibits precisely these qualities, while the tax collector is humble, self-deprecating, and repentant. The "body language" of these two is indicative of their hearts: the Pharisee stands proudly praying to himself, but the tax collector stands some distance away, averts his eyes, and beats his breast.

For some time now the reader has surmised that the Pharisees are self-delusional. On several occasions Jesus has played off their apparent misperception of themselves. They are the elitists of the story, and the fact that they consistently manifest an air of superiority leads the reader to believe that they genuinely do understand themselves as righteous—despite all contrary evidence. Jesus' parable about the Pharisee and the tax collector at prayer reinforces this notion and uses it to ironic effect. The Pharisee thanks God that he is not like other men: extortioners (*harpages*), the unjust (*adikoi*), adulterers (*moichoi*; 18:11). But the reader knows that the Pharisees *are* precisely *harpages* and neglectors of justice, for Jesus has already condemned them as such (see 11:39, 42)! And when the Pharisee gives thanks for not being like "this tax collector," another layer of irony is added. Although he has spoken the truth, its implications for the reader are the reverse of his intentions: he is indeed unlike his fellow supplicant, but in a negative rather than positive way, for he fails to pray with a contrite heart. This ironic self-indictment calls to mind Simon the Pharisee's criticism that Jesus did not realize that a sinner was in his presence. (Jesus did indeed recognize a sinner, but it is Simon himself, rather than the ministering woman; 7:39-47.)

Jesus' conclusion points up the lesson. The tax collector is justified by God; the Pharisee is justified by himself but not by God. Those who exalt themselves will be humbled; those who humble themselves will be exalted. The Pharisees are now clearly cast as paradigms of "the proud in the thoughts of their heart," one of the categories Mary referred to in her oracle of reversal.

Pharisees at the Triumphal Entry (Luke 19:39)

The final reference to the Pharisees in Luke occurs as Jesus enters Jerusalem to the messianic cheers of "the whole multitude of the disciples." At this the Pharisees ask Jesus to rebuke his disciples. The audience does not realize the full significance of this incident until a few verses later (19:44) when Jesus laments Jerusalem's future destruction because it "*did not recognize the time of* [its] *visitation*." The Pharisees who observe—but do not recognize—Jesus as he enters the city embody Jerusalem's failure to recognize its king and its *kairos*.

By this point in the reading process, the reader of Luke has been thoroughly distanced from the Pharisees. They are models of the "seeing but not seeing/hearing but not hearing" theme based on Isaiah's prophecy. Although highly observant, they continually fail to perceive the true significance of what they see and hear. The problem is not with their outward appearances, but with their hearts. Like unmarked graves, they look perfectly innocent on the outside, but inside they are full of filth. Superficial and vain, they are preoccupied with externals, with how things look, to the total neglect of internal, attitudinal righteousness. The list of their deficiencies of the heart is a paradigm of the (anti)values forged by the narrative (pride, self-righteousness, love of money, hypocrisy, injustice, fraud, murmuring, and so forth). In summary, the reader leaves the first half of Luke's narrative with a well-formed and heavily reinforced pejorative image of this leadership group.

THE PHARISEES IN ACTS: THE SIGNIFICANCE OF SEQUENCE

In Lukan studies, conventional wisdom has it that references to Pharisees in Acts are quite positive, or, at worst, ambiguous. In any case, one does not find in this second volume of the Lukan corpus the vituperative criticisms and pejorative caricaturing of Pharisees that appear in the Gospel. Indeed, when evaluated apart from their locations in the narrative flow, these references seem to support the argument that there is a positive dimension to the characterization of Pharisees in Luke-Acts. Our contention in the present chapter is, of course, precisely that the critic must not isolate the Pharisees in Acts from the Pharisees in Luke. Much to the contrary, the image of the Pharisees that the audience builds in Luke strongly affects how they are judged in Acts; therefore, anyone concerned with how the text was heard or read must account for the dynamics of narrative sequence, narrative flow.[24] If one approaches the Pharisees in Acts not with a *tabula rasa*, but with the full-blown and heavily-reinforced image of the group built in reading Luke, the salient Acts passages take on a highly ironical tint that adds nothing positive to the group's character. In fact, what one reads in Acts merely nuances and intensifies some of the negative traits that have already been attributed to Pharisees in the Gospel.

Gamaliel and the Council (Acts 5:34-42)

The reader next encounters a Pharisee early in the narrative about the developing church, during Peter's second clash with the Sanhedrin. A Pharisaic leader named Gamaliel, "well-respected by all the people," demurs when some on the Council are enraged and want to kill Peter and the other apostles (5:33-34). He advises a hands-off policy toward the new movement, arguing as follows:

> "Men of Israel, consider well what you are proposing to do to these men. For some time ago Theudas rose up, claiming to be somebody [important], and about four hundred men joined him; he was killed, and all who followed him were dispersed and came to nothing. After him, Judas the Galilean rose up in

> the days of the census and persuaded people (*laon*) to follow him; he died also, and all who followed him were scattered. So in this case, I tell you, stay away from these men and let them be; for if this plan (*boule*) or work (*ergon*) is of men (*ex anthropon*), it will be overthrown. But if it is of God (*ek theou*), you will not be able to overthrow them—indeed, you might even be found fighting against God." (Acts 5:35-39)

Gamaliel's action is certainly advantageous to Peter and the apostles, but his motivation is hardly admirable. The Sanhedrin's decision is once again based on the fear of possible retribution, not on a sense of justice, or mercy, or even on spiritual insight about the significance of the persons who stand on trial before them. Previously, the Council (including Gamaliel, we presume) had threatened John and Peter but let them go "on account of the people" (Acts 4:25). Here they hesitate to execute their victims for fear of a (remotely) possible confrontation with God. He says in effect, "This new movement will likely hang itself. Let it do so. And if it does not, at least we will have been neutral and so guiltless with regard to it."

Contrary to the common argument, the reader is not impressed by the narrator's description of Gamaliel as *respected by all the people*. The *laos* have proven to be a very fickle lot, backing the opponents of God's agenda as often as they support its proponents (see Kodell 1969). At Jesus' trial, for example, the people stand alongside the high priests and rulers and demand that Pilate have Jesus crucified (Luke 23:13-25). But early in Acts, they are said to be in favor of the growing community of believers in Jerusalem (Acts 2:46-7). The capriciousness of the people is even reinforced ironically in Gamaliel's speech itself: Judas (the false Galilean prophet) got *laon* to follow after him in a revolt, but the entire thing failed. In the eyes of the reader, therefore, the fact that the *laos* respect Gamaliel is not necessarily positive. Indeed, it could very well be deemed a backhanded compliment if the audience remembers that Jesus condemned the Pharisees for "playing to the crowd" rather than pleasing God: "You justify yourselves before men, but God knows your hearts; for that which is highly esteemed among men is detestable before God" (Luke 16:15).

The intended function of the narrator's observation that the people honor Gamaliel is not to upgrade Pharisees, but to explain why the Pharisaic leader carries weight in the Sanhedrin, that is, why the Council listens to him and takes his advice not to murder the apostles. The Council is afraid of the people (Acts 4:2, 21), and thus will take seriously a person of Gamaliel's stature among the masses. To be honored by the populace (*laos*) and respected by the Council, however, is not *ipso facto* to be honored by the narrator or reader, or indeed, by God (see above).

Commentators on Acts have failed to note that the audience's evaluation of Gamaliel is based, at least in part, on a *sygkrisis* (process of comparison and contrast) between the Pharisaic leader and another Council member, Joseph of Arimathea, who also opposed the Sanhedrin. Quite predictably, Gamaliel comes out on the short end of the comparison. The narrator described Joseph as

> . . . a member of the Council, who was a good (*agathos*) and righteous (*dikaios*) man—he had not agreed to their plan or deed—from the Jewish town of Arimathea, and who waited for the kingdom of God . . . ." (Luke 23:50-51)

The distinctions between the two councilors are striking and instructive. In the Gospel passage, the omniscient narrator tells the reader directly that Joseph was both *agathos* and *dikaios*, two traits obviously valued in the narrative. Gamaliel gets no praise from the narrator, save the rather ambiguous note that the people respected him (see above). Furthermore, whereas Joseph is clearly distanced from the Council's purposes and actions *vis-à-vis* Jesus (Luke 23:51), Gamaliel is never absolved of the Council's earlier hostilities against Jesus and the apostles (arresting, trying and threatening Peter and John; Acts 4:1-22). And finally, Joseph is described as waiting for the kingdom of God, a solid indicator of his "insider" status, and a trait notably lacking in Gamaliel's description. In short, the Pharisaic leader suffers in comparison with the Arimathean.

When one considers Gamaliel's speech from the reader's point of view, it takes on overtones of tragic irony (Johnson 1977:197-98). The reader knows that the apostles' witness is *ek theou* (it has been validated by the Spirit) and that their movement is part of a divine plan that cannot be stopped by human opposition. When some Pharisees approached Jesus to warn him about Herod (Luke 13:31), a similar irony resulted, for the reader was already well aware that Jesus' death was under the divine *dei*, not under human control. The Council's deliberations (including Gamaliel's input) regarding the Christian movement in their midst thus appear sadly misguided, presumptuous, even ludicrous. It is richly ironic that here a leader of a group that has "rejected the will of God for themselves" (Luke 7:30) advises others on how not to oppose the will of God concerning the early believers in Christ.[25]

But the tragic irony of the Gamaliel story runs even deeper. The Sanhedrin (including Gamaliel) has twice heard the message of salvation directly from the mouths of God's messengers (Acts 4:8-12; 5:29-32); and yet, they have *not* really heard (understood and accepted) it. Gamaliel's speech betrays this incomprehension, for his words in no way reflect a positive response to what Peter and John have said. He simply ranks their movement among other failed messianic sects of his time and places a large question mark over its fate. He clearly places himself *outside* the movement, and, if his examples are any indicator, Gamaliel believes that it will soon "peter" out. His advice is meant to restrain the Sanhedrin from stoning the apostles, but not to change its mind about their message. In point of fact, the council "takes his advice" (Acts 5:40), orders that the apostles be beaten, and warns them not to speak about Jesus! As Haenchen (1971:258) points out,

> Gamaliel warns the Sanhedrin to leave the Christians strictly alone, lest they should find themselves fighting against God; the others allow themselves to be persuaded—and sentence the Apostles to thirty-nine lashes under which (as Jeremias rightly reminds us) many a prisoner had been known to die.

Later in the narrative (22:1-5), the reader will learn that Saul/Paul, influenced by Gamaliel's strict teaching, and authorized by the Council, set out to kill and otherwise persecute believers in Christ. In short, the picture of Gamaliel and the whole Sanhedrin in Acts is quite negative, and does nothing to improve a reader's evaluation of the Pharisees.

What is glaringly absent from Gamaliel's oration is any sign that he has taken seriously the apostles' witness that God raised Jesus from the dead (Acts 5:30-32). To him this is but another of those messianic movements that dissipate soon after their leaders are removed from the scene. The notion that this movement differs because its leader experienced resurrection is dismissed. For the reader, it seems perfectly fitting that a leader of the Pharisees should showcase such blatant misperception and unreceptivity, for they have consistently been portrayed as those who observe but do not perceive.

As a plot device, therefore, Gamaliel's speech is important: it leads to the freeing of the protagonists which, in turn, allows the action to progress. With regard to the characterization of the Pharisees, however, it only reinforces the reader's understanding of this leadership group as a paradigm of "seeing but not seeing, and hearing but not hearing." In retrospect—after the martyrdom of Stephen, the scattering of the believers, and the spreading of the church to Samaria and Antioch—the audience will perceive in Gamaliel's speech an unwitting, ironic, and paradoxical oracle of church growth: a leader *was* killed, and followers *were* scattered, but instead of dissipating, the movement expanded dramatically.

Pharisaic Believers in Jerusalem (Acts 15:1-5)

Critics who would see in Luke's writing a positive strain in the depiction of the Pharisees place much weight on the fact that certain participants in the Jerusalem Conference are described as "some from the sect of the Pharisees who had believed" (Acts 15:5). From the reader's perspective, however, this information does nothing to erase the deeply-engraved negative image of Pharisees. In fact, when read in context, it actually buttresses their negative characterization.

Several contextual factors must be considered when assessing the Pharisees in this passage. First, and perhaps most important, the Pharisaic believers are said to be the *opposition platform* at the Conference. Countering them are Peter, James and Paul (all of whom have been definitely authorized by the Holy Spirit as divine witnesses). How and why these particular

Pharisees became part of the believing community is never dramatized, and so the reader is at a loss to assess their authenticity. (As we have seen, Luke is very careful to provide documentation for all authorized voices.) Second, the reader has long known the divine will about the major issue of the conference—namely, whether the church should include Gentiles, and, if so, under what conditions (like circumcision or certain Jewish dietary laws; see Acts 10). The reader knows that the Spirit has already been poured out upon Gentiles. Thus, those who obstruct the influx of Gentiles are working at cross purposes with God. Third, the Pharisaic believers' speech betrays a system of values disappointingly similar to that of the Pharisees in the Gospel of Luke, namely *a system that gives priority to externals*. The believing Pharisees hold that "it is necessary to circumcise them [the Gentile believers] and command them to observe the Law of Moses" (Acts 15:5). The reader will consider this yet another instance of the Pharisees' well-established penchant for focusing on and valuing the outside over the inside. Once again, Pharisees stand opposed to those persons who are marginalized but belong to the kingdom; and at the root of their opposition lies an attitude of superiority and an unwarranted stress on appearance and ritual. We never hear from these Pharisees again, for they are allowed no more voice in the debate. Peter and James make lengthy statements to the effect that the Gentiles should be included without having to be circumcised, but the Pharisaic faction remains silent, much as the Pharisees did in the symposia (see above). It is difficult to avoid the conclusion that what the reader learns from all this is that the Pharisees' value-system is wrong whether they are part of the community or not.[26]

One more point needs to be made here: in Luke's story, being counted among the believers is not *necessarily* an indication of a character's righteousness. Ananias and Saphira are prime examples of believers who nevertheless serve as *negative* role models (Acts 5:1-11). So is Simon Magus, the sorcerer who believes and is even baptized by Philip (8:13), but later tries to buy the gift of the Spirit (8:18-19) from Peter! Peter's response is striking: "Your heart is not right before God." So being counted a believer (by oneself or by others) does not automatically signify that one has the Spirit and a clean heart.[27]

Paul's "Pharisaic Defense" at His Trials

On three occasions in his trials at the end of Acts, Paul makes reference to his Pharisaic upbringing as part of his apologia. He utters the first of these references in his defense to the people of Jerusalem (Acts 22:3). Having been beaten and nearly killed by a mob, Paul is rescued by the Roman cohort and allowed to address his persecutors. He claims to have been raised in Jerusalem under the tutelage of Gamaliel, and to have received a strict education in the law of the fathers. Paul's rhetoric is clearly intended to get the crowd of Jerusalemites to identify with him, not to count him as a stranger or outsider. He uses every tool at his disposal to accomplish this, including speaking in Hebrew and associating himself with a crowd favorite, Gamaliel (see 5:34). Here we see a classic case of that familiar figure in Greek story-telling, the wise man who uses his wits to get out of sticky situations in a number of exotic venues (Odysseus comes to mind, but so do the traveling heroes and heroines of the romances who often find themselves in a bind and must rely on their smarts to survive). Paul's comments are so completely conditioned by the dire circumstances within which he utters them that the reader is hardly likely to perceive them as contributing anything (positive or negative) to the characterization of the Pharisees. The people admire Gamaliel, and so Paul uses his connection with that leader to garner the hostile crowd's sympathy.

The next reference (23:1-10) is dramatic and involves actual Pharisees. On trial before the Sanhedrin, Paul insightfully notes that his interlocutors are of two types, Pharisees and Sadducees. Seeking to pit these traditionally antagonistic religious parties against each other, Paul exclaims, "Brothers, I am a Pharisee, a son of Pharisees; I am on trial with respect to the resurrection of the dead." With this short outburst, Paul strongly identifies with one faction and diverts attention from himself by refocusing the debate onto the resurrection of the dead, the very issue that most clearly divided the two parties. Paul's clever ruse works on both groups; they fight each other instead of Paul. The Pharisees on the Council now claim to find nothing wrong with Paul, despite the fact that (so far as the reader knows) they have yet to learn anything about him apart from his claim to Pharisaic lineage.

Given Paul's desperate situation, the reader will take these words about his membership in the Pharisaic party with a grain of salt. In any event, the emphasis of Paul's claim seems to fall on his affiliation through heritage ("a son of Pharisees"), not on the status of his present membership. Furthermore, there is not a shred of evidence which would lead the reader to conclude that the Pharisees on the Council "virtually acknowledge the resurrection of Jesus" (Brawley 1987:90). The narrator makes it crystal clear that the Pharisees are thinking about the *general* resurrection of the dead, whereas Paul, the narrator, and (hopefully) the reader, have in mind the resurrection of Jesus in particular. This is all a clever, irony-laden ploy consisting of partial truths (he never did turn in his membership card, and he does indeed still believe in resurrection), and based on the insight that the Pharisees are susceptible to a display of external religious criteria (lineage, education, membership, doctrinal orthodoxy) but are blind to the deeper truths of the situation. The reader realizes that what Paul fails to tell the Sanhedrin about himself (his conversion, belief in Jesus as Christ, argument that Gentile converts do not have to be circumcised, etc.) is much more significant than what he tells them. Furthermore, the reader is well aware that Paul never talks of his Pharisaism *except* in these desperate situations where such information might help him survive, just as he never mentions his Roman citizenship until he is about to be lashed (22:25-30).

The claim that Paul's reference to his Pharisaic roots casts a favorable light on the Pharisees in Acts would be cogent if the narrative had portrayed Saul as somehow having come to his belief in Christ *because of* his Pharisaic background. Of course, nothing of the kind appears in the story. Here Saul does not begin to see the light through a process of spiritual reflection or reasoning; nowhere is he portrayed as being attracted to this novel movement by similarities between its doctrines and those of Pharisaism (e.g., the resurrection of the dead). Quite to the contrary, Saul repeatedly recounts the story of his call/conversion as a kind of spiritual bludgeoning by the risen Lord. It is clearly not a case of religious insight by an open-minded Pharisee. Indeed, the tale of Saul's conversion plays off the irony of the spiritually-blind Pharisee who cannot see the light until he is blinded by it! Thus there is nothing in this narrative to support the widespread idea that somehow the Pharisees are upgraded by Paul's claim to be one of them.

The entire incident of Paul before the Council has much more to do with the characterization of Paul than with Pharisees. That Paul adapts quite readily to different cultural settings is known to the reader. He is quite willing to take on stances and customs that ingratiate him with the local populace, even if they are not fully representative of his actual position. The narrator informs us, for example, that Paul was very much provoked when he saw all the idols in Athens (Acts 17:16). In his address to the prominent Athenian philosophers, however, his opening line is complimentary rather than critical: "People of Athens, I see that you are very *religious* in all respects" (17:22b). Paul then begins to build a case on the fact that the Athenians worship an Unknown God—"Let me tell you who that is!" The reader knows, of course, that Paul does not believe in the *Agnostos Theos*, but there is enough truth in his declaration to establish a valid link between Paul and the Athenians. The same is true in Paul's Sanhedrin trial. The reader knows that Paul is no longer a dedicated Pharisee. But it is true that he remains one in terms of his lineage, education, and basic eschatological tenets. And why should he not refer to these links in his apologia? This propensity to adapt to diverse environments without betraying his fundamental system of convictions is one of Paul's hallmarks, not just in Acts, but also in the letters:

> To the Jews I became as a Jew . . . to those under the Law, as under the Law, *though not being myself under the Law* . . . to those without law, as without law . . . to the weak I became weak . . . I have become all things to all people. (I Cor 9:20-22; see also I Cor 10:32-33)

The reader realizes that Paul is a Pharisee (in a sense) and yet is no longer a Pharisee. His claim to belong to that party is true, but it is not the whole truth.

Paul's final reference to Pharisaism occurs at the beginning of his defense before Agrippa. One of Paul's preliminary moves is to establish his credentials as an expert in Jewish law. To do so he recounts both his upbringing in Jerusalem and the fact that he lived as a Pharisee (26:4-5). In this more controlled trial, Paul refers to his Pharisaism in the *past* tense (*ezēsa pharisaios*). He will go on to relate his call experience and the dramatic changes it wrought in his life and self-identity. It is clear that Paul's use of his connection with the Pharisees depends on the situation in which he finds himself (earlier to identify with the Pharisees on the Council, here to establish his legal credentials), and not on any felt need to define himself as a Pharisee in general.

In conclusion, Paul's references to himself as a Pharisee do not alter the reader's deeply-engraved image of Pharisees. All of these references are strongly conditioned by their context in the trials of Paul before Jews. Furthermore, the Pharisees who appear at Paul's Sanhedrin trial are superficial and misperceiving, just like the Pharisees in the Gospel. And like Jesus before him, Paul is able to advance his cause by playing off these deficiencies in those who would put him to the test (recall how Jesus trapped the Pharisees with their self-righteousness in Luke 15).

The derogatory image of the Pharisees developed in the first half of Luke's narrative is so nearly indelible that little short of a direct and unequivocal affirmation of that group by a highly authoritative voice (e.g., the omniscient narrator, an archangel, or the risen Lord) would serve to upgrade them in the second half of the story. As we have seen, that does not happen. Readers come to Acts already distanced from and suspicious of the Pharisees, a prejudice that conditions all of their encounters with that group in the story of the church's beginnings. Even seemingly benign or positive references to Pharisees are thus read ironically or with distrust born of experience. When evaluated from this angle, Acts does not redeem the Pharisees; indeed it reinforces some negative traits already attributed to them in the Gospel.

CONCLUSION

The reader of Luke-Acts builds a complex, yet consistent and coherent image of the Pharisees. This group is integral to three of the primary rhetorical strategies of the text: (1) recognition and response; (2) the reversal of status; and (3) the division of characters into insiders and outsiders. And in each of these, the Pharisees are firmly situated at the negative end of the spectrum of *dramatis personae*.

The Pharisees are the observers *par excellence* of God's will as manifested in Jesus and others. Nevertheless, they continually fail to recognize it. They therefore embody the theme of "seeing but not seeing, and hearing but not hearing." The cause of their spiritual obtuseness is the condition of their "hearts." All of the negative values of the text are demonstrated in their actions and thoughts: pride, love of money, injustice, hypocrisy, lack of repentance, murmuring and so forth.

Although exalted in their own minds, and esteemed by certain others, the Pharisees find disfavor with God. Thus they are prime examples of how the proud, mighty, and rich are humbled while the humble, weak, and poor are exalted—the reversal of roles already predicted in the infancy narrative.

Finally, the Pharisees oppose Jesus and the other messengers of God. In this they belong to those in Israel who see Jesus as a "sign to be opposed." By the end of the story, they are clearly grouped with the outsiders, while sinners, tax collectors and the poor are classified as insiders.

Luke's caricature of the Pharisees is meant to mold audience evaluation of the primary actions and characters of the narrative. In other words, it coaches the reader's reading (i.e., seeing and hearing) of the story. The Pharisees serve as the most consistent example of how *not* to apprehend the account of "things fulfilled among us." The audience is thus distanced from the Pharisees and encouraged to repudiate their point of view and the value-system that shapes it.[28]

5

HERODTHE FOX: METAPHOR AND CHARACTERIZATION

INTRODUCTION

Jesus has "resolutely set his face toward Jerusalem" (Luke 9:51) and is well into his journey there when some Pharisees come to him with a warning: "Go and depart from here for Herod wishes to kill you" (13:31). Jesus replies at length:

> "Go tell this fox, 'Behold, I cast out demons and perform cures today and tomorrow, and on the third day I am brought to an end.' But it is necessary that I journey on today and tomorrow and the next [day], for it cannot be that a prophet should perish outside Jerusalem. Jerusalem, Jerusalem, killer of the prophets and stoner of those sent to her, how often did I wish to gather your children together as a hen [gathers] her brood under her wings, but you would not have it. Behold your house is left to you. And I say to you, you will not see me until you say, 'Blessed is he who comes in the name of the Lord.' " (13:32-35)

This remarkable passage is widely considered an interpretive crux of Luke's so-called travel narrative, for it falls precisely at the midpoint of that section and forcefully expresses its main themes.[1] But it is also recognized as being enigmatic. What are the "three days" to which Jesus twice refers, and what does he mean by *teleioumai* (vs. 32)—"I am completed," or "I shall be killed," or "I shall reach my goal?" Furthermore, what does Jerusalem's "house" (*oikos*) denote? More broadly, how are we to link Jesus' description of his itinerary (in vss. 32-33) to his lament over Jerusalem (vss. 34-35)? The object of this chapter is to shed some light on one of the less notorious and yet important interpretive issues raised by the passage: How did Luke's Greco-Roman audience understand Jesus' reference to Herod (the Tetrarch) as *te alopeki taute* ("this fox")? Clearly, our answer to this question will not solve all of the hermeneutical problems in the passage. We shall see, however, that discernment of how readers processed this terse metaphorical epithet near the beginning of Jesus' long retort to the Pharisees provides one key to the semantic integrity of the entire saying.

METAPHOR AND CHARACTERIZATION

Jesus' reference to Herod as fox is deceivingly simple. Most interpreters have failed to perceive, much less grapple with, the complex hermeneutical issues concerning both characterization and metaphor that are raised by this short epithet. The temptation is to treat it simply as a rather straightforward philological issue to be resolved with little more than lexicographical legwork. The task involves determining the dominant figurative sense of "fox" in ancient Jewish or Greco-Roman parlance, and then substituting that sense for *alopex* in Luke 13:32. What Jesus *actually* means is that Herod is cunning, sly, and devious,[2] or perhaps that he is weak, insignificant, and worthless,[3] or rather that he is destructive, dangerous, and rapacious.[4] Luke's Jesus chooses to say in a more ornamental or indirect manner what he could have expressed more literally and directly. The critic's task involves simply choosing the "correct" literal substitute for the figure of speech used by Jesus.

Such *substitutive* approaches quite obviously fail to explain how the metaphor functions, however, for they produce a number of discrete readings, each of which has been touted as definitive by one or another critic. This diversity of readings by interpreters using essentially the same data underscores the reality that even "simple metaphors" like this one are actually quite elusive and require specialized treatment. Indeed, recent studies of metaphor warn against precisely this kind of substitutive handling of these polyvalent tropes so common within biblical studies. Literary theorists and linguists alike now see metaphors as complicated linguistic phenomena that pose unique problems for the reader as well as the critic.

Metaphor as Interaction: Max Black Reconsidered

Perhaps the most prominent figure in modern metaphor studies is the philosopher of language, Max Black (1962; 1979). His theory of metaphor provides a convenient, widely-recognized reference point for our observations on the subject. Building on the insights of I.A. Richards, Black (1962:25-47; 1979:19-43) develops what he terms an *interaction* theory of metaphor.[5] In contrast to "substitution" approaches which see metaphors as simply decorative replacements of literal statements, interaction theories maintain that metaphors bring into perpetual and creative tension two different systems of implications (ideas or "associated commonplaces").[6] A primary subject (Herod) and a secondary subject (fox) are actually semantic fields that, when juxtaposed in metaphor, produce special insights and connotations which cannot be adequately expressed in a literal paraphrase such as "Herod is cunning." Indeed, these unique meanings or effects cannot be conveyed by any means other than metaphor, for metaphor "imposes an extension of meaning" that is apprehended only when two different semantic systems are juxtaposed. A metaphor expands the meaning potential of both its subjects (fox and Herod) and remains somewhat open, polyvalent, mysterious, elusive.

This is not to suggest, however, that metaphor is completely indeterminate or unstable and, therefore, that every reading of a metaphor must be deemed equally valid. Black's interaction theory hardly falls prey to radical indeterminacy or relativity. Indeed, it is precisely one of Black's goals to demonstrate that metaphor can and does communicate specific meanings or connotations. It is at this very point, however, that his suggestive model needs some adjustment, clarification, and amplification. How do we determine "the meaning" of a metaphor?

The Reader and Metaphorical Interaction

What reader-response critics find distressing in interaction theories such as Black's is a certain formalism that sees texts as autonomous and autotelic, as whole objects whose parts produce meaning by interacting among themselves. According to reader-response theory, on the contrary, metaphor's subjects do not themselves interact, but rather are caused to interact by the reader or hearer. In essence, a metaphor is only an invitation to the audience to draw analogies and forge meaningful connections between two distinct semantic systems (signified by two subjects). From this view, metaphors confront the audience with an indeterminacy, a question mark. Readers produce meaning, and thus our focus must shift from authorial intention (What did Luke and/ or Jesus mean by the epithet?) or text *per se* (How do these words interact?) to how readers recognize and process metaphors.[7]

Metaphor and Narrative Context

Black also fails sufficiently to account for context and its vital role in determining metaphorical meaning. Such an oversight is understandable when one realizes that his goal is to determine the "truth value" of isolated metaphorical assertions (that is, their trustworthiness as propositions). Only obliquely does Black mention (1962:29, 43) the fact that a given social or literary context may well adjust the hearer's configuration of the secondary subject of the metaphor. But the fact that context helps determine the shape of the semantic fields involved in a metaphor is a very important insight and thus should be central to any discussion of how these tropes function (Stern 1931:129-61; Booth 1979:51-53; Tolbert 1979:48-50; Kjärgaard 1986:39-42). If a tale consistently depicts lions as timid, fickle, weak creatures, for example, then the statement "Richard is a lion," encountered by the reader at the end of the story, has a very different meaning effect than if this famous metaphor is isolated and the conventional wisdom that lions are valiant, aggressive, and strong is brought to bear.

Furthermore, the *primary* subject of the metaphor may also be reconfigured by literary context, a possibility of which Black is seemingly unaware. After all, if we say "Richard is a lion," it is important for our audience to know whether we are referring to Richard I, King of England, or Richard Nixon. The context tells a reader which Richard is indicated. Context may also alter readers' perceptions or evaluations of the royal crusader or of the former president, in which cases the metaphor itself will be apprehended differently.

Metaphors confront readers with a gap or indeterminacy which the audience attempts to resolve by "consistency building," the conscious or unconscious drive to fit textual data together in an optimally consistent and coherent pattern (Iser 1974:383-84; 1978:16-17, 118-34). In this process, the reader chooses possibilities that are compatible with other information within the story as it has been actualized up to that point. More specifically, one opts for answers that are "simplest and most probable," "create the maximal relevance among diverse features," and "bring together more elements than alternative hypotheses" (Sternberg 1985:187).

When confronted by metaphor, the reader looks to the context for guidance both in configuring the semantic systems represented by the primary and secondary subjects (Herod and fox), and in the formation of hypotheses about how the two interrelate. Some ideas in each of these semantic fields will be foregrounded, and others will be suppressed as less relevant or applicable (e.g., the fact that foxes are furry and Herod has a brother named Philip; Luke 3:1). Of course, the reader's choices remain hypotheses, with higher or lower degrees of probability depending on how much information or narrative guidance is available. As reading progresses beyond the metaphor, the reader continues to look for further information by which to confirm or readjust his or her initial configuration and "bridging" of the metaphor's discrete systems of ideas.

Previous treatments of Jesus' metaphorical epithet for Herod have simply failed to take into account the very information that was designed to guide the reader in processing the metaphor. That is, interpreters have overlooked or devalued narrative context as a determining factor in understanding this figure of speech. Such inattention to contextual data bearing on Luke 13:32 has been due in large part to the historical critical (atomistic) methods that have been employed. Apart from a few references to how the saying summarizes important themes in the travel narrative, little or no effort is made to investigate possible links between this episode and broader patterns of characterization in the story. Luke 13:31-35 is in fact usually treated in isolation from the rest of Luke, for it is regarded as sitting rather uncomfortably in its present setting. The redactor has awkwardly tied it into the narrative at this juncture with a typical Lukan "at that very hour"(13:31a); and, at the end of the episode, the scene shifts immediately to a seemingly unrelated symposium at the house of a Pharisaic leader. In short, from a redactional point of view, there does not appear to be much editorial paste holding the passage in place.

Even more significantly, perhaps, redaction critics consider the passage itself to be little more than a pastiche of materials cobbled together by slight redactional insertions and adjustments. The setting (the Pharisee's approach and warning) is derived from L or is by the redactor's own hand. One or both sayings in verses 32b-33 (on the "days" of Jesus' journey) might be from either L or the redactor. The lament over Jerusalem (vss. 34-35) is from Q, and may well have been linked to the previous saying by the catchword "Jerusalem."[8] Because critical attention has been focused on such source issues, the question of how a reader "works" the passage in its present configuration and within its greater literary grid has gone both unasked and unanswered.

If, in fact, context is so important for understanding how a metaphor functions, then our task is *to reconstruct the narrative frames* that guide the reader in evaluating Jesus' epithet for the Tetrarch. This involves retracing the reader's sequential imaging and construction of Herod up to Luke 13:32. This characterization is most important to our equation, for it tells us how the reader has configured the semantic field that is represented by the name Herod thus far. This set of information about the Tetrarch, along with any narrative information concerning foxes, constitutes the essential framework within which readers process the metaphor.

Metaphor and Extratext

There is a further complicating factor, however, which Black and other theorists have treated. Readers bring to a metaphor not only contextual (intratextual) information, but also conventional extratextual knowledge. As we have seen, the reader draws on both kinds of information throughout the reading process. Extratextual data or expertise is especially useful for resolving tensions and filling gaps in the text. Whereas the reader is able to construct Herod from plentiful narrative indicators, he or she will find it necessary to rely heavily on the extratext to fill out the second subject, fox. That is, conventional ideas about foxes in life and literature help to *prestructure* this system of ideas for readers. If, for example, certain traits (e.g., cleverness and cruelty) of foxes were commonly attributed to human beings, then those traits would be foregrounded, for Herod is obviously a human. Other fox-like traits (e.g., pointy ears) would be suppressed, although not eliminated from consideration. The system of ideas represented by the word fox was thus not totally amorphous; rather it was shaped and limited prior to the reading of the story. It is important to know how such semantic systems are shaped, for different cultures tend to fashion them variously. And, of course, as the shape of a term evolves with time and culture, the metaphor of which it is a part changes. In modern American usage, for example, the word fox is often used metaphorically with regard to a sexually attractive person ("She's a fox!"). It would be misleading to read such an implication back into the semantic field of *alopex* in Greco-Roman times. But what *were* the conventional semantic options for the term in late Hellenism? Here is where classical philology comes into play in our interpretive endeavor.

Interpreting Ancient Metaphor

A summary of the argument thus far is in order. Interpreting Jesus' oblique reference to Herod involves much more than a basic lexicographical study of *alopex* in ancient literature (though the latter is obviously a necessary part of the process). The epithet uttered by Jesus is metaphorical, and thus it calls on the reader to compare and draw analogies between two semantic fields, one signified by the word fox, the other by the name Herod. Directing the audience's efforts meaningfully to relate these different and somewhat amorphous "systems of associated commonplaces" are (1) narrative context and (2) the extratext. These provide frames for narrowing interpretive options, and so help the reader to achieve a degree of certainty in attempting to resolve the indeterminacy posed by the metaphor. Such frames guide us both in reconfiguring and in relating the two semantic fields of this trope. The reader evaluates and ranks ideas or connotations within these two fields in terms of their applicability and appropriateness *vis-à-vis* the frames of context and extratext. By context we mean primarily the characterization of Herod up to Luke 13:32. The salient extratext is the reader's repertoire of knowledge about foxes and their use in contemporary literature.[9] Finally, we must keep in mind that the reader's attempts to resolve the metaphor's indeterminacy are hypothetical and thus subject to change as reading progresses. Although the gap opened up by the metaphor will never be entirely filled, the audience will keep on trying to bridge it as new data becomes available. In light of all this, our tasks are clarified: we must reconstruct how Herod the Tetrarch has been characterized in Luke's gospel prior to Jesus' epithet, and we must reconstruct the contemporary semantic field of *alopex*. Only then can we begin to understand how the reader works the metaphor.

HEROD THE TETRARCH IN LUKE

By the time Jesus refers to him in Luke 13:32a, the Tetrarch is no longer simply a semantic blank for the reader. The audience has already developed a very definite and consistent—if somewhat flat—image of the Galilean potentate.[10]

Introducing the Earthly Powers That Be

Readers first encounter Herod at 3:1, in a list of political and religious rulers in power at the beginning of John's ministry.

> In the fifteenth year of the reign of Tiberias Caesar, when Pontius Pilate was governor of Judea, and *Herod was tetrarch of Galilee*, and his brother Philip was tetrarch of the region of

> Iturea and Trachonitis, and Lysanias was tetrarch of Abilene, in the high-priesthood of Annas and Caiaphas, the word of the Lord came to John, the son of Zacharias, in the desert (Luke 3:1-2).

This exhaustive synchronic list of the powers that be is not just an example of Luke showing off his erudition or exactitude (Loisy 1924:134); neither is it just a signal that a new narrative phase has begun. Rather, it introduces the reader to potentates who may very well have a role to play in the upcoming tale. But not every ruler mentioned is of equal significance to the audience, for the text has already specified three locales as major arenas in which the divinely ordained action will take place: Galilee, Jerusalem, and Judea. Thus the rulers of those territories—Pilate, the high priests, and Herod—command greater attention and engender a much higher level of expectation than do the others (indeed, the other figures are never again mentioned in the story). In Luke 1-2, the protagonists and their families have been solidly linked to Judea and Jerusalem. In addition, intertextual allusions to these areas in the Septuagint have been pointed and unmistakable, engendering within the reader the notion that they will be places of destiny. Pilate and the high priests in Jerusalem are thus quite likely to play important roles as the story progresses and as the protagonists carry out their missions in these domains (Darr 1987:202-203).

For similar reasons, the reader finds the reference to Herod as Tetrarch *of Galilee* especially interesting. It was in Nazareth of Galilee that the angel Gabriel announced the birth of Jesus to Mary (1:26). And the fact that Galilee is the home of Jesus, Mary, and Joseph is emphasized several times (2:4; 39; 51). This region is clearly one of the major arenas of divine activity, and so its ruler may well be of some consequence to the story.

So Herod becomes a focus of attention, and the reader begins to construct his character with care. Two pieces of family information are derived from the list itself. First, a Herod has already been mentioned (1:5), a fact that could cause some confusion were not the two potentates distinguished by their titles (*basileus* and *tetrarches*). Nevertheless, the reader would presume some familial relationship between the two. And second, we learn that the Tetrarch has a brother named Philip, who holds a similar title. A character is beginning to emerge from a mass of discrete information, although his image is still faint at this point.

Among the rulers listed by Luke, Herod is certainly the most fully construed, and, therefore, in the mind of the reader, seems more likely to play a continuing role. Reader speculation on that role is constrained by the narrative in two ways. First, John and Jesus have already been cast as charismatics; they are not a part of the hierarchical power structures of Galilee and Judea. Though he is the son of simple and "humble" people, Jesus demonstrates his charisma as a child, amazing the teachers in the temple with a wisdom far beyond his age. As we noted in Chapter 3, John is cast as the prophet of the Lord (1:17, 76; 3:2b). Their potency derives from neither heredity nor bureaucracy, but from the Spirit. As we shall see more clearly in our next chapter, this characterization of Jesus and John raises a specific set of expectations involving the antagonistic interaction of charismatics and rulers. That is, the reader is already primed (through extratextual convention) to anticipate that John and Jesus will clash with the authorities in certain stereotypical ways. In short, the reader draws on related conventions from the Septuagint and from Greco-Roman culture: the ubiquitous "prophet versus king" interaction in the scriptures, and the "philosopher versus tyrant" syndrome in Hellenism. Here it suffices to point out that the reader already anticipates some conflict between the charismatic protagonists and their political and religious overlords.

Second, the reader's expectation that there will be tensions between the Lord's messengers and earthly powers is reinforced by the text. Through Mary, the Holy Spirit has already declared that "He [God] has brought down rulers from thrones, and has exalted those who are humble" (1:52). This reversal of fortunes not only casts aspersion on rulers, but foreshadows conflict between these authorities and "the humble" ones God chooses.[11] Confrontation is in the making.

John the Baptist Versus Herod the Tetrarch

The reader does not have long to wait for the conflict. When the Galilean tetrarch is next encountered—sixteen verses later—it is evident that he is playing the role of wicked king opposite John's prophet. Both are stock characters.

> So with many other exhortations he [John] preached to the people; but when Herod the Tetrarch was reproved by him concerning Herodias the wife of his brother and concerning all of the evil things which Herod had done, he added this also to them all—he locked John up in prison. (3:18-20)

The passage is notoriously opaque, full of gaps. One assumes that the brother referred to is Philip the Tetrarch (3:1) but the precise nature of the Galilean Tetrarch's *harmartia vis-à-vis* his brother's wife is not clarified. "All the other evils that Herod had done" also remain unspecified. Largely through John's speech, however, the narrative has established a basic definition of evil as the selfish abuse of power, position, privilege, or possession (see our discussion of John's preaching in Chapter 3). The reader is strongly inclined, therefore, to suppose that Herod's sins are of this nature.

The extratextual framework also provides guidance here. John is simply doing what many of his prophetic predecessors did. Like Moses confronting Pharaoh, or Nathan confronting David concerning Bathsheba, or Elijah censuring Ahab and Jezebel, so John confronts Herod and (we suppose) Herodias (Ernst 1977:147). The description of Herod's evil echoes the brief evaluative formulae for wicked kings in the Deuteronomistic History. Compare the Septuagint's curt evaluations of Ahab, for example, with that of Herod in Luke (Schürmann 1969:184; 3 Reigns = 1 Kings).

> *epoiesen* Achaab to *poneron* enopion kyriou
> (Ahab did evil in the sight of the LORD; 3 Reigns 16:30);
> Achaab hos eprathe *poiesai to poneron*
> (Ahab, who sold himself to do evil; 3 Reigns 21:25);
> panton hon *epoiesen poneron* ho Herodes
> (all the evil which Herod did; Luke 3:19).

Herod is now definitely characterized as the stereotypical wicked ruler who is confronted by the prophet. His incarceration of John is fully in keeping with this developing pattern (e.g., Micaiah's imprisonment by Ahab). At this point, then, the reader constructs Herod as a malevolent ruler who opposes the messengers of God and has both the power and the will to harm them.

"Who Then is This?"

Following the short notice of John's imprisonment, the scene shifts rapidly to the baptism of Jesus and then to his mission in Galilee. The reader is left wondering about John's fate and about the Tetrarch's potential interaction with Jesus. Not until 8:3 is Herod mentioned again; there, the wife of his steward is reported to be one of the women who follow Jesus throughout Galilee. These are ominous words indeed. Can it be long before the evil Tetrarch learns of this new—and even more threatening—charismatic in his realm? The answer is soon provided.

> And Herod the Tetrarch heard of all that was happening, and he was utterly perplexed because it was being said by some that John had been raised from the dead, and by some that Elijah had appeared, and by others that a prophet of old had risen. And Herod said, "I beheaded John; who then is this concerning whom I hear such things?" And he kept trying to see him. (Luke 9:7-9)

This startling passage tells the reader several things about Herod. He is inquisitive, curious and highly conscious of persons and events within his jurisdiction. He is one of those characters who hear much about Jesus but fail to comprehend his significance and true identity. He wishes "to see" Jesus, but, of course, he will never be able truly to perceive who Jesus is (we discuss the climactic confrontation between Jesus and Herod below, in Chapter 6). Most shocking to the reader, however, is the information that Herod has beheaded John. The Tetrarch's first words, "I beheaded John," are all the reader ever learns of John's tragic demise in this gospel. Unlike Mark and Matthew, Luke appends no explanation of how and why John was killed. The notions that the Tetrarch had a grudging admiration for John, that Herodias was really to blame in that she plotted and entrapped him, that somehow Herodias got her daughter to dance for Herod and his cohorts, that

Herod still hesitated to kill the Baptist even after he had promised to do so, and that he was plagued by a guilty conscience after the deed was done—all these are absent from Luke's narrative. In this account there is no trace of the weak, indecisive "king" (see Mark) who is manipulated by his scheming "Jezebel," and then fears divine retribution. Here Herod is not portrayed as a paranoid tyrant who fearfully (mis)identifies Jesus as John *redivivus* (Mark 6:14-29); instead, he radically dissociates the two: "I beheaded John; who then is this about whom I hear such things?" In Luke's narrative world, Herod assumes complete responsibility for John's death and exhibits no remorse, no guilt, no fear, no weakness, no doubts or second thoughts. And this characterization is consistent with the Lukan narrator's evaluation of him in 3:18-20: he is the evil but powerful political opponent of the Lord's messengers. And now his baleful gaze has shifted to another prophet, Jesus.

This, then, is the rather stark and flat characterization of Herod that the reader has constructed prior to Luke 13:31. In the light of this malevolent image, the Pharisees' report about Herod wanting to kill Jesus is hardly surprising. Rather, it reinforces the idea that the Tetrarch is wicked and fully capable of preying on the messengers of the Lord.

ALOPEX IN LUKE AND THE EXTRATEXT

There is much (intra)textual information to guide a reader's construction of Herod the Tetrarch, the primary subject of Jesus' metaphor. But what of its secondary subject, fox? Would something in Luke's story lead the audience to reformulate the conventional associations of that term? That is, are foxes depicted in unusual ways in the narrative, so that the reader might have construed an unconventional image of those animals? The story does not provide a unique, specialized frame in this case. The word *alopex* (in its plural form) occurs at only one other point, where Jesus laments, "Foxes have holes, and birds of the air have nests; but the Son of man has nowhere to lay his head" (Luke 9:58). This reconfirms general knowledge about the natural habits of foxes; it therefore does nothing to establish an idiosyncratic set of implications to be associated with this animal.

With reference to the secondary subject (*alopex*), therefore, the reader is forced to access extratextual information about the attributes commonly associated with foxes in life and literature. Philological research in the Koine has largely reconstructed this particular system of associated commonplaces.[12] The data we have suggests that foxes were quite familiar to the inhabitants of the ancient Mediterranean world. Besides commonly-known natural facts about foxes (they live in holes, are doglike, have fur, are agile and quick, sport bushy tails, etc.), there were some conventional figurative applications of the term fox. It seems that of all the traits attributed to foxes, four were seen as comparable to human characteristics.

The first of these characteristics was intelligence. The fox was regarded as an exceptionally smart animal and was depicted in many fables as the wisest of all beasts. In this sense, then, the fox's intelligence was a virtue to be emulated by humans. A second common notion, however, was that the fox's sagacity was perverted in some sense. Too often the wisest of the beasts used his mental capacities not to promulgate wisdom, but rather for illicit, self-serving, and harmful purposes. Thus foxes were often portrayed as devious, sly, mischievous, cunning, and crafty, always attempting to get what was not theirs by right. Dio Chrysostom, for example, could ask concerning some infamous political connivers, "Philip . . . Lysander . . . is Archilochus' crafty fox any different?" (Discourses 74.15; quoted by Downing 1988:180). In short, the fox was commonly considered to be intelligent, although both positive and pejorative connotations attended his sagacity.

Third, foxes also suggested inferiority, weakness, and cowardice. A fox-like person lacked resolve, the ability to carry through with threats or plans. Behind this unfavorable connotation lay a stock (unfavorable) comparison of fox to lion (brave, strong, superior). For example, a Roman proverb went, "When people are at home they tend to think of themselves as lions, but in public they are just foxes" (Petronius, *Satyricon* 44; quoted by Danker 1988:265).

A fourth trait attributed to foxes was the inclination toward destructiveness and rapacity. This pejorative notion was probably based on the actual experiences of farmers and herdsmen who often lost crops and livestock to these common predators. In the LXX we read of foxes that ruin vineyards (Cant 2:15a), and prophets who, like desert foxes, undermine the security of Israel (Ezek 13:4-5; the image is not clear—perhaps they dig under its foundations as foxes dig in city ruins). In Neh 3:35b (LXX) Tobias (an Ammonite) asks concerning the Jews who have recently returned from exile to rebuild Jerusalem's walls, "Shall not a fox go up and pull down their wall of stones?" This seems to be a double-layered saying: the wall is so fragile that a fox could knock it down, and Tobias will be the "fox" to do it! And in *1 Enoch's* allegorical vision recapitulating Israel's history, the foxes who maraud the special flock (i.e., Israel) stand for the Ammonites.[13] Foxes and jackals also were associated with the utter desolation of cities in whose ruins they dwelled:

> For this has grief come; our heart is sorrowful: for this our eyes are darkened. Over the mountain of Zion, because it is made desolate, foxes have walked therein. (Lam 5:17-18)

In summary, the system of implications associated with foxes was rather large and diverse. It included data on the anatomy and habits of foxes, as well as a more specialized subset of abstract notions about their intelligence, disposition, and status *vis-à-vis* other animals. Foxes were alternatively perceived as wise, tricky, cunning, wily, deceitful, inferior, base, of little or no concern or consequence, cowardly, greedy, rapacious and destructive. Such traits made the fox a favorite subject of figurative applications to human beings. Given the paucity of linguistic data extant from that period, however, it is not possible to determine whether one or another of these figurative applications was so predominant as to be considered normative. In the absence of further data, we are obliged to rank all of these linguistic options as equally applicable. (If one dominated, then the reader would naturally go to that one first.) We must assume, therefore, that in every case where *alopex* is used figuratively, the reader depended heavily on context to determine which, if any, of these senses applied.

HEROD AS FOX IN LUKE 13:32

How then does the reader process the metaphorical epithet in Luke 13:32? First, the reader must recognize that Jesus is indeed speaking figuratively. Taken literally, his command—"Go tell this fox"—is nonsensical, for foxes neither speak nor understand human speech. Jesus is obviously referring to a person. By simple (even unconscious) deduction, therefore, readers shift from the literal to the figurative mode of understanding. Once this initial change is effected, the reader begins immediately to shape the secondary subject (fox) so that applicable elements within that system of implications are foregrounded. Conventions in the figurative use of "fox" are thus highlighted, but common knowledge of foxes' anatomy and natural habits are suppressed. Of course, the latter are not eliminated entirely. Still, it is highly unlikely that Jesus is referring to someone's physical attributes (e.g., "Go tell this pointy-nosed so-and-so . . .").

The reader's second cognitive move involves identifying just who is the object of Jesus' epithet. He does not refer to Herod by name, but, as we have already argued, the immediate context makes it very clear that the Galilean Tetrarch is in mind. He cannot be referring to the Pharisees for he uses the singular (*alopex*), and no other likely candidates for Jesus' retort are available. Jesus receives a threat and responds to the threatener.

But what, precisely, is Jesus' opinion of Herod? The text is silent on this matter. Although Jesus has long been in the domain of the Tetrarch, he has not actually interacted with him, nor has he made any previous comments about him. Confronted by this large gap, the reader assumes that Jesus' view of Herod is in line with the Tetrarch's characterization up to this point in the narrative. And this is a logical assumption to make, for Jesus is firmly set as a *privileged character*, that is, one who knows what the reader and the narrator know about other characters, and who is fully in agreement with the narrator's assessment of events and personages. No contrary indicators disrupt that harmony of viewpoint in these verses. The reader presumes, therefore, that when the Lukan Jesus refers to Herod, he has in mind the same portrait of the Tetrarch that the reader has constructed in reading the story thus far. In turn, this image constitutes the interpretive frame essential for narrowing the semantic options for the metaphor in question. That is, Herod's depiction through Luke 13:31 is a governing factor in the reader's assessment and ranking of the potential implications of "fox."

Having identified Herod as the primary subject, the audience concludes that Jesus' metaphorical epithet is pejorative. Nothing in Herod's characterization thus far demonstrates laudable wisdom on his part. Indeed, what one finds is precisely the opposite. It would be counterintuitive to conclude that Jesus wishes to praise the intellect of a tyrant who has murdered "the greatest born of woman" (7:28) and threatened to kill the "son of the Most High" (1:32). Reader expectations, shaped by what has transpired in the story, narrow the range of semantic options to those which are negative.

Is Jesus' metaphor meant primarily to castigate the Tetrarch as devious, cunning, and wily? Plummer (1914:349) argued for this option and even added a confident assessment of Herod's motivation and state of mind: "Herod's craftiness lay in his trying to get rid of an influential leader and a disquieting preacher of righteousness by a threat which he did not have the courage to execute. He did not wish to bring upon himself a second time the odium of having slain a prophet." Against this interpretation, it should be noted that nowhere else in Luke-Acts is Herod portrayed as either cunning or troubled by public opinion (over his slaying of John), or again, as in any way lacking the courage or will to act on his convictions. The traits and motives alleged by Plummer derive not from *this* narrative, but rather from Josephus' dramatic accounts about Antipas' (a name never used for Herod in Luke) machinations and resultant public resentment, and from the other gospels where Herod is portrayed as a vacillating, guilt-ridden, and frightened monarch. In Luke's narrative world, the Tetrarch displays none of these traits, and therefore the reader is not likely to rank the connotation of cunning highly in attempting to understand Jesus' metaphorical epithet.

A more attractive option is that Jesus is simply calling his ruler weak and insignificant. The sense of the passage would then be that the threat on Jesus' life is hollow because Herod has not the status, power, or courage to carry it out. Fully confident in his own superior status and the sanctity of his mission, Jesus is free to disregard Herod. Taking this tack, one modern critic (Grimm 1973:114-16) even claims to detect here cryptic intertextual allusion casting Jesus as the lion of David over against Herod as the Saulian fox.[14] While Jesus is surely denying that the Tetrarch will kill him, however, it does not necessarily follow that Jesus considers his overlord weak and ineffectual. The reason why Jesus will not die in Galilee is not because his would-be executioner is incapable or lacks resolve, but rather because such an event would not fit into the divine plan (13:33). Jesus is destined to die in Jerusalem. Furthermore, an assessment of Herod as inconsequential or cowardly is inconsistent with his image as constructed to this point by the reader. In light of his execution of the Baptist, it can hardly be said that this overlord lacks either the will power or real power to carry out his agenda. He cannot be ignored. Once again, he is not (in *this* story) the timid, hen-pecked person who agonizes over his actions and is easily swayed by the opinions of others. These images, which are drawn from Josephus and the other gospels, too often have led critics to put undue emphasis on this understanding of the metaphor (e.g., Hoehner 1970:347).

The final fox-like trait—the inclination to destroy what is valuable but vulnerable—is very attractive to the reader, for it is perfectly congruent with the frame of Herod's characterization thus far in Luke's story. Of all the connotations associated with foxes, *malicious destructiveness* stands out as most applicable to the Tetrarch. He has beheaded John and is now intent on murdering Jesus. Foregrounded in the reader's mind, therefore, is the image of the malevolent predator, the rapacious marauder, the destroyer of vineyards and livestock. Upon hearing of Herod's threat, Jesus pegs the Tetrarch as a varmint in the Lord's field, a murderer of God's agents, a would-be disrupter of the divine economy.[15]

By using the dual frames of Herod's characterization in Luke and of the conventional figurative uses of *alopex*, the reader can come to tentative conclusions about the meaning of

Jesus' epithet. At this point, the reader's hypothesis is that the primary thrust of Jesus' comment is to identify and condemn this Galilean tyrant as one of the earthly powers who oppose the implementation of the divine plan by destroying God's agents. The possibilities remain, of course, that Jesus is also characterizing Herod as cunning and inconsequential, though these options are somewhat suppressed. In other words, the reader cannot entirely dismiss these as semantic possibilities for the metaphor. The notion that Jesus is praising the Tetrarch's sagacity is quickly eliminated from consideration. Although not foregrounded in this case, other elements of the *alopex* system of implications (e.g., natural habits, behavior, or anatomical features) continue to hold potential for the evolution of Herod's image as the story progresses. Having identified Herod as a fox, the reader will (consciously and unconsciously) continue to look for ways in which the Tetrarch is foxlike. The metaphor's tension endures; as reading progresses, the audience searches for information that would confirm, supplement, alter, or even negate their initial understanding of Jesus' epithet.

The hypothesis that Jesus' primary intent is to characterize Herod as malicious destroyer is reinforced in the rest of Jesus' lengthy saying (13:32b-35). The reader draws an (implicit) analogy between Herod's threat to kill Jesus and Jerusalem's role as killer of prophets. *This* killer (Herod) will not kill him, but *that* one (Jerusalem) will, even as it has murdered other prophets. This implicit analogy may very well explain the unusual choice of demonstrative pronoun in Jesus' epithet for Herod. Since Herod is not present when the reference is made, one expects Jesus to call him *that* (*ekeine*) fox. Instead, Jesus calls him *this* (*taute*) fox, thus raising the specter of another—more distant—predator lying in wait.

But the analogy is carried to still another level: Jerusalem herself will be the victim of a bloodthirsty marauder. When Jesus laments, "how often did I wish to gather your children together as a hen [gathers] her brood under her wings, but you would not have it" (13:34b), the imagery is that of a hen defending chicks against attack by a predator. Jesus does not specify the predator, but the reader immediately thinks of the fox, for it was a common predator of livestock and chickens and it has just been mentioned by Jesus.[16] Thus, part of the connective tissue binding together this seemingly discontinuous passage is the reiterated imagery of predatory foxes (Herod, Jerusalem, Rome) that threaten vulnerable prey (Jesus, the prophets, the children of Jerusalem). The images are etched indelibly in the reader's mind and spawn other images; even the reference to Jerusalem's future desolation—"your house is left to you"—elicits the connotations of foxes living in the ruins of decimated cities.

The metaphor Jesus creates will remain vital. Though readers strongly expect Herod to continue his role as evil destroyer, the other attributes of the fox might also emerge as his character is developed in the narrative. Jesus has tagged him as a fox, and so he might very well exhibit cunning, or cowardice, or even some of the natural characteristics of the varmint not usually applied to humans. That is for the reader to discover as the work unfolds.

6

TETRARCH AND EXTRATEXT

INTRODUCTION: HEROD AND THE RHETORIC OF BOLDNESS

Our approach to characters and characterization in Luke-Acts stresses the significance of the original extratextual repertoire (= extratext). This store of conventional knowledge was not simply a convenient magazine of ornamental imagery, but was an important factor in the production of literary meaning. The characterization of Herod the Tetrarch provides a good case study of how the extratext enabled the audience to construct characters and thereby to experience their rhetorical effects.

Much of the rhetoric in Luke's narrative is designed to mold readers into ideal *witnesses*. There are, of course, two essential criteria for being a reliable witness: one must (1) carefully and insightfully perceive the events in question; and (2) report what one has seen and heard to others. It is not enough simply to be a witness *of*; one must also bear witness *to*. In this study, we have devoted much attention to the rhetoric of perception—how readers are persuaded to become ideal witnesses *of* "the things that have been fulfilled." We have said little, however, about how readers of Luke-Acts are inspired to become brave and outspoken witnesses *to* what they have "seen and heard" (i.e., what they have read).

That one of the story's primary goals is to transform a mere *reader* into a bold *teller* is obvious. It begins by lifting up as exemplars the "eyewitnesses" who faithfully reported everything they had seen and heard, and ends with Paul (in Rome) "preaching the kingdom of God, and teaching about the Lord Jesus Christ with all boldness (*parresias*), unhindered" (Acts 28:31). Between these two poles lie numerous examples of protagonists who declare their faith despite hostile listeners (Luke's story has much more the flavor of the martyrdom genre than do the other New Testament narratives; see Talbert 1983). It is quite clear, then, that the narrative not only demands to be read (witnessed) in a particular way, but also seeks to be retold (witnessed to) by its readers.

Perhaps the most explicit passage urging boldness to witness is the prayer of the early community in Jerusalem. When Peter and John are miraculously let out of prison, they go to their friends and report that the Sanhedrin has ordered them neither to preach nor teach in the name of Jesus. The community responds by praying that God grant them boldness (*parresia*) to speak the word.

> . . . they lifted their voices together to God, saying, "O Sovereign, it is you who formed the heaven and the earth and the sea and all that is in them, who, by the mouth of David, our father and your servant, by the Holy Spirit, said,
>
> > 'Why did the Gentiles rage, and the peoples plot in vain? The kings of the earth came up, and the rulers were gathered together (*synechthesan*) in one location against the Lord and against his anointed.'
>
> For truly, in this city were gathered together (*synechthesan*) against your holy servant Jesus—whom you anointed—Herod and Pontius Pilate both, along with the Gentiles and the peoples of Israel, to do whatever your hand and plan had predestined to occur. And even now, O Lord, take note of their threats, and grant that your servants may speak your word with all boldness (*meta parresias pases*) . . ." And when they had prayed, the place where they had gathered was shaken, and all of them were filled with the Holy Spirit, and began to speak the word of God with boldness (*meta parresias*). (Acts 4:23-31)

There can be no doubt that readers are here being encouraged to witness courageously along with the community. What may not be so obvious to critics, however, is that this rhetoric of boldness began to develop much earlier in the narrative. Although the term *parresia* does not appear in the Third Gospel, by the time readers encounter the community prayer early in

Acts, they are steeped in the ideal of boldness. In this chapter, we shall explore how this rhetoric of *parresia* develops in the story prior to the community prayer, and how that development helps the audience to understand that supplication. Our thesis is tripartite: (1) John the Baptist and Jesus serve as prototypes of *parresia*; (2) Herod functions as their foil (a fact that—at least in Jesus' case—is signalled in the community prayer itself); and (3) the characterization of all three (and of the relationships among them) depends heavily on conventions in the Septuagint and Greco-Roman culture. We turn initially to a survey of these extratextual phenomena.

CHARISMATIC VERSUS RULER IN ANCIENT MEDITERRANEAN LITERATURE AND LIFE

Reconstructing the Ancient Extratext

Many difficulties attend the charting of extratexts, be they modern or ancient. Because extratexts are, by definition, *assumed* knowledge, they are rarely codified (Alter 1981:47-49). We cannot expect to find many abstract definitions of conventions which the people of the time (authors, readers, and critics alike) took for granted. And with regard to an ancient extratext, we are not able to establish the contours of a repertoire by conducting a poll. Rather, we must *infer* an extratext from the past solely on the basis of extant literature. Even that culture's *social* conventions are now largely filtered through its *literary* legacy, a fact that many modern sociologists have simply disregarded. And what remains of Greco-Roman literature cannot be considered fully representative of that great period's extratext. We cannot be sure, therefore, how widespread or long-lived or well formulated a convention was. Furthermore, our endeavors to recover ancient literary conventions are unavoidably plagued by a certain circularity of reasoning: we see something interesting in the text; we then go to contemporary literature to determine whether it is part of a pattern; and finally, if we are satisfied that it is indeed reflective of a convention, we use that convention as a framework for interpreting the work in question.

For all of these reasons, then, our maps of Luke's extratext must be considered largely provisional (direct quotation from the Septuagint would be an exception to this caveat). Nevertheless, a search for the ancient extratext is not always fruitless; and our sense of the hermeneutical value of such knowledge should conquer our reservations about attempting to recover it.[1]

In looking for extratextual factors that may have influenced the characterization of John, Jesus, and Herod (and the relations among them), we begin with a very firm fix on the time of writing and on the general cultural milieu of Luke's reader (see Chapters 1 and 2 above). Then we adopt a rather broad rubric for how these three powerful figures interact in the story. A survey of salient passages reveals that Luke depicts the relationships between John and Herod, and Jesus and Herod, as conflicts between charismatic and ruler (i.e., institutional authority figure). The Baptist and Jesus are clearly charismatic in that their authority derives not from heredity or bureaucracy, but rather from their unusual gifts of mind and spirit. Herod's authority is based on the position he holds, an inherited tetrarchate buttressed by Rome's bureaucracy. What we see, then, is a typical example of what Max Weber defined as the perennial clash between charisma and institution (see Darr 1987:139-42 for more on Weber's categories).

Once we have defined the perimeters of our search and identified a suitable heuristic device, we sift the literary remains of Greco-Roman culture with the charismatic-versus-ruler rubric. We cannot chronicle the entire search process here. It must suffice to note that two well-entrenched conventional patterns emerge: (1) within Greco-Roman literature in general, the prevalent juxtaposition of "philosopher against tyrant" comes to light; and (2) in the LXX the stereotypical motif of "prophet versus king" appears. These two quite similar patterns formed part of the repertoire that the competent reader of Luke-Acts brought to bear in constructing the Tetrarch as a character, especially in terms of his relationships with John and Jesus. Luke's references to the Tetrarch would have triggered within the reader a certain set of expectations derived from the reader's familiarity with these two conventional ways of portraying charismatics and institutional rulers. In what follows we shall describe these patterns and their functions more fully.

Philosopher Against Tyrant in Greco-Roman Culture

The type-scene in which a wise man confronts a tyrant was as prevalent in Greco-Roman literature as the show-down at high noon is in American movies and popular novels. In these stock scenes a philosopher of some stripe (the category had become very broad by the end of the first century C.E.) plays the protagonist, while a ruler, generally portrayed as a powerful tyrant, plays the antagonist. The interaction between these two types consists of a charged and hostile confrontation. Despite being vulnerable to torture and/or death, the philosopher invariably exhibits the Cynic-Stoic ideals of self-sufficiency (*autarkeia*), self-control, and boldness (*parresia*). When threatened by the tyrant, the sage retorts wittily and wisely, or takes the occasion to expound his philosophy, or, in some cases, to showcase preternatural gifts. Sometimes the tyrant is won over by the philosopher; more often, the wise man becomes a martyr. In either case, the ideal of resistance to tyranny is upheld and the tyrant fails to get what he seeks—ultimate control over the sage. These suspenseful, melodramatic, agonistic scenes with stock characters were extremely popular in Greco-Roman culture and affected the way philosophers behaved in actual life. Indeed, the image of the traveling philosopher (usually a Cynic or Stoic) who confronted and reproached local rulers was so common as to be a cliché in the Roman world of the late first century (MacMullen 1966:59-60). No self-respecting sage could afford not to confront the nearest tyrant. The conflict between philosophers and tyrants became the subject of essays (e.g., Epictetus' "How Ought We to Bear Ourselves Toward Tyrants?" and Dio Chrysostom's "Diogenes, or, On Tyranny"), anecdotes, exempla, chreiai, and especially the idealizing biographies of philosophers.[2]

Perhaps the favorite subject of chreiai and exempla of these sorts was Diogenes of Sinope, the morose sage who tended to upset social conventions. The most famous tale about Diogenes' behavior toward rulers concerned his run-in with Alexander the Great. When Alexander comes to Corinth, Diogenes does not deign to visit him; instead, Alexander comes out to see the sage, who just happens to be sunbathing. When the great conqueror asks him whether he wants anything, Diogenes replies, "Yes. I wish that you would step out of my sunlight." Alexander is so impressed with the sage's sense of himself that, rather than punishing him, he admires him.[3] Perhaps more pertinent to our study, however, are the chreiai that depict Diogenes as the "censor of tyrants." Two examples follow.

> Dionysius the Stoic says that after [the battle of] Chaeronea he [Diogenes] was seized and dragged off to Philip [of Macedon], and being asked who he was, replied, "A spy upon your insatiable greed." For this he was admired and set free.
>
> Perdiccas having threatened to put him to death unless he came to him, "That's nothing wonderful," quoth he, "for a beetle or tarantula would do the same." Instead of that he would have expected the threat to be that Perdiccas would be quite happy to do without his company.[4]

Notable in these short narratives are the threat against the philosopher's life, and the invective using animal imagery—stock material from the arsenal of Stoic rhetoric that appears in Jesus' epithet for Herod (Luke 13:31).

The tyrant versus philosopher convention, developed on Greek soil, proved a popular means of expressing opposition to tyranny throughout the Greco-Roman world. Roman senators, Alexandrian Jews and Greeks, and a host of philosophical schools used this formula in one way or another.[5] The Jewish story of Eleazar and the so-called Seven Sons who oppose and are executed by Antiochus (in IV Macc) is testimony to the widespread influence of this Hellenistic convention (MacMullen 1966:84). Here Jewish protagonists are dubbed "philosophers;" they "antiphilosophize against the tyrant" (8:15); and, each in turn, they demonstrate their *parresia* and *autarkeia*. Written *circa* 37-41 C.E., the work is a dramatic diatribe with definite signs of Stoic influence. Pious reason is sovereign over the emotions (1:1-6; 2:6; 6:31; passim), and the best way of proving it is to recount the heroism of those who "died for the sake of virtue" (Hadas 1953:91, 147). And, as usual, the point is made that the tyrant has physical control over the heroes but can never dominate their reason. In the climactic scene, Antiochus plays the tyrant role to perfection: he tests and tempts the victims; he asks paradigmatic leading questions; and he responds in typical ways to their answers and conduct (he is very impressed and uses the martyrs as examples for his troops, we are told). The narrator interprets the entire incident allegorically: the confrontation was a sacred *agon* whose referee was virtue, and whose contestants were Eleazar and the Seven Sons; the tyrant was the adversary, and all the world were the spectators (19:11-16).

The conventional confrontation of philosopher and tyrant was so commonplace (and apparently so abused) by the end of the first century C.E. that Lucian could satirize it in his famous story of "The Passing of Peregrinus." In that tongue-in-cheek tale, poor Peregrinus, the would-be philosopher, travels all the way to Rome hoping to gain glory and to establish his status as a true sage by confronting the Emperor himself. Lucian reverses convention by depicting the Emperor not as a despot but as a "mild and gentle" old man who just wants to be left alone. When Peregrinus persists in condemning and annoying the Emperor anyway (just to fulfill the conventional expectations), he is finally expelled from Rome by a lesser official. At this turn of events, the "simple folk" hail Peregrinus as hero. Thus Peregrinus the (pseudo-)philosopher gets the recognition he craved, albeit in ironic fashion.[6]

The functions of this ubiquitous topos are quite obvious and have already been touched on. First, a confrontation with tyranny seems to have been a veritable *sine qua non* for philosophers; and they were often compared on this score ("How did the founders of *your* school do when it came to opposing despots?"). Philostratus says as much in writing about Apollonius of Tyana:

> I am aware that the conduct of philosophers under despotism is the truest touchstone of their character, and am in favor of inquiring in what way one man displays more courage than another . . . so I must first of all enumerate all the feats of wise men in the presence of tyrants which I have found worthy of commemoration, and contrast them with the conduct of Apollonius. For I think it is the best way of finding out the truth. (Book VII, 1)

Philostratus then recounts a number of instances when philosophers confronted tyrants, and in each case argues that Apollonius' acts were superior. At another point in this biographical account, the author recounts a story about Apollonius leading a band of young disciples toward Rome and certain conflict with Nero. The band is met and warned by one of their kind who is retreating from the capitol. Instead of fleeing, however, Apollonius welcomes the chance to confront the Emperor, deeming it an opportunity to test his disciples to see "which of them are philosophers and which of them prefer some other line of conduct than that of philosopher" (Book IV, 37). Confronting the tyrant was obviously a litmus test (perhaps *the* litmus test) for the sage, and thus, tales about how philosophers behaved in these dire circumstances were embellished and multiplied.[7] The import for our study is that a hellenistic reader would expect a charismatic figure to confront and upbraid the local despot.

Second, the confrontation scene provided the sage a dramatic stage for exhibiting the virtues of *autarkeia* and *parresia*. These Cynic-Stoic ideals form the ethical substructure of virtually all of the philosopher-versus-tyrant stories. Often, the moral lesson is taught by simple ironic contrasts between the behavior of sage and tyrant. The despot may well have full physical control of the situation, but he lacks self-control. Despite being vulnerable to the tyrant, the sage maintains full inner control. To sharpen the contrast, the tyrants are usually drawn rather flatly as paranoid and vindictive, driven to cruelty by a lust for power and fear of losing it. Dio Chrysostom provides a convenient description:

> Every one of them calls to mind the deaths of [other] tyrants and all the conspiracies that have ever been formed against them; he imagines that they are all coming his way, and is as terror stricken as if he were doomed to all those deaths; and he is always wanting to look on every side and to turn around, as though he might be struck from any quarter. (6:53; Mussies 1972:343)

Dio's definition certainly seems applicable, at least in part, to Luke's Herod, who carries on a perplexed interior monologue about John and Jesus as potential enemies (Luke 9:6-9).

Third, these scenes are entertaining and effective forums to showcase teachings and/or charismata, for validating a wise man's claim to divinity, or for refuting charges lodged against him. (It seems that followers of a later time often used such scenarios to stage a powerful apologia for their erstwhile leader, and thus to authenticate their own identity *vis-à-vis* various authorities and other, more powerful, groups.)

It is impossible to determine the extent to which the common philosopher versus tyrant story may have become a formal literary genre. Nevertheless, as Musurillo (1954:239) remarks, "whether or not these scattered tales ever crystallized into a definite literary form, there is good reason to suppose that the portrait of the *vir bonus et sapiens* resisting the tyrant became a stock motif in the rhetorical and philosophical schools, especially in the Roman period." What we are dealing with, then, was probably not a rigidly formulated literary phenomenon restricted to a kind of literature, but rather a stock situation (or type scene) that involved stereotyped characters behaving in conventional ways and with typical results. The Greco-Roman reader of the first century *expected* the charismatic protagonist (in whatever literary genre) to confront the tyrant and exhibit certain qualities in doing so. It is this convention that lies behind the depiction of Herod and his relationships with John and Jesus, and so forms the pertinent context of expectations affecting their characterization.

Prophet Versus King in the Septuagint

In his study of the plague narrative of Exodus, Martin Buber (1946:63) insightfully places the conflict of Moses and Pharaoh against the backdrop of a pattern, a situation "which recurs again and again from Samuel to Jeremiah, a situation in which the *nabi'* penetrates into history again and again and operates therein. It is the great refrain of Israel's history: prophet versus king." The ubiquity of this pattern is underscored by a short listing of the more famous antagonists: Moses/Pharaoh, Samuel/Saul, Nathan/David, Elijah/Ahab; Micaiah ben Imlah/Ahab, and Jeremiah/Jehoiakim. This convention is most noticeable in the Deuteronomistic History with its stark alternatives—Yahwism or idolatry. In these stories the "prophets represent the deuteronomistic ideology and mark . . . how far short of it a particular king may fall. The importance of this conflict motif can be seen in the fact that the reign of so many kings is punctuated by . . . angry prophets denouncing some act or attitude of a king" (R. P. Carroll 1981:136).

Although these common episodes vary widely in details, they tend to include certain elements and follow a rather set pattern of development. And although the prophet is the protagonist in these stories of conflict, most of the accounts are set within a larger, quite rigid chronological and theological framework that focusses on the monarchs of Israel and Judah. The opening formula for such tales is usually "in the reign of [king x], the word of the Lord came to [prophet y]." The king in question is invariably evaluated negatively by the reliable narrator. Typical is 3 Reigns (= 1 Kgs) 16:30: "And Ahab did that which was evil in the sight of the Lord, and did more wickedly than all that were before him." These remarks then set the stage for the prophet's confrontation with the king.

The impetus for confronting the king comes from *outside* the prophet. He is seized by *to rhema tou theou*, which functions both as message and motivator. The prophet himself is often portrayed as physically, socially, or emotionally unsuited to the task at hand (e.g., Moses' speech impediment, Amos' lowly social status). Such diminutions of the messenger highlight the effectiveness of the "word of the Lord" which empowers and motivates the prophet. In this sense these conflict stories differ sharply from the philosopher versus tyrant tales in Greco-Roman culture. The biblical narrator does not hesitate to point out the human frailty of the prophets and their dependence on something beyond themselves. Self-control and self-reliance (*autarkeia*) are not highly valued in these narratives. Thus we see Elijah fleeing from Ahab and his wicked wife Jezebel, and Micaiah ben Imlah falsifying his prophecy to avoid upsetting Ahab and Jehoshaphat.

Inevitably, the prophet must confront the king and deliver a divine oracle condemning the monarch's behavior and attitudes and spelling out certain consequences. The prophet "enters history" (to use Buber's term), for his warnings invariably have national or international import. When prophets confront kings in the LXX, it is never simply a matter of personal morality, for these tales are always freighted with salvation-historical significance. The very survival of a people depends on what happens in these tense and dramatic confrontations.

In delivering his oracle, the prophet often performs wonders and signs to establish the efficacy of the "word" he speaks, as well as to authenticate his credentials as a genuine messenger of the Lord. These miracles are not performed simply to dazzle, or to idealize (or divinize) the prophet himself. They are done only in the service of the divine word.[8]

The prophet's oracle, accusation, threat, or sign most often elicits a hostile response from the king who then refuses to heed the Lord's will. Sometimes the king's displeasure with the message carries over to the messenger, and, as a consequence, prophets are jailed, pursued, or otherwise persecuted.[9] However, what we find very often is that the king is ambiguous about the seer. Sometimes the king (e.g., Pharaoh, Saul, David, Jeroboam, Ahab) even humbles himself in the face of the prophet's power. The prophet's actions and words provoke not just the king, but also his advisors—Moses must face the sorcerers of Pharaoh's court, Elijah battles Ahab's prophets of Baal on Mount Carmel, Micaiah is slapped and ridiculed by Zedekiah, and Jeremiah is opposed by Hananiah. And finally, an account of the fulfillment of the seer's oracle is often appended to the story of conflict between prophet and king.

The short account of the nameless seer (*anthropos tou theou*) who confronts King Jeroboam at the altar of Bethel (3 Reigns [= 1 Kgs] 13:1-10) exhibits many of the conventions of the prophet versus king story sketched above. The prophet comes *en logo kyriou* (13:1) to the idolatrous altar that Jeroboam had set up (3 Reigns 12:25-33 establishes Jeroboam's wickedness and 3 Reigns 13:33-34 furnishes the typical formulaic, negative evaluation of him). In the king's presence, the prophet delivers an oracle predicting the monarch's overthrow, the death of his priests, and the appearance of a sign; the latter is to be a miraculous splitting of the altar (13:2-3). Upon hearing these threatening words, the king stretches out his hand and orders that the prophet be seized. Instantly the king's hand withers and the altar is split. Then the stricken monarch is humbled and must beg the man of God to restore his hand, which he does. In this tale we thus see in short order: an emphasis on the word of the Lord, the delivery of an oracle, a threat by the king against the prophet, a miracle, a sign, and reversal of status as the king is humbled before the prophet.[10]

Lukan scholars have firmly established that Luke's portraits of John the Baptist, Jesus, and the disciples are colored largely from the palette of prophetic materials in the Septuagint.[11] And it is highly likely that the significant "supporting" actors in Luke-Acts have received their shading from the same source. After all, characters are shaped primarily in relation to other figures in a narrative. If John, Jesus, and the others are truly prophets (in the Septuagintal sense) then they must confront certain kinds of antagonists—false prophets, recalcitrant Israelites, and evil rulers.

In conclusion, the interpreter of Luke-Acts must be aware of two somewhat similar sets of extratextual conventions that affect the characterization of Herod the Tetrarch. Both the septuagintal "prophet versus king" pattern and the Greco-Roman "philosopher versus tyrant" convention pit charismatics against wicked rulers in ways that showcase and idealize the charismatic's gifts and/or message. Both feature climactic confrontation scenes in which the charismatic proves the ruler's superior in some way. As Hellenism increasingly influenced Judaism, the ancient prophets came to be seen by some Jews as martyred philosophers, a notion that finds a certain corroboration in the tales about their resistance to evil kings (Fischel 1947; Schoeps 1950). In both traditions the litmus test of the charismatic was a confrontation with a hostile ruler, and so it was natural that analogies were drawn between these two kinds of stories. Sirach's way of eulogizing Moses (ca. 180 BCE) would thus very probably have been appreciated by Gentile and Jew alike: "[And the] Lord glorified him *in the presence of kings*" (45:3). In any event, these two somewhat analogous phenomena form the extratextual backdrop against which the reader constructs the Tetrarch and his charismatic opponents in Luke-Acts.

JOHN, JESUS, AND HEROD IN LUKE-ACTS

In light of both the extratextual repertoire described above and the depictions of John and Jesus in the birth narratives, the introduction to John's ministry in Luke 3:1-2 is clearly meant to be understood by the reader as the beginning of another tale of a prophet in Israel. As we saw in Chapter 5, Pilate and Herod stand out among the many potentates listed in 3:1 because their domains have already been identified as territories in which the drama of salvation will unfold. John's reintroduction to the reader (3:2b) leaves no doubt that he is to be understood as a prophet: *egeneto rhema theou epi Ioannen ton Zachariou huion* ("the word of God came to John son of Zacharias") is obviously based on the introductory formulae for prophetic ministries in the LXX (it is an almost exact replica of Jeremiah 1:1a).[12] The allusions to the LXX trigger a whole set of expectations about John's relation to and interaction with a ruler. Readers anticipate conflict with one or another of the rulers listed in 3:1, and Herod is the most likely candidate since he has been most fully construed.

The audience's suspicions are quickly confirmed when, within a few paragraphs, the narrator relates that John confronted Herod and was jailed for his audacity (3:18-20). This passage is opaque in several ways. What, precisely, was the nature of John's charge against Herod and Herodias? Which of Herod's brother's is/was her husband (the reader likely thinks of Philip, since he was the one mentioned in 3:1)? What were the many other "evil things that Herod had done?" The reader is able to answer such questions in a very general sense on the basis of intratextual and extratextual data, but no precise answers are forthcoming. John's message implicitly defines evil as abuse of power, position, and possessions, and so the reader infers that the Tetrarch's infractions have to do with such abuses. Once again, the description of Herod as doer of evil (*poneron*) resonates with the short negative evaluations of rulers in the Deuteronomistic History (e.g., 3 Reigns [= 1 Kgs] 16:30). As Nathan confronted David concerning Bathsheba, and Elijah confronted Ahab about Jezebel, so John confronts the Tetrarch concerning Herodias and a host of other abuses. The scenario provided by the narrator is only a sketch, but it is enough to confirm Herod as the wicked king of the Septuagintal prophet versus king pattern. Absent from all this, of course, is a dramatization of the climactic scene of confrontation itself, a lacuna whose significance we have already discussed (see Chapters 3 and 5). In summary, the lack of a scene of confrontation deprived John of an idealizing forum, and denied Herod the opportunity to exhibit a more appealing side (either by showing regret or being the victim of a plot by Herodias). In the (truncated) Lukan version of the story, Herod is starkly evil.

The Tetrarch is next brought to the reader's attention by an oblique reference in a list of names of women who accompany Jesus on his preaching tour of Galilee (8:2-3). The narrator points out that one of these women, a certain Joanna, is the wife of Herod's manager (*epitropos*). Besides adding to the reader's store of data on the Tetrarch's personal life, this remark serves as a reminder that *Herod* remains *in power in Galilee* and may well be interested in a second prophetic figure in the realm (Fitzmyer 1981:698). As far as the reader knows, John is still in Herod's prison—a place that almost certainly could hold more than one prisoner. That the wife of Herod's steward is now a member of Jesus' entourage makes it highly likely that the Tetrarch knows about, or will soon know about, Jesus.

Very soon (at 9:7-9), the reader learns that Herod has heard about Jesus and is very perplexed (*dieporei*, Luke 9:7) because of the various opinions that people express about this new prophet's identity. Herod's inner turmoil and suspicions about Jesus elicit the conventional image of the tyrant as one who is always looking over his shoulder, suspicious of everyone as a potential assassin or usurper (see, e.g., Dio Chrysostom's vivid description above). John is now completely off the scene. Although others may believe Jesus to be John *redivivus*, Herod radically dissociates them (see Chapter 3) and frankly admits to having beheaded the Baptist. The focus now shifts ominously from the relationship between John and Herod to that between Jesus and Herod. Lest the reader miss these developments, the narrator observes that the Galilean tyrant *kept trying to see*

Jesus (9:9b). Already the die has been cast: Herod, who thus far has played the role of evil king in the Septuagintal sense, will continue as the primary antagonist of those who carry out the divine agenda. But elements of the Greek tyrant have begun to color the Tetrarch's image also. The reader expects that Herod and Jesus will be in conflict, and is in suspense as to the outcome.

Luke 13:31-35, which we have examined quite carefully in the preceding chapter, intensifies the suspense surrounding Jesus and Herod, and plays off of the philosopher versus tyrant conventions even more directly.[13] Jesus' retort and its metaphorical epithet directed at Herod, the focus on the protagonist's inner fortitude and boldness, and the emphasis on the charismatic's martyrdom all evoke the familiar Greco-Roman conflict scenes.

As Dibelius recognized (1965:162-63), this passage is similar in form to a chreia, which he defined as "a short pointed saying of general significance, originating in a definite person and arising out of a definite situation" (156). Introduced with a short question, personal remark, or review of the circumstances within which the saying was uttered, chreiai focused attention on the utterance itself which, in turn, revealed the wit, wisdom, or spirit (the *ethos*) of the speaker.[14] Chreiai were thus a favored medium for capturing the essence of honored persons from the past (Dibelius 1965:156). In Luke 13:31-35, the Pharisees' delivery of the Tetrarch's threat is the "definite situation" which prompts Jesus' defiant, yet poignant, reply: he will indeed die the death of a prophet/philosopher, but his death and the events leading up to it will not be determined by the likes of Herod.

Jesus' response to Herod's threat must have sounded familiar to Greco-Roman readers who had heard many chreiai about legendary philosophers. Remember, for example, Diogenes' response in a similar situation.

> Perdiccas having threatened to put him to death unless he came to him, "That's nothing wonderful," quoth he, "for a beetle or a tarantula would do the same." Instead of that he would have expected the threat to be that Perdiccas would be quite happy to do without his company.

Once again, the primary function of such stories was to highlight the charismatic's *autarkeia* and *parresia*, the virtues so dear to Cynic-Stoic philosophy. Through this (peculiarly Lukan) scenario, Jesus and Herod are firmly—and suspensefully—linked in the mind of the reader. It can be only a matter of time now before the two meet face to face. The Lukan Herod thus adds elements of suspense and conflict that serve to maintain reader interest and build the dramatic connective tissue that binds the work together.

Jesus Before Herod (Luke 23:6-12)

The anticipated confrontation between Jesus and Herod occurs in the midst of the passion narrative.

> But when Pilate heard [them referring to Galilee], he asked whether the man was a Galilean, and upon learning that he was of Herod's jurisdiction, he sent him to Herod, who was himself in Jerusalem in those days. And Herod was very glad (*echare lian*), for he had desired to see (*thelon idein*) him, and he was hoping (*elpizen*) to see some sign performed by him. And he asked him many questions; but he answered him nothing. And the chief priests and the scribes stood by, accusing him vehemently. And Herod and his soldiers, after treating him with contempt and mocking him, dressed him in gorgeous apparel and returned him to Pilate. And Herod and Pilate became friends with one another that very day; for before this they had been at enmity with each other.

This unusual passage is replete with gaps which the audience tries to fill with information gleaned from text and extratext.[15] We shall not attempt to treat all of the interpretive issues that arise in this scene, for the scope of this chapter will not allow it.[16] Rather, our focus will be restricted to four factors that augment and shape reader comprehension of the enigmatic encounter between Herod and Jesus: (1) the repertoire of charismatic versus ruler conventions reconstructed above; (2) the text's rhetoric of perception; (3) intertextual linkage with Isaiah; and (4) Herod's characterization up to this point, especially the fact that Jesus has tagged him as a fox.

Although sketched only briefly, this encounter between

Jesus and Herod bears the unmistakable traits of a martyrology. All of the typical *dramatis personae* make their appearance: the forceful tyrant with his demeaning questions (23:9); the vulnerable but composed prophet; the false but nevertheless vehement accusers, castigating the victim from the sidelines (vs. 10); and the menacing, mocking military men who are only too ready to carry out the will of the tyrant (vs. 11). What is strikingly absent from the type scene, however, is the charismatic's dramatic self-defense through word or deed. The extratext leads the audience to expect strongly that Jesus will use this arena to manifest his teachings, powers, and divine identity. The demagogue's court provides the forum *par excellence* for the revelation of a protagonist's virtues, wisdom, doctrine, and/or supernatural abilities. This is the conventional moment for Jesus to climax his ministry by publicly revealing the true nature of his mission and its divine source. Jesus failed to give an unambiguous apologia before the Sanhedrin and Pilate; the reader hopes strongly that he will do so now. But he neither says nor does anything. The convention has been defamiliarized (to use Iser's term), and the audience seeks meaning in this novelty. Why does Jesus not respond?[17]

The reader can draw upon many sources of information to deal with this perplexing development. The first source to be accessed is what has been read thus far, that is, the work itself. Herod's characterization provides certain clues as to why Jesus now fails to speak or perform a sign. In Luke 23:8, the narrator reports in almost hyperbolic fashion the deep desire of Herod to witness the charismatic about whom he had heard so much. Close readers cannot help but notice the unusual aggregation of verbs of perception in this verse:

—"he was glad when he *saw* Jesus"
—"for he had wished *to see* him"
—"because he had been *hearing* about him"
—"and was hoping to *see* some sign"

This verse not only connects the present event with previous episodes involving Herod (9:7-9; 13:31-35), but also indicates to the reader that the current confrontation should be understood in terms of the by now familiar "seeing and hearing" rhetoric. Herod neither *sees* a sign nor *hears* a sound from Jesus. The visual and acoustic vacuum created by Jesus' lack of response mirrors the spiritual imperceptivity of Herod and the accusers. Their blatant abuse of power assures that they will not see or hear—literally or figuratively—anything from Jesus. When asked earlier by the Council to say whether he was the Christ, he answered, "Even if I do tell you, you will not believe, and if I ask a question, you will not answer" (Luke 22:67-68). There is no need to sow seed on obviously unreceptive soil (see Luke 8:9-15). Those who, like Herod, are wicked and unrepentant, and seek signs simply out of curiosity or to test Jesus, receive only the "sign of Jonah" (virtually a non-sign) or a call to repent (Conzelmann 1960:192). The Tetrarch serves as the ironic embodiment of all of the rulers Jesus referred to in an aside to his disciples:

> Blessed are the eyes which see the things you see, for I say to you that many prophets and *kings wished to see* the things which you see, *and did not see, and to hear* the things which you hear, and *did not hear.* (Luke 10:23-24)

What blocks spiritual vision is not just distance in time, but an attitude of the heart. Simply *wishing* to see is not sufficient to guarantee true vision.[18]

There is, of course, an intertextual dynamic at work here as well. The author is drawing on Isaiah for both the seeing-hearing rhetoric (Isaiah 6:9-10) and the suffering servant imagery:

> He was oppressed and he was afflicted,
> Yet he did not open his mouth;
> Like a lamb that is led to the slaughter,
> And like a sheep that before its shearers is silent,
> So he did not open his mouth. (53:7)

Isaiah provides the author with (1) the materials to explain why there are some in Israel who will never be able to perceive Jesus as *to soterion tou theou*, and (2) the model of the righteous one who remains silent under persecution. That the latter is intended is quite clear from the fact that Luke's Jesus has already used a quote from Isaiah 53 to explain his predicament.

At the meal just before his arrest, Jesus claims that he will fulfill Isaiah 53:7, "he was classed with criminals" (Luke 22:37; Soards 1985a:42). The combination of the recalcitrance of Israel's leaders on one hand, and the necessity of Jesus' death as part of God's salvific plan on the other, help the reader make sense of the strange scene in Herod's court. There is much irony here, for what Herod cannot perceive (but what readers must) is that a divinely inspired event is indeed taking place in his presence, although it is not the type of thing he so strongly hopes to see. Jesus' *parresia*, his bold witnessing, is manifested precisely in his silence, for it testifies to his identity as the suffering but silent Messiah.

For Greco-Roman readers, Jesus' resolute silence in the face of tyranny is an example of *autarkeia*, or strong self-control.[19] Jesus clearly places himself above Herod and his petty curiosity. Jesus and the reader know that something much greater is at hand. The sign of all signs is about to take place, but not here in the presence of the Tetrarch of Galilee. Jesus mounts no defense, and refuses to perform a spectacular deed. Nonetheless, he conducts himself in an admirable manner. The narrative has broken the convention that calls for the protagonist's charismata and genuine identity to be publicly verified in the tyrant's court. This forces the audience to look elsewhere (i.e., ahead) for a climactic recognition scene in which the protagonist will be fully revealed and authenticated to the other characters in the story. In the Lukan narrative, the full revelation of Jesus will occur in the appearance of the Lord to the disciples after the resurrection. Jesus' resurrection (the meaning of which is revealed in scripture and the breaking of the bread; Luke 24:26-46) finally opens the eyes of his disciples to understand fully his status and function in God's plan; and it is to the resurrection that they will witness in Acts.

Although Pilate and Herod refuse the pressures of the Jewish leaders to condemn Jesus, neither one of these rulers is depicted in a flattering light. Pilate does indeed declare Jesus righteous (or innocent) three times in this account. But what critics often fail to note is that this very insistence on Jesus' lack of guilt makes the Roman governor's "delivering up" of Jesus to the mobs that much more heinous in the eyes of the reader. Pilate is quite convinced that Jesus is innocent, and yet hands him over to those who are intent on seeing him crucified. This can be no one's idea of the upright judge and ruler. In like manner, Herod's return of Jesus to Pilate (Luke 23:11), with its implication that Herod had found nothing worthy of death in the defendant (Luke 23:15), does nothing to rehabilitate the Tetrarch. Legal technicalities aside, the immediate impression is that Pilate handed Jesus over to the Tetrarch in order "to free himself of an awkward case" (Hoehner 1970:88), and that Herod returned him to Pilate for the very same reason.

Herod's cruel and cunning handling of Jesus' hearing reminds the reader of the fact that Jesus has already called this ruler a fox. Like a fox that has cornered its helpless prey, Herod plays a vicious game with his victim. Hoping to be entertained, the ruler badgers and mocks Jesus in the attempt to get him to strike or to perform interesting feats. Herod is still a wicked and formidable opponent, but he is also *crafty* enough to realize when it is time to end the "fox and hen" game. After joining his soldiers in an impromptu round of mocking and insulting Jesus, Herod remands him to Pilate. Why should he take the responsibility for Jesus' death when it appears that others are perfectly willing to shoulder it? Besides, by siding with Pilate in finding Jesus innocent, he will make inroads with the powerful Roman governor. The narrator tells us that Herod's gamble paid off: he avoided direct responsibility for the death of Jesus, and yet, by mirroring Pilate's indecision (both turn Jesus over rather than protect him) and backing him on Jesus' innocence, he makes a powerful friend. In essence, the two become colleagues in capitulation.[20]

The Community Prayer for *Parresia* (Acts 4:23-31)

Herod is next referred to in the Jerusalem believers' prayer near the beginning of Acts. In their petition, the community sets up parallels among three situations: (1) the dramatic scene David envisions in Psalm 2; (2) the trial of Jesus; and (3) their own predicament. The details of Psalm 2:1-2 are linked allegorically to certain of the phenomena of Jesus' trial: the Gentiles = the

Roman soldiers; the peoples = the people of Jerusalem (the tribes of Israel); the kings = Herod; the rulers = Pilate; and, of course, the anointed of the Lord = Jesus.[21] In turn, all of these enemies correspond to the rulers, elders, scribes, and high priests who threaten the nascent community in Jerusalem (4:5-6). That such correspondences are intended to be inferred by the reader is clearly indicated by the repetition in each case of the term *synachthenai* to describe the assemblage of antagonists (4:5, 26, 27). The Jerusalem church is to be viewed as the latest link in a typological chain; and as the most recent of the "Lord's anointed" (Pentecost!) they face opposition just as David, the prophets, John, and Jesus did.

One of the effects of this typology is to force the audience to reassess the trial of Jesus in terms of Psalm 2:1-2. Herod and Pilate have already been linked together by the narrator's remark that they became friends on the day of Jesus' trial; this linkage anticipates and supports the community's claim that these leaders were *allies*.[22] A somewhat discordant note is struck, however, in that both Pilate and Herod found Jesus innocent in Luke's account of the trials. These rulers did *not* "gather against the Lord and his anointed." Indeed, Pilate even made some efforts to liberate Jesus.[23] But this is hardly the major gap it has been made out to be by so many interpreters, especially as regards Herod. The idea that Herod is an antagonist of the divine agenda has been so well established that the reader easily reimages his role in the trial as inimical to Jesus. Moreover, Herod and his soldiers *did* act in a hostile manner toward Jesus, mocking and humiliating him before sending him back to Pilate.

The effect of Acts 4:23-31 is to identify Herod as the archetype of those before whom the "anointed of the Lord" are tried. This passage establishes Herod as part of a pattern which has roots in the scriptures and finds its completest form in Jesus' trial. And the reader understands it to be a pattern that will be reiterated whenever the Lord's anointed witness to "what they have seen and heard." The community has already drawn this analogy between its own predicament and that of Jesus at his trial. The pattern will likely continue to be repeated. In this sense, then, the petition of the community is anticipatory. There will be many more Herods, and Pilates and chief priests, and councils, and accusers, as the message and messengers of the kingdom spread throughout the empire. Soon another Herod (King Agrippa I) will "lay hands on" members of the church (Acts 12:1). He will execute James (John's brother) and, when he sees that his action pleases some of his people, he will imprison Peter in hopes of parading him before the crowds at Passover (Acts 12:2-4). It is near the end of Acts, however, that the pattern is evoked most clearly. Paul's trial before the Roman governor Festus and King Herod (Agrippa II) echoes unmistakably the earlier trial of Jesus before Pilate and Herod the Tetrarch.

Jerome Neyrey's (1985:89) comment that "the trials of the apostles in Acts are continuations of the trial of Jesus in the Gospel" is a somewhat hyperbolic, yet insightful, tribute to the fact that the confrontations between protagonists and tyrants are intentionally and meaningfully paralleled in the story. The lesson is quite clear: confrontations with "Herod" are unavoidable if one is to be a true witness, that is, one who perceives correctly and testifies with *parresia* to what one has seen and heard.

EPILOGUE

One of the common complaints about reader-oriented criticism is that it so focuses on readers reading that authors and writing are neglected. It is hardly coincidental that those who make this complaint are invariably authors. No one relishes the notion that once our writing is published, we lose control of it and it takes on a life of its own. The poignancy of separation between author and text is particularly acute for one who, like myself, writes a book that strongly endorses reader criticism. By doing so, I have implicitly bracketed myself, the author, out of the picture. What counts most now is how you, my audience, understand the text that I have produced. Besides, experience teaches that authors are not necessarily the most astute critics of their own writing. And yet fairness demands that a writer (who is also part of the audience) be allowed the initial assessment of what he or she has authored. Epilogues were invented for just such a purpose.

My foray into the complexities of Lukan characterization has convinced me that Harvey was correct in asserting that characters are contingent on context. But what Harvey failed to recognize is that "context" is much more complex even than the "complicated structure of artificially formed contexts" in the text (1965:31). The definition of context must be broadened to include *the reader reading*, a fact that formalist biblical critics (e.g., poeticists and narratologists) still have not grasped adequately. Of course, including the reader in the interpretive equation complicates our task considerably. Questions about the identity and activities of readers are difficult to answer with precision, and yet they must not simply be ignored. It is at this point that the present study makes a contribution to research on Lukan characters, for it lays out and demonstrates the value of a reader-response model that is appropriate to Luke-Acts.

Readers construct characters, but critics construct readers; and both of these constructive behaviors are strongly conditioned by social and cultural factors (extratextual repertoires). In our post postmodern age, it is impossible to dismiss such influences and bury our heads in "the text alone." Readers to whom critics refer are heuristic constructs that inevitably mirror the persons who construe them. Though this aspect of my work is best assessed by others, I have had some insight as to how and why I imaged the reader as I did. The fact that my interpretation focusses so much on *witness* as an interpretive key, for example, is probably not a coincidence; rather, it grows out of my own experience as the son of Christian missionaries to West Africa. Modern missions tend to view themselves as extensions of Acts, and place a premium on the proclamation of the gospel in hostile environments. This does not mean, of course, that I am reading things *into* the narrative, but only that my reader has many of my predilections and so processes the text in ways that other critics and readers may not.

The reader will always be *my* reader. But that fact does not, indeed should not, preclude attempts to reconstruct the extratext presupposed by the author of Luke-Acts. In other words, we cannot ignore the distance between ourselves and the original readers of this ancient narrative. Although we can never recover it in full, the intended (authorial) reader's cultural repertoire remains the optimal extratext for understanding Luke's story. Those who fancy themselves literary critics but not historians cannot contribute much of value to our knowledge of Lukan character. The historical task must be reshaped, however, for our purpose differs from that of traditional (historical-critical) biblical research. We do not seek to reconstruct the development of pre-gospel traditions, but rather to recover the conventional knowledge and skills requisite for a competent reading of the finished text. "The reader" will always be a hybrid of that world and our world, but this is as it should be.

Finally, my definition of the interpretive context for Lukan characters includes an explanation of reading as an activity. The critic must pay attention to the processes by which readers bring the text to life. If the true object of our inquiry is not static, but consists of readers reading, then we are obliged to take into account factors like retrospection and anticipation, consistency-building, sequence, and identification. Without reference to such factors, it has been well-nigh impossible for gospel scholars and secular critics alike to provide cogent explanations of just what constitutes (intratextual) context. When interpreters bracket the reader reading and focus solely on a text, they overlook the very mechanism by which the textual data are to be ordered, evaluated, supplemented, and related. Disregarding the reading process, some recent literary studies of the gospels handle textual information with little discernible—or defensible—logic or consistency, and so produce highly questionable results.

In conclusion, this study of Lukan characterization charts a hermeneutical course between the doldrums of strict formalism and the maelstrom of total relativism. If, as I have argued, literary characterization is a function neither of the audience nor of the text alone, but rather of the dialogue between them, then methods that neglect or downplay either factor are inadequate. Audiences, whether real or fictional, are variable; and thus, the characters they build will differ. Absolute claims by critics concerning *the* (one and only) meaning of Lukan personae are specious.

To acknowledge the variability of readers and the consequent diversity of characterization, however, is not to assert that all readings are equally valid or worthwhile. The literary historical approach developed herein features two control factors. Schematic though it may be, the text remains a constant in the interpretive equation. It thus serves as the prime criterion for narrowing the range of acceptable readings. Granting priority to the repertoire of the original readers helps us to reduce the spectrum of viable options even further. It seems to me that some such system, which maintains a delicate balance between pluralism and constraint, is necessary in our age of hermeneutical excess.

NOTES

NOTES TO INTRODUCTION

[1]Here I adopt a rather broad definition of character as any figure or group in a literary work. Characterization refers to the process by which characters are formulated, depicted and developed. In accord with the modern critical consensus, I understand the third gospel and Acts to be two volumes of a single work by the same unknown author. The name Luke is sometimes used when referring to that author. This usage is for the sake of convenience only; no specific historical data (e.g., the notion that Luke was a companion of St. Paul) is to be inferred from it. In any case, we have access only to the *implied* author, not the real author of the text.

[2]Of course, this is not to say that redaction critics have failed to contribute any insights concerning characterization and other literary phenomena in Luke-Acts. We can learn much from the work of scholars such as Cadbury (1927, 1955), Brown (1977), and Fitzmyer (1981, 1985), especially in terms of first century Greco-Roman literary culture and how it relates to Luke-Acts. The fact remains, however, that the traditional historical methods simply are not designed for the study of character and characterization, and therefore tend to produce little in this regard.

[3]Moore rightfully warns gospel critics that, "if we are not to remain perpetual dilettantes in our literary criticism of the Bible, we must be prepared to read long and hard in critical theory" (1989:178). Although highly appreciative of some aspects of recent literary criticism of the gospels, Moore's study is in great measure an indictment of the many who have *not* "read long and hard."

[4]The hazards of using New Criticism on Luke-Acts are well documented in Charles H. Talbert's insightful critique (1988:137-38) of Robert C. Tannehill's literary study of the third gospel (1986). As Talbert demonstrates, one cannot address with cogency such subjects as the shape and rhetoric of the narrative without also appealing to its original context of literary conventions.

The best overview and critique of the denial of history by modern and postmodern theorists is Lentricchia's *After the New Criticism* (1980); strong arguments against the widespread antihistorical bias are also found in Said (1983:3-4; 26-39). One of the most influential postmodern biblical scholars to argue for the abandonment of historical context (which he characterizes—or perhaps, caricatures—as the "transcendentalized *Sitz im Leben,* assumed to be independent in principle of attempts to reconstruct it") is Moore (1989:172). Similar sentiments have been expressed by McKnight (1988:150): "A reader-oriented approach acknowledges that the contemporary reader's 'intending' of the text is not the same as that of the ancient author and/or the ancient readers. *This is not possible, necessary, or desirable*" (emphasis added).

[5]Meir Sternberg (1985:10-11) makes the same observation concerning those who would treat ancient Hebrew narrative without reference to its original cultural context. None are willing to set aside the ancient Hebrew and work exclusively in a modern language. As Sternberg notes, this is the Achilles' heel of the antihistorians.

[6]This is not to deny the value of later readings in other milieux. But if we, as *critical* interpreters, are to take Luke-Acts on its own terms, we cannot in good faith ignore the simple fact that it is a narrative from a very different time and place. The questions of the extent to which we can bridge this gap, and of how we should attempt to bridge it, pose difficulties, but do not in any way absolve us from the task itself.

[7]Literary studies by Tannehill (1986, 1990), Dawsey (1986a, 1986b), and Gowler (1989) shed light on discrete aspects of Lukan characterization, but few would consider them to be well-grounded in literary theory. Tannehill and Dawsey virtually ignore broader methodological issues and exhibit little interest in or knowledge of the contemporary theoretical landscape. Gowler shows a greater awareness of literary theory, and even begins to develop one that shows promise; however, he allows sociological categories quickly to overwhelm and obscure literary concerns, and, as a result, his approach remains only partially formed. For example, Gowler notes correctly that a critic must evaluate not just the text, but also the reader and the activity of reading ("Any attempt to evaluate characters apart from the actual reading of the text runs the risk of reductionism" [1989:54]). He fails, however, either to frame or adopt a theory of reading. Gowler also realizes that we should attempt to reconstruct the framework of cultural conventions that are presupposed by Luke-Acts (something Tannehill and Dawsey seem to ignore). He makes some insightful contributions on this score, but his reconstructions are devoted almost exclusively to social scripts rather than to *literary* conventions. The contributions of these three critics and others will be utilized and evaluated at appropriate points throughout this study. At this juncture we need only point out that research on Lukan characterization remains in the embryonic stage; suggestive studies have appeared, but no one has developed a satisfactory (theoretically-sound, text-specific) approach.

An excellent example of the type of approach I call for here is found in Mary Ann Tolbert's recent investigation of the second gospel (1989). This groundbreaking study delineates and applies a method that is attuned to the "context of conventions" in first century Greco-Roman culture and well-rooted in ancient and modern literary theory. What Tolbert designates a "literary historical" approach proves extremely effective in solving narrative riddles that have plagued Markan scholars for centuries. Robert L. Brawley's study of Luke (1990), which treats Lukan characters and other narrative phenomena according to categories developed by Roland Barthes, came into my hands too late to use or evaluate in the present study.

NOTES TO CHAPTER 1
READING READERS READING LUKE-ACTS

[1]Abrams (1953:6) provides a convenient typology of aesthetic theories. He classifies different approaches by their tendency to focus on or emphasize one of four factors in the interpretive equation: (1) the work itself (objective theories); (2) the author or artist (romantic theories); (3) the universe or nature (mimetic theories); or (4) the reader or audience (pragmatic theories).

[2]For thorough discussions of this central problem and of various responses to it, see Freund (1987:134-56) and Darr (1987:20-39).

[3]Fitzmyer (1981:684-6) provides a fine digest of all the historical-critical grapplings with this interpretive problem.

[4]Suleiman (1980:23-24) makes similar observations about Iser.

[5]The presently popular metaphysical skepticism which holds that there really is no such thing as a stable textual entity out there is ultimately self-defeating. To speak of interpretation is to assume the existence of a critic and an object of criticism. While theorists may make the ontological claim that a text as such does not exist, they are obliged to posit the existence of just such an entity in order to do meaningful criticism. For example, Stephen Moore, an admirer of Stanley Fish's "text in the reading community" approach and an advocate of postmodernism, is forced to conclude that while "epistemologically the text is an abyss, praxically it spills over with properties" (1989:128). As Freund (1987:152-54) points out, the subject-object dichotomy refuses to go away, no matter how much critics might rail at it.

[6]On Iser's puzzling use of the reader both as part of the text's *Appelstruktur and* as a creative respondent to it, see Freund (1987:142-47) and Holub (1984:84-85).

[7]On readers as heuristic constructs of the interpreter, see Mailloux (1982:202-205) and Suleiman (1980:11).

[8]Iser certainly recognizes the need to take the cultural conditioning of readers into account; he even calls for an effort to reconstruct the norms and values of the original readers of texts from the past (see, e.g., 1978:152). But he largely fails to treat either author or audiences as culturally conditioned (Lentricchia 1980:149; Suleiman 1980:25-26).

Seymour Chatman has probably done more to popularize the notion of an inscribed reader (which he calls an *implied* reader) than any other theorist. Careful inspection of Chatman's theory, however, reveals the same ambiguity we detected in Iser's model. According to Chatman (1978:151) the elements of the "narrative communication situation" include real author, implied author, narrator, narratee, implied reader, and real reader; but "only the implied author and implied reader are immanent to a narrative . . . . The real author and real reader are outside the narrative transaction as such, *though, of course, indispensable to it in an ultimate practical sense*" (emphases added). For a discussion of the strong influence of this "immanence" model within gospel criticism, see Moore (1989:46).

Wayne Booth, one of the earliest advocates of the notion of an inscribed (unconditioned) reader, has since shifted away from that position: "I now see that . . . I must make problematic the sharp distinction I once made between flesh-and-blood authors and implied authors and between the various readers we become as we read and *the actual breathing selves we are within our shifting cultures*" (1983:415).

[9]The term extratext is more precise than the term context, for the latter is commonly used to refer to both what lies outside the text and to specific areas within the text (e.g., the context of a verse is a larger passage such as a chapter). In this study, extratext will refer to the cultural environment of reader and/or critic.

[10]Important theoretical contributions to our understanding of extratextual repertoires and their functions have been made by Jauss (1970), Culler (1975), Mailloux (1982), Rabinowitz (1987), and Jackson (1989).

[11]On the identification and significance of type scenes in biblical literature, see Alter (1981:47-62). On Luke's use of the symposium, see Steele (1984:379-394).

[12]Perhaps the most confident and specific reconstruction of this kind has been done by LaVerdiere (1980:xiii-xviii). He avers that Luke wrote for third-generation Gentile Christians who knew Mark and Q, had their origins in the Pauline mission, resided in "missionary communities" radiating from Antioch in Syria, lived in urban social settings, and were troubled with loss of identity because of frictions from within and persecutions from without! The hazards involved in such attempts to reconstruct the author's so-called community are well-catalogued by Johnson (1979).

[13]My reader, for example, will inevitably share some traits that reflect my cultural horizon as a white, Anglo-Saxon, male, Protestant, American, middle-class, heterosexual, married, father, and teacher at a Jesuit university in New England. For insightful comments on the inevitable subjectivity involved in referring to readers, see Fowler (1983:46-49).

[14]See Culpepper (1983:7-8, 205-227) for similar conclusions with regard to the quest for John's reader(s).

[15]Jackson (1989:88-89) insightfully likens the interpreter's exercise of historical imagination to the historical novelist's fictional recreation of ancient cultural environments. It should be noted that there is *some* continuity of values and tradition in Western culture, and, therefore, that it is not as difficult for us to transport ourselves imaginatively into Luke's context as it would be for say the Sawi tribespeople of Irian Jaya (see above).

[16]For an exhaustive survey of kinds of literature extant at the time the gospels were written, see Aune (1987:11-157).

[17]H.J. Cadbury once observed: "I do not know where one can get so many illustrations of the idiom and ideas of the author of Acts in 150 pages as in the love story of his near contemporary, Chariton of Aphrodisias" (1955:8). For a comparative study of Acts and Chariton's work, see Edwards (1987).

[18]The so-called God-fearers (*sebomenoi*; Acts 10:2 and 17:4) may well have been Gentiles who were attracted to Judaism and who practiced at least some of its tenets and lifestyle. Although not considered fully Jewish, the God-fearers would probably have been quite familiar with Jewish scripture and tradition.

[19]The differences between hearing and sight-reading a story have been much discussed recently (Kelber 1983). It is quite true that most of Luke's audience would have been hearers, not readers *per se*. However, the differences in how these groups appropriated the narrative are, from the perspective of pragmatic theory, much overemphasized. As Moore (1989:84-88) points out, reader-response criticism, with its emphasis on sequential actualization of texts comes nearest of all the literary methods to reconstructing how a text was heard. In short, my reader could also be thought of as a hearer.

[20]Esler maintains that a reader must come to the text with

> a large amount of knowledge to do with Jesus' proclamation of the gospel, otherwise he [Luke] would need to explain such expressions as 'the Son of Man' and 'the Kingdom of God,' and to provide at least some background information on some of the parables, the beatitudes, the apocalyptic discourses and the Lord's Supper. (1987:25)

A reader well-versed in the LXX, however, would hardly find these terms and literary forms unfamiliar, and the text of Luke-Acts provides plenty of guidance to define their Christian usage. The notion of a neat, somewhat isolated community for each of the evangelists is highly questionable, but seems to be dying a hard death within the discipline. (It is easier to conceive of Matthew and John writing to a narrowly-defined group than to image Luke's audience that way.)

All of this brings up another important point concerning the level of competence necessary for reading. It is not necessary to assume that the reader must know everything about each culture or institution mentioned in order to be a good reader. Many cultural phenomena can be adequately understood through analogy. It is not necessary, for example, for the reader to know all about sects of Judaism, for the various Hellenistic philosophical schools served as adequate analogies. Indeed, Luke seems to model the encounters of Jesus with the Pharisees on the scenario of philosopher versus sophists (Brawley 1987:86). Similarly with the temple cultus: the Greco-Roman audience, no matter where it was situated, would have had salient analogies for such things as sacrifice, purifications, the taking of vows (see Paul's Nazirite vow in Acts 21), and the like.

[21]The reading process as I understand it is very much akin to the "interactive model" of human cognition that prevails in the field of cognitive psychology. According to this theory, the human subject makes use of both new information and conventional knowledge to construct meaning in any given situation. In the words of W. John Harker, "constraints on meaning emanating from both the text and the reader's conceptual knowledge interact to produce a construction of meaning deriving from both information sources" (1989:471).

[22]The critic can examine the processing of textual data at any level—individual words, sentences, scenes, episodes, etc.

[23]Literary critics of the gospels, and especially narrative critics, have distinguished themselves from historical critics on this very point—"we have a holistic view of the text, they have a fragmented view" (see the introduction to this study). This is true, but is often misunderstood. Much of Stephen Moore's recent survey of literary criticism in the gospels (1989) documents how the notion of holism dominates the field; it also points out the flaws in this understanding of texts. However, Moore goes too far in the opposite direction, arguing so strongly for the notion of an inconsistent, gapped, even self-undermining narrative, that he fails to account for the audience's proclivity to weave it all together, that is, to concretize it into a coherent *work*.

[24]The story is found in Luke 7:36-50; see translation and comments above.

[25]Some of my readers may desire a more precise guide to the location of my theory on the current literary critical map. My model lies between formalism (New Criticism, structuralism, and their more recent offspring, narratology) and constructivism (as represented by Fish [1980] and certain of the deconstructionists [e.g., Moore 1989]) in that it both assumes the reality of the text, and denies that the text alone is the locus of meaning. Rather, meaning is produced by the interaction of the text and the reader. In this sense I concur with Iser; though the text is not the locus of meaning *per se*, it does offer an ordered set of stimuli to the reader. My understanding of the rhetoric of texts is based largely on the insights of Wayne Booth (1983), who has amply demonstrated the many ways in which texts manipulate us. Where my approach goes beyond Iser and Booth is in its insistence on the relevance of social and literary convention (or extratext) for the reading process. In this sense, my model leans toward the non-formalist end of the critical spectrum (i.e., meaning is due, at least in part, to the cultural situation of the reader). I am informed in this sector of my model by the work of such theorists as Mailloux (1982) and Rabinowitz (1987). Finally, following such critics as Jauss (1970:19) and Culler (1975), I maintain that the original extratextual repertoire of the text remains the *optimal* (but not the only possible) frame for its critical interpretation. In summary, I have collapsed the author (or authorial intention) into the text (as implied author) and the extratext (or history) into the reader.

NOTES TO CHAPTER TWO
BUILDING LUKAN CHARACTERS

[1]*The Poetics*, 6:19. A fuller discussion is found in 6:7-21.

[2]Kermode (1979:75-78) provides an overview of the argument over whether plot or character is primary. For further discussion of this issue in modern theory, see Walcutt (1966:6-19), Springer (1978:24-26), and Burnett (1985:39).

[3]Kermode (1979:81-98) interprets several figures in Mark's passion narrative as being essentially identified with their plot functions (e.g., Pilate = Judge). Each has little being for the reader apart from a simple function. Culpepper (1983:102) follows Kermode in this regard. Not all critics, however, are amenable to the reduction of characters (even typed characters) to themes or plot devices (see Springer 1978:23; and Docherty 1983:xii).

[4]The classic treatment of this geographical pattern is, of course, that of Conzelmann (1960:18-27). Unlike his sources, Luke carefully avoids locating John in Judea (20), and does not depict Jesus in the

region of the Jordan subsequent to his baptism (19). Conzelmann is surely correct here, but because he disregards the infancy narrative, he fails to connect these observations on the geographical settings of ministry with the earlier rhetoric which subordinates John to Jesus. For criticisms and modifications of Conzelmann's treatment, see Wink (1968:48-51) and Bachmann (1980: 123-55). Whether or not we agree with Conzelmann that the Baptist is absolutely isolated from Jesus or that this schema indicates an idiosyncratic salvation-historical pattern is irrelevant here. That in some sense geography is brought to bear in the shaping of the relationship between these two characters in Luke's story is patent.

[5]The insight that readers "construct" characters is quite new to critical theory, and few theorists have begun to chart its interpretive potential. On reader construction of characters, see Docherty (1983: xiii-xiv), Kermode (1979:77-78), and Burnett (1985:40). Strict attention to sequence—or, more accurately, to successive reading activities—is the primary factor that sets our approach apart from most other critical methods (see Resseguie 1984:317).

[6]On how a character's choices affect characterization, see Aristotle, *The Poetics*, 6:24, and Springer (1978:32). On behavior or actions, see Springer (1978:24-27). On interior monologues and speech, see Scholes and Kellogg (1966:177-79) and Springer (1978: 27; 41-44).

[7]The second chapter of Docherty's study is devoted entirely to the roles of names and naming in narrative. Besides a short and provocative study by Dawsey (1986b), Luke's utilization of names has not been analyzed. Dawsey shows that the narrator and characters in Luke-Acts are very consistent in their use of names and titles for Jesus and one another. This naming helps guide the assessment of relationships among characters.

[8]The terms "flat" and "round" were first used to designate the poles of this character continuum by E.M. Forster (1927:67-78). For a pertinent discussion of various ways of describing how we categorize characters, see Burnett (1985:49-53).

[9]One complexity of Luke-Acts, of course, is that the major agent—God—remains "offstage." The divine will is expressed in and through the omniscient narrator, Jesus, and, especially, the Spirit.

[10]On this issue and the debates it has engendered, see Fleck (1984:21-41), Hochman (1985:1-58), and Burnett (1985:38-41).

[11]Burnett (1985:40).

[12]It is such speculation, of course, which fuels the writing of further narratives concerning these characters. In this regard, Walcutt (1966:8) cites a book titled *The Girlhood of Shakespeare's Heroines.* As Kermode (1979:98-9) demonstrates, the natural tendency to wonder about characters' "other lives" is a prime reason for the growth of the gospel narratives.

[13]In an extremely suggestive essay, Scholes and Kellogg (1965: 82-105) have demonstrated and explained the distinctions between illustrative and representative narrative, and how these two modes evolved in Western literary tradition.

[14]For recent trends in genre scholarship, see Aune (1987) and Pervo (1987). For the linking of character to genre, especially in classical studies, and for a negative assessment of the results of the recent quest for gospel genre, see Burnett (1985:42). Kennedy (1984: 33) takes away much of the motivation for identifying specific genres for the gospels when he states that, "In general, identification of genre is not a crucial factor in understanding how rhetoric actually works in units of the New Testament" (see also 97-98).

[15]See Kermode (1979:162-3), who notes that "discussions of the gospels as genre seem not to have benefitted from the interest of secular critics in genre theory."

[16]This conclusion—but not the means of reaching it—is not much different from that reached long ago by Bultmann (in ET, see 1976:374-75).

[17]"Luke" stands for the implied author.

[18]These adjectives define various aspects of a point of view in narrative: psychological—the Lukan narrator is omniscient in that "he" provides inside views of others' thoughts, emotions, intentions, and motives that no human observer could; spatial—the narrator appears in all scenes and is sometimes in two places at once; temporal—the story is told in the past tense; ideological—the narrator is reliable in that his perspective is always borne out in the text and he always speaks in accord with its norms. In other words, he fully represents the implied author. For an excellent discussion of these aspects of point of view, as well as for bibliography, see Culpepper (1983:20-34).

We would be remiss not to mention Dawsey's controversial work on the Lukan narrator (1989), although it is deeply flawed in its assumptions and method. Dawsey argues that the narrator and Jesus are at odds on essential issues like christology and eschatology. The conflict between these authoritative "voices" in the story is intended, at least initially, to confuse the reader, to evoke irony (the know-it-all narrator gets Jesus wrong), and ultimately to persuade the reader to abandon the narrator's view and take up that of Jesus. This is not the place for a full-blown rebuttal of Dawsey's study, but a few observations are in order. First, it is wholly inadequate and misleading to characterize and evaluate the narrator (or any figure) solely on the basis of speech (Tannehill 1986:7). Second, Dawsey exhibits no sense of the reading dynamics of a work, dynamics that would largely mitigate his findings that Jesus and the narrator do not always say the same things. Readers can and will coordinate these two authoritative voices (which are not, in fact, nearly so distinct as Dawsey presents them). Third, Dawsey imports a modern literary agenda (confusion and ambiguity, dear to the heart of modern and post-modern literatures) into an ancient narrative. And finally, Dawsey's work is not grounded in literary theory; he virtually ignores all of the significant work on narrators and point of view done within the past thirty years. Interaction with that research would almost certainly lead to the revision of Dawsey's opinions. Sheely (1988) builds a worthy case for the reliability of the Lukan narrator.

[19]Upon reading the prologue with its first-person narration, the reader may well question the narrator's reliability (on this see Sternberg 1985:86). However, any such doubts are quickly and consistently dispelled by the rest of the narrative in which the narrator functions as a wholly reliable, omniscient, omnipresent guide. Wayne Booth (1983: 150) calls the issue of person "perhaps the most overworked distinction" in theory on narration. He goes on to say (151) that *function* is a more important issue and that first-and third-person narrators can function quite similarly and authoritatively.

[20]The few exceptions consist of angelic appearances, voices from heaven, visions, and so forth.

[21]In a provocative and insightful essay (1987), Joseph Tyson argues that Luke has a "utilitarian" view of scripture. "It is authoritative where it is useful, especially in the prophetic section, and when it is correctly interpreted. It is irrelevant at those points where God has provided subsequent alteration or annulment" (630).

[22]Although some scholars have noted Luke's stress on seeing and hearing (e.g., Dillon 1978:133, 147, 217; Karris 1985:87-88, 109-113; 1986:66-67; Hamm 1986:457-77), the ubiquity and import of his "rhetoric of perception" has yet to be fully appreciated or understood within the Lukan studies guild.

[23]See Rabinowitz (1987:58-64) on how first and last sections of a literary work "scaffold" expectations and interpretations.

[24]For a lengthy study of the use of this Isaianic passage in Judaism and early Christianity, see Evans (1989). It is certainly the primary "apologetic" text behind Luke's narrative arguments for the rejection of Jesus by the majority of Jews.

[25]See Rabinowitz (1987:62) on how final sentences or sections help order our interpretations of the entire work. On the ending of Acts and its relations to the rest of the narrative see Dupont (1984: 457-511), and Moessner (1988b).

[26]For the importance of this oracle in interpreting figures in Luke-Acts, see Tannehill (1986:40-44).

[27]The rise and fall of characters in the narrative is linked to yet another pattern which is previewed for the reader in Mary's oracle (Luke 1:51-53): "He has shown his strength with his arm, he has scattered the proud in the imagination of their hearts, he has put down the mighty from their thrones, and exalted those of low degree [or, the humble]; he has filled the hungry with good things and the rich he has sent away empty." Reversal of status is then fleshed out in the rest of the story, with the Pharisees becoming a prime example of the proud and rich being excluded (or, better, excluding themselves) from God's *basileia*.

[28]Plutarch's *The Parallel Lives* is the most famous example of this technique. On *sygkrisis* and its relevance for John and Jesus in Luke 1-2, see George (1970). It may well be that readers would have seen the juxtaposition of certain apostles (Peter/Philip and Peter/Paul) functioning in the same way as Jesus/John here.

NOTES TO CHAPTER THREE
RECAPITATING JOHN THE BAPTIST

[1]The most influential treatments of John in Luke are by Conzelmann (1960) and Wink (1968). Both studies approach the text from a redaction critical perspective, and—despite contrary claims—both bracket Luke 1-2 off from the rest of the narrative. Conzelmann, after claiming to do a holistic reading (". . . our aim is to elucidate Luke's work in its present form, not to enquire into possible sources or into the historical facts which provide the material" [1960:9]), firmly dismisses Luke's infancy stories as foreign material that is inconsistent with what follows (118, 172). Wink looks at the infancy stories in depth, but also fails to analyze them in conjunction with the rest of Luke-Acts. In fact, his two major sections are headed "John the Baptist in the Body of Luke's Gospel," and "John the Baptist in the Lukan Infancy Narrative" (1969:42-58 and 58-82). Despite some remarks about certain consistencies between these two bodies of material, Wink has effectively walled them off from each other.

[2]Most recent treatments of John the Baptist in Luke-Acts have been either strictly historical in nature ("What can these accounts tell us about the real Baptist?"—see e.g., Becker 1972 and Reumann 1972) or redactional ("What sources on the Baptist did Luke have available, how did he edit them, and what might that tell us about the editor's understanding of John?"—see Bachmann 1980 and Fitzmyer 1989). The latter evince some literary insight, but still fragment the text (there is a John of Q, a John of Mark, a John of L, and so on) and tend to focus almost exclusively on the issue of whether Luke's John

should be understood as the last of the prophets or as the forerunner and herald of Jesus (a question raised by Conzelmann's work). To my knowledge, no one has treated John as a character within a coherent narrative.

[3]Like Mary in 2:19 and 51b, the neighbors are *performative* rather than simply informative figures. That is, their cognitive and evaluative efforts are to be emulated by readers. At these points they stop (along with the characters), ponder, treasure, and ask certain leading questions. On performative characters in narrative, see Rabinowitz (1987:55). The phenomenon of secondary characters serving as *focalizers* (that is, serving to narrow interpretive options and direct the reader) has been investigated by Lanser (1981:140-48). Davis (1982: 226) also notes that Mary's pondering has strong implications for reading.

[4]Similar emphasis on names and/or naming is given to only a few other characters, all of whom are pivotal: Jesus, Simon/Peter (6:14), and Saul/Paul (Acts 13:9). The tale about Zacharias not believing Gabriel is a rhetorical strategy aimed at the reader: those who do not believe these oracles will suffer the consequences!

[5]Fitzmyer (1981:319-20) contends that a "Baptist source" which Luke used here identified John with Elijah and that Luke chose not to modify it. Strong arguments against the identification of John with Elijah in Luke 1:17 are made by Dubois (1973:165-6) and Wink (1968:42-5).

[6]The parallel scenes of Luke 1-2 have often been noted, but seldom have the implications of this structuring been treated. The usual concerns have been with sources and structures (How should the scenes be divided?) rather than with effects. An exception is George (1978) who investigates the rhetoric of the passage.

[7]That all three episodes involve financial matters is hardly coincidental. Throughout Luke's work, attitudes toward money determine one's ability to recognize and respond to the divine. One thinks immediately of the rich young ruler, the older brother in the parable of the gracious father, and the spiritual blindness of the Pharisees (attributed—at least in part—to their "love of money").

[8]In Mark it is clearly implied that John is Elijah (Mark 1:6 and 9:9-13). Matthew removes all doubt by having Jesus state that John was Elijah (Matt 11:14 and 17:10-13). In chapter 3 and following, Luke consistently deletes many of the links between John and Elijah from his sources. His reasons for doing so are not necessarily eschatological (i.e., to remove the Elijah *redivivus* motif and thus expunge the idea of an imminent eschaton) as Hans Conzelmann argues. They may rather be typological/christological; more than any other evangelist,

Luke models Jesus' activities on those of Elijah and Elisha. Perhaps because of this, Luke chooses not to identify John, exclusively with Elijah although John too is depicted as Elijianic in some ways. For similar arguments see Wink (1966:42-5).

[9]The verb *euaggelizo* should be rendered "preached" rather than as "preached the good news" (Conzelmann 1960:63 n. 1; Fitzmyer 1981:172-74, 463, 475). For a different opinion see Wink (1968:52).

[10]Our full discussion of this convention appears in Chapter 6.

[11]Whether or not one agrees with his method and/or results, Conzelmann's work (1960) has done much to raise awareness of Luke's tendency to distinguish among periods in the history of salvation. Luke's review of "things that have been fulfilled among us" does appear to be divided into certain phases, each with its own authority figures, geographical setting, and chronological perimeters. It is not so clear that Conzelmann was correct about the contours of these phases, however. If one includes the birth narratives, as we have, then the pattern must shift away from Conzelmann's strict separation of John and Jesus into distinct epochs. Given our findings, it seems best to view the entirety of the period dramatized by Luke as under the aegis of the Holy Spirit: how, when, and to whom the Spirit is given are the determining factors in delineating the progressive phases within this overarching period. Contra Conzelmann, then, even John belongs to this epoch, for he too receives the Holy Spirit—albeit *in utero* and through interaction with the unborn Jesus. Each phase is consequent on the previous one and yet is carefully marked off from it. For example, Jesus' ascension removes him from the scene so that the apostles in Jerusalem can receive the Spirit at Pentecost and begin the next phase of the story. Herod's imprisonment of John functions in the same way—to remove John before Jesus' ordination by the Spirit in preparation for his upcoming ministry, the next phase of the story. Although John's message is essentially that of the prophets, it gains new significance because it falls within the new age of the Spirit which was announced by Gabriel and initiated at Jesus' conception in Luke 1. We shall pay more attention to these matters below, in our discussion of Luke 16:16.

[12]As these carefully balanced phrases reveal, the characterization of John in Luke is more complex and nuanced than certain redaction critical treatments allow. For example, Conzelmann's work (1960:21-27), which has influenced all subsequent discourse on the issue, seems to presuppose only two rigid and exclusive categories for John. For Conzelmann and others, he must be either the eschatological forerunner (as in pre-Lukan tradition) and so part of the new epoch, or simply a prophet (as Luke supposedly attempts to depict him) and thus part

of the old era. Wink (1968:54) correctly points out that "Conzelmann is so intent upon emphasizing the manner in which Luke has eliminated eschatological motifs from the forerunner idea that he fails to recognize that Luke does not eliminate the forerunner idea itself, but reconceives it in terms of the delayed parousia and the present Lordship of Christ." Similar observations are made by Oliver (1964:203) and Bachmann (1980:133-134, 154).

[13]This implies strongly that John is the *Elias redivivus* of the passage Jesus quotes. Fitzmyer (1981:671) correctly maintains that this passage undermines Conzelmann's arguments that Luke did not consider John a forerunner of Jesus.

[14]See our detailed discussion of this important passage in Chapters 1 and 4; see also Kilgallen (1985).

[15]For full bibliography and discussion of Herod's question and its placement, see Darr (1987:249-54).

[16]On the extratextual conventions involved and how the reader would process the trial scenes, see Chapter 6.

[17]A reader-response approach buttresses the conclusion of those commentators (e.g., Fitzmyer 1985:1115-6) who understand John as a transitional or bridging figure playing crucial roles in both of these epochs of salvation-history.

[18]On the reader's drive to build consistency, see Chapter 1. I am not denying that tensions and opacity plague this text. My goal, however, is to reconstruct the reader's moves—no matter how questionable they may be from a critical standpoint—to build a consistent story from seemingly disparate data. Käsemann (1982) provides a very full elucidation of the interpretive problems in the passage, as well as some creative solutions that are not far from our own.

NOTES TO CHAPTER FOUR
OBSERVERS OBSERVED: THE PHARISEES

[1]An early draft of this chapter was presented to the Literary Aspects of the Gospels and Acts Group of the Society of Biblical Literature (1989).

[2]For similar sentiments see: Tyson (1978:144-50; 1983:303-327; 1984:574-83); Tiede (1980:14 and 87; 1986:142-51); Tannehill (1986:130-41); Moessner (1988:21-46); and Powell (1990:93).

Garrett (1989) rightly reminds us that the conflict is wider than this, however, for it involves the supernatural *agon* between God and Satan, angels and demons. But the dramatic focus rests on the struggle among the various *human* factions; the basic conflict of the story is thus situated on the human plane. Everything else is background.

[3]Both Sanders (1987) and Brawley (1987), for example, hold that Luke's portrayal of the Pharisees is ambivalent, but Brawley tends to find much more on the positive side of the ledger (91-2) than does Sanders. Much of the criticism that follows is directed at the work of Brawley and Sanders because their studies are both comprehensive and representative of standard positions within the Lukan studies guild. Sanders' chapter on the Pharisees is derived directly from his essay in the Saunders *festschrift* (1985).

[4]Gowler's "socio-narratological" approach certainly goes beyond redaction-criticism and provides many literary as well as sociological insights about the Pharisees in Luke-Acts. But while Gowler claims to focus on the reader reading, he in fact provides no theoretical framework for understanding the sequential process of reading. Without such a framework, one lacks the necessary guidelines for ordering and evaluating discrete textual data, and so the results are skewed. It is little surprise, therefore, that Gowler's overall argument (the Pharisees are bad in Luke but good in Acts) ends up essentially where earlier studies have. Gowler's latest work (1991) did not come into my hands in final draft form before this book was sent to press; my comments are thus based on an earlier draft the author was kind enough to send to me, and on personal correspondence. In this chapter, I answer his criticisms of my position (as voiced in my paper of 1989) at the appropriate points, but I have not attempted to interact with the entirety of his treatment of the Pharisees.

[5]In one of the most influential and prudent commentaries in recent years, for example, Fitzmyer (1985:1030) reiterates the common opinion: "One must recall that for Luke Christianity in the long run is a logical sequel to Pharisaic Judaism (see the end of Acts) . . ."

[6]Even if one takes a redaction critical approach, however, it is difficult to maintain the argument that the redactor favors the Pharisees, for he has clearly *added* harsh, negative traits and incidents found in none of the sources. Examples: Luke's narrator accuses the Pharisees of being "lovers of money" (*philargyroi*); the parable of the Pharisee and the tax collector at prayer (Luke 18:9-14); and the note that at the triumphal entry the Pharisees attempt to quiet Jesus' disciples from praising him. Brawley, and others who wish to show that the editor was trying to upgrade the Pharisees, have not presented cogent arguments as to why negative "Lukan additions" such as this appear in the text.

[7]This is clearly the ultimate agenda for both Brawley and Sanders; it is so ingrained as the primary goal of biblical study that they and others do not even feel obligated to justify its validity.

[8]This argument is very similar to the one we mounted above in

Chapter 1 with reference to the issue of the author's purpose and how that related to the identification of an audience.

[9]The reader is already aware of the spiritual significance of these three locales, for they have been tagged as the primary stages upon which the divine drama will be played out (Darr 1987: 202-205).

[10]Sanders (1985:156-7) and Fitzmyer (1985:1030) argue along these lines. Even on redaction critical grounds, however, this is a weak argument, because Luke obviously has a *stylistic* preference for narrowing Mark's general references by the use of *ti* or *tines*. Furthermore, Luke is hardly consistent in this regard: he often refers to "*the* Pharisees" (as in the very next scene) even when they are being depicted in a bad light. He will also write *tines pharisaioi* at 13:31, a passage Sanders regards as portraying the Pharisees positively. If Sanders' logic were to be followed, then one would have to distance such "good" behavior from the group also. Sanders makes much of the fact that in Luke, only a single Pharisee (implicitly) criticizes Jesus for not washing his hands (11:37-38), whereas in Mark this criticism is delivered by "the scribes and Pharisees from Jerusalem." What Sanders neglects to mention is that the lone Pharisee in Luke's story represents the entire group, as Jesus' reply makes clear: "You *Pharisees* [pl.] clean the outside . . ." (11:39). In short, Sanders ignores the dynamics of consistency-building and coherence by which a single figure can represent the entire group in a particular instance.

[11]The juxtaposition of characters with similar expertise or talents leads the reader to compare and contrast them (e.g., John and Jesus). On this syndrome, see Harvey (1965:52) and Springer (1978:189-90).

[12]For a full study of the murmuring motif in the wilderness traditions, see Coats (1968). One of the murmurings against Moses ("Who made you a ruler and a judge?" Acts 7:38) is recounted in Stephen's speech indicting his audience for not having accepted Jesus as the Christ. In essence, the wilderness generation serves as a prototype for those of "this generation" who also observe the great acts of God but do not recognize them as such.

[13]The characterization of John and his disciples climaxes late in the story (Acts 19:1-7), when Paul finds a group of about twelve of the Baptist's followers in Ephesus. When he informs them of Jesus, they respond immediately and are baptized with the Holy Spirit.

[14]The observation that at certain points Jesus seems to be depicted as an ideal philosopher in Luke-Acts is insightful, and certainly merits further comparative research. Such study would almost certainly throw more light on the characterization of the Pharisees also (i.e., as stereotypical opponents of philosophers). Brawley has already done some research along these lines. He points out (1987:86) that Jesus' accusations that

the Pharisees are lovers of money and that they "justify themselves" may well have been *topoi* of philosophers' attacks on the sophists.

[15]For suggestive applications of social categories to these accusations against the Pharisees, see Moxnes (1988:109-126), and Gowler (1989a; 1991). Saldarini (1988) has produced an excellent, up-to-date study of the real Pharisees which can shed some light on their literary depiction as well.

[16]See Chapter 5 below for a fuller investigation of Herod's characterization up to and including this important passage.

[17]For a full study of the Pharisees' characterization here, and how it has been interpreted by biblical scholarship, see Darr (1987: 255-64). The basic interpretive positions have been that: (1) the threat on Jesus' life is fabricated by the Pharisees in a vain attempt to get him out of their territory (Denaux 1973:261-68); (2) the threat is authentic and the Pharisees are simply trying to aid Jesus (Rese 1975:209-215); and (3) the report of Herod's threat is reliable, but the Pharisees are using it to get rid of Jesus and his troublesome ministry (Plummer 1914:348-49; Marshall 1978:570-71). The first reading fails to comprehend how negatively Herod has been depicted thus far, and the second fails to account for the totally negative portrayal of the Pharisees to this point. The final option is closest to what the reader would have hypothesized based on narrative development to this point.

[18]On the connection between Luke 13:23-30 and the Pharisees dining with Jesus, see also J. T. Carroll (1988b:615).

[19]It is worth re-emphasizing that there may well be a great difference between the meaning of these parables in Jesus' actual historical ministry and in the artificially-constructed narrative context within which they are now found. My purpose is to recover what the reader (not the historian) does with these brief stories in their present textual environment. While it may be misleading (historically) to allegorize Jesus' parables, that is precisely what this narrative urges its audience to do.

[20]On possessions in Luke-Acts, Luke Johnson's dissertation (1977) is still valuable. For more recent work on the subject see Pilgrim (1981) and Moxnes (1988).

Those who would see in the author an advocate of Pharisees are strongly contradicted by this reference. Brawley (1987:86) attempts to ameliorate its venom by pointing out, rather disingenuously, that (1) this may be a conventional accusation, and (2) the Pharisees actually do Luke a favor by providing him with a contrast against which he sets Jesus off to advantage (1987:86)! Aside from these rather weak arguments, Brawley simply ignores this strident—and uniquely Lukan—accusation against the Pharisees. Sanders' claim (1985:155-56) that the accusation "is without basis in the Gospel or the Acts," is patently false. As we have seen, the Pharisees are described at both 11:37-54 and 14:1-24 as having some serious problems related to wealth. Thus, this criticism cannot be passed off as isolated and/or inexplicable due to the lack of contextual support. Contra Sanders on this point, see also Moxnes (1988:151).

[21]For a recent, well-balanced literary interpretation, see J. T. Carroll (1988a:71-87). Carroll includes a good survey of critical studies of these verses as well.

[22]We need not enter the mire of modern debates about Lukan eschatology here. Suffice it to say that the reader understands the kingdom to be manifested already in Jesus' person and works. The kingdom has been announced, and people are forcing their way into it (16:16). When Jesus and the disciples preach and heal, the kingdom is said to come upon, or to come near, people (10:9, 11).

[23]While novel, this interpretation is not without parallel. It is similar to one way some ancient scholars (e.g., Tertullian) and some modern commentators (e.g., Cadbury) have understood this troublesome clause: "the kingdom of God is *within your grasp*, or *within your reach*." See Fitzmyer (1985:1161-63) for bibliography and basic philological options here.

A perceptive reader might also see here a pun on the inside/outside rhetoric of the narrative. The Pharisees do not see what is "within them" (that is, *within their ken*) because of what is within them (that is, in their hearts). Interestingly enough, the Gospel of Thomas presents this saying in such a way as to promote just such a meaning (exteriority *and* interiority). Logion 3 reads:

> Jesus said, "If your leaders say to you, 'Behold, the kingdom is in heaven,' then the birds of heaven will precede you. If they say to you, 'It is in the sea,' then the fish will precede you. Rather, *the kingdom is within you and it is outside you.* When you know yourselves, then you will be known, and you will understand that you are children of the living Father. But if you do not know yourselves, then you dwell in poverty, and you are the poverty."

[24]The assumption behind all of this is that Luke and Acts were two parts of a single narrative. This remains conventional wisdom in the field despite some provocative critiques.

In a recent work on the Pharisees (1991), Gowler takes issue with my treatment of the materials in Acts (based on my 1989 paper), while praising my handling of the Pharisees in Luke. Gowler lauds my criticism of Ziesler *et al.* for reading Acts back into Luke, but then accuses me of committing a similar gaffe by reading Luke into Acts. The obvious answer to this (illogical) criticism is that reading Luke first and Acts second is the *right* (intended, normative) way to proceed if we agree that the two are part of a single narrative. Gowler's critique is further weakened by his simultaneous—and contradictory—approval of my sequential treatment of the Gospel, and castigation of my continuing of such with Acts. The accumulation of character does not stop at the end of Luke, but continues on into Acts. For some reason, Gowler does not seem willing to acknowledge the hermeneutical significance of this fact. As we mentioned above, Gowler (see 1989:54) recognizes the necessity of taking readers and reading into account, but he does not build a theoretical framework for assessing the effect of these factors. To reiterate, neglect of narrative sequence leads inevitably to a distortion of character. Gowler's book will contribute much to our understanding of the social aspects of the Pharisees' portrayal. However, in shielding the Pharisees of Acts from the Pharisees in Luke, he is perpetuating a seriously-flawed convention of Lukan interpretation.

[25]I owe this insight to conversations with Abraham Smith.

[26]Some critics have pointed out that in Acts 15:22, "the whole church" cooperates with the apostles and elders in sending delegates and a letter to Antioch informing them of the decision to include the Gentiles without circumcision. Although the reader might well understand the Pharisaic believers to be party to this dispatch, the fact is that they have been bludgeoned by authority in the debate. We never again hear their side of the argument, and we do not know exactly how the decision sits with them. Like those Pharisees who attend the symposia in Luke, these Pharisees are not given a voice to validate their position. It is difficult, therefore, to credit them even for simple acquiescence.

[27]Note that once again, faulty attitudes about money crop up as a primary source of evil, even within the believing community.

[28]Those who hope to find in Luke's portrayal of Pharisees a late first-century apologia for peaceful coexistence between Jews and Christians will find no encouragement here. But then again it is wrong—and indeed quite dangerous—to presume that groups like the Pharisees in Luke's story world correspond to real Jews, then or now. Our own agendas, no matter how ideal, should not be read back into this ancient narrative, or distortion will result.

NOTES TO CHAPTER FIVE
HEROD THE FOX

[1]See, e.g., Conzelmann (1960:65); Talbert (1974:51-56); Rese (1975:208); Fitzmyer (1985:1029); and Moessner (1989:155-56).

[2]Plummer (1914:349); Easton (1926:221); and Fitzmyer (1985:1031).

[3]This seems to be the preferred option among critics. See Hoehner (1972:347); Parker (1987:203); Danker (1988:265).

[4]Leaney (1988:209). This interpretation seems to have the fewest modern proponents.

[5]The foundational work by Richards is found in two studies (1936; and, with Ogden, 1936). Soskice (1985) explores the implications of an interaction theory of metaphor (which she adapts and renames the interanimation theory) for theological discourse. The interaction approach has also influenced the interpretation of the synoptic parables (e.g., Kjärgaard 1986:94-105).

[6]In the course of his work Black uses all of these phrases to denote the semantic fields juxtaposed in a metaphor.

[7]Black (1979:29) acknowledges that his earlier work (1962) was misleading in this regard.

[8]Fitzmyer (1985:1027-38) provides a full discussion of the issues related to the prehistory of this passage.

[9]See the definition of the reader in Chapter 1. I assume—rather safely, I believe—that specific data on the historical Herod, little more than a petty Galilean Tetrarch, was not a part of the (general Hellenistic) reader's extratextual repertoire.

[10]The context makes it quite clear that Herod is the object of Jesus' remark, despite the fact that Jesus himself never names the Tetrarch specifically. We discuss this more fully below.

[11]Brown (1977:363) correctly notes that Luke 1:52 functions proleptically, for in Acts 4:24-27 Herod and Pilate are declared to be the enemies of the Lord and of his anointed.

[12]Hoehner (1970:343-47) conveniently draws together most of the extant evidence on the meanings and usages of the word fox in Greco-Roman times.

[13]Commentators on Luke 13:32 have failed to take note of the references to foxes in this pseudepigraphical book; see *1 Enoch* 89:10, 42, 43-49, 55. It is interesting that foxes are associated with hostile Ammonites in both the Nehemiah and *1 Enoch* passages cited here.

[14]Though intriguing, Grimm's argument requires far too much of the reader. In order to make the connection that Grimm detects, for example, one must realize that the name Saul is much like the Hebrew term for fox (*shaul*). As Fitzmyer correctly notes, Grimm's contrast is "farfetched," especially since a lion is never even mentioned (1985:1031).

[15]Ironically, this option has been the least favorite of the modern commentators on Luke.

[16]Atomistic methodologies have largely shielded critics from perceiving the overarching predator/prey imagery in this passage. For an exception, see Verrall (1908/09:353).

NOTES TO CHAPTER 6
TETRARCH AND EXTRATEXT

[1] For a fuller discussion of the problems confronting the would-be reconstructor of ancient extratexts, see Darr (1987:128-33 and 177-82).

[2] Classical scholars have long recognized that stories about philosophers confronting tyrants constitute one of the most common identifiable literary patterns from Greco-Roman times. The following is a sampling of some important modern literature on the subject: Nock (1933:193-202); Dudley (1937:18, 123-85); Sayre (1938:112-14); Toynbee (1944:43-58); Hoistad (1948); Starr (1949:20-29); Musurillo (1954:236-46); Alfoldi (1958); Hadas and Smith (1965); MacMullen (1966:46-94); Strauss; (1968); Döring (1979). Some biblical scholars have been aware of this pattern (e.g., George 1970:157; Munck 1977:330; and Talbert 1983:103-104) and have sensed its import, but have not followed through on how it would have affected the reading of the gospels.

[3] See Sayre (1938) for a comprehensive study of Diogenes and his depictions in later eras. Sayre includes a long discussion of the Alexander anecdote (see 11, 83-85, and 102-113).

[4] Quotes from Diogenes Laertius (1925), VI, 43-44.

[5] We cannot catalog all the examples here, of course. For a much fuller discussion of philosopher against tyrant, see Darr (1987:144-80).

[6] The point here is that Lucian could play off a well-known extratextual convention—philosopher versus tyrant—to make his satire work. Indeed, satire always depends heavily on the extratextual repertoire for its effect on the reader.

[7] Although we are not doing a genetic tracing of the origins of this convention here, we would be remiss if we did not note the strong influences of the Socrates story on these subsequent tales of resistance to despotism.

[8] The fact that some scholars (e.g., Childs 1974:146) have tried to draw a sharp distinction between the "prophet as wonder-worker" and the "prophet as messenger," and have assigned them to very different epochs in the history of tradition, does not really bear on our discussion, for both kinds of prophetic activity were fully mixed in the stories as Luke's audience had them.

[9] Surprisingly, none of the prophets about whom we read are killed as a consequence of confronting a king.

[10] Longer prophet versus king stories are found in the plague narrative of Exodus and the Elijah Cycle of 3 and 4 Reigns (= 1 and 2 Kings)—both Elijah and Micaiah versus Ahab. For a full-scale treatment of the Micaiah story and its import for prophetic narrative, see De Vries (1978).

[11] The literature on this subject is voluminous. We can cite only a

sample: Hastings (1958:50-75); Swaeles (1964); Hinnebusch (1967); Wink (1968:42-44); Hammer (1970); Brown (1971); Dubois (1973); Franklin (1975:67-69); Hausman (1976); Minear (1976); Johnson (1977:58-59); Büchele (1978:91-92); George (1978); Tiede (1980); Moessner (1983; 1989).

[12] The synchronic listing of rulers is found in both the LXX (Jeremiah 1:1-3; Isaiah 1:1; Hosea 1:1) and Greek history-writing (Thucydides 2:2, Polybius 1:3, Josephus *Antiquities* 18:106). When John is introduced with *to rhema tou theou*, however, reader focus shifts primarily to the Septuagint as the most appropriate extratextual backdrop for the story. For examples of this formula in the LXX, see 1 Reigns (= 1 Sam) 15:10; 2 Reigns (= 2 Sam) 7:4; 24:11; 3 Reigns (= 1 Kgs) 12:22; 20:28; 4 Reigns (= 2 Kgs) 20:4; Micah 1:1; Zechariah 1:1; and Ezekiel 1:3.

[13] This is not to deny, of course, that the general pattern of prophet versus king from the Septuagint is evoked here: Jesus himself refers to the killing of *prophets* (13:33-34), though the killer is identified as "Jerusalem," not wicked kings. Several scholars have attempted (with little success) to trace parallels between this episode and specific tales of prophetic conflict in the LXX. Plummer (1914:349) and Loisy (1924:373-74) point to Amos 7:10-17, the story of Amos' argument with Amaziah, the priest of Bethel. Denaux (1973:283) is convinced that the story of Jezebel sending a messenger to threaten Elijah with death for killing the prophets of Baal (3 Reigns [= 1 Kgs] 19:1-2) is the model for this account. Grimm (1973:114-17) sees here a recasting of King Saul's pursuit of David (1 Sam 23:9-13). None of these speculations, however, are convincing, for the parallels they hypothesize are either too far-fetched, or break down at crucial points (Darr 1987:270-4).

[14] For a recent and excellent study of *chreiai* and gospels, see Robbins (1983). Robbins shows that symbolic actions could take the place of sayings in chreiai, and that this form was amazingly flexible (students were asked to rewrite *chreiai* in at least eight different ways for various stylistic and rhetorical purposes).

[15] The questions raised by this pericope have long occupied critics. Why does Pilate send Jesus to Herod, and why does Herod remand Jesus to Pilate? What kind of questions did Herod ask of Jesus? What accusations did the high priests and scribes bring against him? Why did the Tetrarch and his soldiers mock Jesus, and what is the significance of the "gorgeous apparel" they put on him? What was the basis of the enmity between Herod and Pilate, and why did the events of this day make them friends? See Soards (1985b:344) and Buck (1980:165) for similar observations about the difficulties of the passage.

[16] For full-scale redactional studies of Luke 23:6-12, see Müller (1979), Buck (1980), and Soards (1985b). For a literary treatment of Jesus before Herod, see Darr (1987:278-305).

[17] Commentators have provided many and varied answers to the question. For a summary and bibliography see Soards (1985a:41-3). Is Jesus' silence meant as a symbolic condemnation for Herod's murder of John? Or does it reflect the breakdown of communication between Jews (= Herod) and Christians (= Jesus) in the latter years of the first century (Buck 1980:176)? Perhaps Luke felt obligated to use the "silence motif" simply because it was already so set in Christian tradition (Müller 1979:126-8). Or, again, are we to understand that Jesus is forcing Herod's hand, to make him find Jesus guilty?

[18] If we are correct, then Müller's argument that Luke is here attempting to make Herod out to be an "expert witness" (i.e., because he was interested in Jesus and had heard much about him) is unfounded.

[19] Soards (1985a:43) recognizes that there was a Greco-Roman tradition of nobility in the face of death, but he fails to locate it in the philosopher versus tyrant motif popularized by Stoics.

[20] As has often been noted, a major effect of Luke's passion is to shift the preponderance of blame for Jesus' death to Jewish leaders and the crowds they incite. This notion is summed up in a speech by Paul at Pisidian Antioch: "For those who live in Jerusalem, and their rulers, recognizing neither him nor the utterances of the prophets which are read every Sabbath, fulfilled these by condemning him" (Acts 13:27). Note how the fault is not blamed on maliciousness but on failure to perceive.

[21] See our translation at the beginning of this chapter. The correspondences traced here have long been noted by critics; see, e.g., Haenchen (1971:227).

[22] Dibelius (1915) rightly saw Luke:23:12 as the mental link between the trial and Acts 4:27. Dibelius' interest, however, was in tracing the author's creative process (from the Acts passage with its scriptural reference back to the gospel), whereas our goal is to trace the reader's process from the trial forward to Acts. For further redactional research on the passage (much of which points to Lukan composition of the entire episode) see Holtz (1968:53); Rese (1969:94-97); and Schneider (1980:354-5).

[23] This inconsistency has often been noted (e.g., Conzelmann 1963:37), and forms one of the major arguments against Dibelius' theory that the editor used the traditions found in Acts 4:25-28 to construct Luke 23:6-12 (see Rengstorf 1958:264).

BIBLIOGRAPHY

Abrams, M. H. 1953. *The Mirror and the Lamp: Romantic Theory and the Critical Tradition.* New York: Oxford Univ.

——. 1981. *A Glossary of Literary Terms.* New York: Holt Rinehart & Winston.

Alfoldi, A. 1958. "Der Philosoph als Zeuge der Wahrheit und sein Gegenspieler der Tyrann." *Scientiis artibusque* 1:7-19.

Alter, R. 1981. *The Art of Biblical Narrative.* New York: Basic.

Aristotle. 1953. *The Poetics.* Loeb Classical Library. Cambridge, MA: Harvard Univ.; London: Heinemann.

Aune, D. E. 1987. *The New Testament in Its Literary Environment.* Philadelphia: Westminster.

Bachmann, M. 1980. "Johannes der Täufer bei Lukas: Nachzügler oder Vorläufer?" In *Wort in der Zeit: Neutestamentliche Studien [Fest.* Rengstorf], ed. W. Haubeck & M. Bachmann. Leiden: Brill.

Becker, J. 1972. *Johannes der Täufer und Jesus von Nazareth.* Neukirchen-Vluyn: Neukirchener.

Berlin, A. 1983. *Poetics and Interpretation of Biblical Narrative.* Sheffield: Almond.

Black, M. 1962. "Metaphor." In *Models and Metaphors: Studies in Language and Philosophy.* Ithaca: Cornell Univ.

——. 1979. "More About Metaphor." In *Metaphor and Thought*, ed. A. Ortony. Cambridge: Cambridge Univ.

Booth, W. C. 1974. *A Rhetoric of Irony.* Chicago: Univ. of Chicago.

——. 1979. "Metaphor as Rhetoric: The Problem of Evaluation." In *On Metaphor*, ed. S. Sachs. Chicago: Univ. of Chicago.

——. 1983. *The Rhetoric of Fiction.* 2nd ed. Chicago: Univ. of Chicago.

Brawley, R. L. 1978. "The Pharisees in Luke-Acts: Luke's Address to Jews and His Irenic Purpose." Ph.D. diss., Princeton Theological Seminary.

——. 1987. *Luke-Acts and the Jews: Conflict, Apology, and Conciliation.* Atlanta: Scholars.

——. 1990. *Centering on God: Method and Message in Luke-Acts.* Louisville: Westminster/John Knox.

Brown, R. E. 1977. *The Birth of the Messiah: A Commentary on the Infancy Narratives in Matthew and Luke.* New York: Doubleday.

Buber, M. 1946. *Moses.* London: Phaidon.

Büchele, A. 1978. *Der Tod Jesu im Lukasevangelium: Eine redaktionsgeschichtliche Untersuchung zu Lk 23.* Frankfurt: Knecht.

Buck, E. 1980. "The Function of the Pericope 'Jesus before Herod' in the Passion Narrative of Luke." In *Wort in der Zeit* [see Bachmann 1980].

Bultmann, R. 1976. *The History of the Synoptic Tradition.* New York: Harper & Row.

Burnett, F. W. 1985. "Characterization in Matthew: Reader Construction of the Disciple Peter." Unpub. paper presented to the Literary Aspects of the Gospels and Acts Group of the Society of Biblical Literature.

——. 1990. "Characterization and Reader Construction of Characters in the Gospels." In *Listening to the Word of God* [Blackwelder *Fest.*], ed. B. L. Callen. Anderson, IN: Warner.

Cadbury, H. J. 1927. *The Making of Luke-Acts*. New York: MacMillan.

——. 1955. *The Book of Acts in History*. London: A. & C. Black.

Carroll, J. T. 1988a. *Response to the End of History: Eschatology and Situation in Luke-Acts*. Atlanta: Scholars.

——. 1988b. "Luke's Portrayal of the Pharisees." *CBQ* 50:604-21.

Carroll, R. P. 1981. *From Chaos to Covenant: Prophecy in the Book of Jeremiah*. New York: Crossroad.

Chatman, S. 1978. *Story and Discourse: Narrative Structure in Fiction and Film*. Ithaca, NY: Cornell Univ.

Childs, B. S. 1974. *The Book of Exodus: A Critical, Theological Commentary*. Philadelphia: Westminster.

Conzelmann, H. 1960. *The Theology of St. Luke*. New York: Harper & Row.

Coats, G. 1968. *Rebellion in the Wilderness: The Murmuring Motif in the Wilderness Traditions of the Old Testament*. Nashville: Abingdon.

Cox, P. 1983. *Biography in Late Antiquity: A Quest for the Holy Man*. Berkeley: Univ. of California.

Culler, J. 1975. *Structuralist Poetics: Structuralism, Linguistics and the Study of Literature*. Ithaca, NY: Cornell Univ.

Culpepper, R. A. 1983. *Anatomy of the Fourth Gospel: A Study in Literary Design*. Philadelphia: Fortress.

Danker, F. 1988. *Jesus and the New Age. A Commentary on St. Luke's Gospel*. Philadelphia: Fortress.

Darr, J. A. "'Glorified in the Presence of Kings": A Literary-Critical Study of Herod the Tetrarch in Luke-Acts." Ph.D. diss., Vanderbilt Univ.

——. 1989. "Observers Observed: The Pharisees, The Reader, and the Rhetoric of Characterization in Luke-Acts." Unpub. paper, Literary Aspects of the Gospels and Acts Group, Society of Biblical Literature.

Davis, C. T., III. 1982. "The Literary Structure of Luke 1-2." In *Art and Meaning: Rhetoric in Biblical Literature*, eds. D. J. A. Clines, D. M. Gunn, A. J. Hauser. Sheffield: JSOT.

Dawsey, J. M. 1986a. *The Lukan Voice: Confusion and Irony in the Gospel of Luke*. Macon, GA: Mercer Univ.

——. 1986b. "What's in a Name? Characterization in Luke." *BTB* 16:143-7.

Denaux, A. 1973. "L'hypocrisie des Pharisiens et le dessein de Dieu: Analyse de Lc., XIII, 31-33." In *L'Évangile de Luc: Problèmes littéraires et théologiques*, ed. F. Neirynck. Gembloux: Duculot.

De Vries, S. J. 1978. *Prophet against Prophet: The Role of the Micaiah Narrative (I Kings 22) in the Development of Early Prophetic Tradition*. Grand Rapids: Eerdmans.

Dibelius, M. 1915. "Herodes und Pilatus." *Zeitschrift fur die neutestamentliche Wissenschaft* 16:113-126.

——. 1965. *From Tradition to Gospel*. New York: Scribner's.

Dillon, R. J. 1978. *From Eye-Witnesses to Ministers of the Word: Tradition and Composition in Luke 24*. Rome: Biblical Institute.

Dio Chrysostom. 1932. *Works*. Loeb Classical Library. 5 vols. London: Heinemann; New York: Putnam's Sons.

Diogenes Laertius. 1925. *Lives of Eminent Philosophers*. Loeb Classical Library. 2 vols. London: Heinemann; New York: Putnam's Sons.

Docherty, T. 1983. *Reading (Absent) Character: Towards A Theory of Characterization in Fiction*. Oxford: Clarendon.

Donahue, J. 1988. *The Gospel in Parable: Metaphor, Narrative, and Theology in the Synoptic Gospels*. Philadelphia: Fortress.

Döring, K. 1979. *Exemplum Socratis: Studien zur Sokratesnachwirkung in der kynisch-stoischen Popularphilosophie der frühen Kaiserzeit und im frühen Christentum*. Wiesbaden: Steiner.

Downing, F. 1988. *Christ and the Cynics: Jesus and Other Radical Preachers in First-Century Tradition*. Sheffield: JSOT.

Dubois, J.-D. 1973. "La figure d'Élie dans la perspective lucanienne." *Revue d'Histoire et Philosophie Religieuses* 53:155-176.

Dudley, D. R. 1937. *A History of Cynicism From Diogenes to the 6th Century A.D.* London: Methuen.

Dupont, J. 1984. *Nouvelles études sur les Actes des Apôtres*. Paris: Cerf.

Easton, B. 1926. *The Gospel According to St. Luke: A Critical and Exegetical Commentary*. New York: Scribners.

——. 1955. "The Purpose of Acts." In *Early Christianity: The Purpose of Acts and Other Papers*, ed. F.C. Grant. London: SPCK.

Edwards, D. R. 1987. "Acts of the Apostles and Chariton's *Chaereas and Callirhoe*: A Literary and Sociohistorical Study." Ph.D. diss., Boston Univ.

Epictetus. 1926. *The Discourses as Reported by Arrian, the Manual, and Fragments*. Loeb Classical Library. 2 vols. London: Heinemann; New York: Putnam's Sons.

Ernst, J. 1977. *Das Evangelium nach Lukas*. Regensburg: F. Pustet.

Esler, P. F. 1987. *Community and Gospel in Luke-Acts: The Social and Political Motivations of Lucan Theology*. Cambridge: Cambridge Univ.

Evans, C. A. 1989. *To See and Not Perceive: Isaiah 6.9-10 in Early Jewish and Christian Interpretation*. Sheffield: JSOT.

Fischel, H. A. 1947. "Martyr and Prophet (A Study in Jewish Literature)." *Jewish Quarterly Review* 37:265-280; 363-386.

Fish, S. 1972. "Literature in the Reader: Affective Stylistics." *New Literary History* 2:123-162.

——. 1980. *Is There a Text in This Class? The Authority of Interpretive Communities*. Cambridge, MA: Harvard Univ.

Fitzmyer, J. A. 1981. *The Gospel According to Luke I-IX: Introduction, Translation, and Notes*. Garden City, NY: Doubleday.

——. 1985. *The Gospel According to Luke X-XXIV: Introduction, Translation, and Notes*. Garden City, NY: Doubleday.

——. 1989. *Luke the Theologian: Aspects of His Teaching*. Mahwah, NJ: Paulist.

Fleck, J. 1984. *Character and Context: Studies in the Fiction of Abramovitch, Brenner, and Agnon*. Chico, CA: Scholars.

Forster, E. M. 1927. *Aspects of the Novel.* New York: Harcourt, Brace & World.

Fowler, R. 1985. "Who is 'the Reader' of Mark's Gospel?" *Semeia* 31:5-23.

Franklin, E. 1975. *Christ the Lord: A Study in the Purpose and Theology of Luke-Acts.* Philadelphia: Westminster.

Freund, E. 1987. *The Return of the Reader: Reader-Response Criticism.* London & New York: Methuen.

Garrett, S. 1989. *The Demise of the Devil: Magic and the Demonic in Luke's Writings.* Minneapolis: Augsburg Fortress.

Gasque, W. 1975. *A History of the Criticism of the Acts of the Apostles.* Tübingen: Mohr (Siebeck).

George, A. 1970. "Le parallèle entre Jean-Baptiste et Jésus en Luc 1-2." In *Mélanges Bibliques en Hommage au R. P. Béda Rigaux,* ed. A. Descamps & R. P. A. de Halleux. Gembloux: Duculot.

——. 1978. "Par le doigt de Dieu (Lc 11,20)." In *Études sur l'oeuvre de Luc.* Paris: Gabalda.

Ginsberg, W. 1983. *The Cast of Character: The Representation of Personality in Ancient and Medieval Literature.* Toronto: Univ. of Toronto.

Gowler, D. B. 1989a. "A Socio-Narratological Character Analysis of the Pharisees in Luke-Acts." Ph.D. diss., Southern Baptist Theological Sem.

——. 1989b. "Characterization in Luke: A Socio-Narratological Approach." *BTB* 19:54-62.

——. 1991. *Host, Guest, Enemy and Friend: Portraits of the Pharisees in Luke and Acts.* New York: Lang.

Grimm, W. 1973. "Eschatologischer Saul wider eschatologischen David: Eine Deutung von Lc. xiii 31ff." *Novum Testamentum* 15:114-133.

Hadas, M. 1953. *The Third and Fourth Books of Maccabees.* New York: Harper & Brothers.

Hadas, M. & M. Smith. 1965. *Heroes and Gods: Spiritual Biographies in Antiquity.* New York: Harper & Row.

Haenchen, E. 1971. *The Acts of the Apostles: A Commentary.* Philadelphia: Westminster.

Hamm, D. 1986. "Sight to the Blind: Vision as Metaphor in Luke." *Biblica* 67:457-477.

Hammer, R. A. 1970. "Elijah and Jesus: A Quest for Identity." *Judaism* 19:207-218.

Harker, J. 1989. "Information Processing and the Reading of Literary Texts." *New Literary History* 20:465-481.

Harvey, W. J. 1965. *Character and the Novel.* Ithaca, NY: Cornell Univ.

Hastings, A. 1958. *Prophet and Witness in Jerusalem: A Study in the Teaching of Saint Luke.* Baltimore: Helicon.

Hausman, R. A. 1976. "The Function of Elijah as a Model in Luke-Acts." Ph.D. diss., Univ. of Chicago.

Hinnebusch, P. 1967. "Jesus, the New Elijah, in St. Luke." *The Bible Today* 31:2175-82; 32:2237-44.

Hirsch, E. D., Jr. 1988. *Cultural Literacy: What Every American Needs to Know.* New York: Vantage Books.

Hochman, B. 1985. *Character in Literature.* Ithaca & London: Cornell Univ.

Hoehner, H. 1970. "Why did Pilate Hand Jesus Over to Antipas?" In *The Trial of Jesus* [Moule *Fest.*], ed. E. Bammel. London: SCM.

——. 1972. *Herod Antipas.* Cambridge: Cambridge Univ.

Hoistad, R. 1948. *Cynic Hero and Cynic King: Studies in the Cynic Conception of Man.* Uppsala: Lund Blom.

Holtz, T. 1968. *Untersuchungen über die Alttestamentlichen Zitate bei Lukas.* Berlin: Akademie.

Holub, R. C. 1984. *Reception Theory: A Critical Introduction.* London & New York: Methuen.

Horace. 1929. *Satires, Epistles and Ars Poetica.* Loeb Classical Library. London: Heinemann; Cambridge, MA: Harvard Univ.

Ingarden, R. 1973. *The Literary Work of Art: An Investigation on the Borderlines of Ontology, Logic, and Theory of Literature.* Evanston: Northwestern Univ.

Iser, W. 1972. "The Reading Process: A Phenomenological Approach." *New Literary History* 3:279-299.

——. 1974. *The Implied Reader: Patterns of Communication in Prose Fiction from Bunyan to Beckett.* Baltimore & London: Johns Hopkins Univ.

——. 1978. *The Act of Reading: A Theory of Aesthetic Response.* Baltimore & London: Johns Hopkins Univ.

Jackson, J. de J. R. 1989. *Historical Criticism and the Meaning of Texts.* London & New York: Routledge.

Jauss, H. R. 1970. "Literary History as a Challenge to Literary Theory." *New Literary History* 2:7-38.

Johnson, L. T. 1977. *The Literary Function of Possessions in Luke- Acts.* Missoula, MT: Scholars.

——. 1979. "On Finding the Lukan Community: A Cautious Cautionary Essay." *Society of Biblical Literature Seminar Papers.*

Josephus. 1965. *Jewish Antiquities: Books XVIII-XIX.* Loeb Classical Library. Cambridge, MA: Harvard Univ.; London: Heinemann.

Karris, R. J. 1985. *Luke: Artist and Theologian; Luke's Passion Account as Literature.* Mahwah, NJ: Paulist.

Käsemann, E. 1982. *Essays on New Testament Themes.* Philadelphia: Fortress.

Kelber, W. H. 1983. *The Oral and the Written Gospel: The Hermeneutics of Speaking and Writing in the Synoptic Tradition, Mark, Paul, and Q.* Philadelphia: Fortress.

Kennedy, G. A. 1984. *New Testament Interpretation Through Rhetorical Criticism.* Chapel Hill & London: Univ. of North Carolina.

Kermode, F. 1979. *The Genesis of Secrecy: On the Interpretation of Narrative.* Cambridge, MA: Harvard Univ.

Kilgallen, J. J. 1985. "John the Baptist, the Sinful Woman, and the Pharisee." *JBL* 104:675-9.

Kjärgaard, M. S. 1986. *Metaphor and Parable: A Systematic Analysis of the Specific Structure and Cognitive Function of the Synoptic Similes and Parables qua Metaphors.* Leiden: Brill.

Kodell, J. 1969. "Luke's Use of *Laos*, 'People,' Especially in the Jerusalem Narrative (Lk 19,28-24,53)." *CBQ* 31:327-343.

Lanser, S. 1981. *The Narrative Act: Point of View in Prose Fiction*. Princeton: Princeton Univ.

LaVerdiere, E. 1980. *Luke*. Wilmington, DE: Glazier.

Leaney. A. 1988. *A Commentary on the Gospel According to St. Luke*. Peabody, MA: Hendrickson.

Lentricchia, F. 1980. *After the New Criticism*. Chicago: Univ. of Chicago.

Loisy, A. 1924. *L'Évangile selon Luc*. Paris: Émile Nourray.

MacMullen, R. 1966. *Enemies of the Roman Order: Treason, Unrest, and Alienation in the Empire*. Cambridge, MA: Harvard Univ.

Mailloux, S. 1977. "Reader-Response Criticism?" *Genre* 10:413-31.

——. 1982. *Interpretive Conventions: The Reader in the Study of American Fiction*. Ithaca & London: Cornell Univ.

Malina, B. J. 1989. "Dealing With Biblical (Mediterranean) Characters: A Guide for U.S. Consumers." *BTB* 19:127-141.

Marrou, H. I. 1956. *A History of Education in Antiquity*. London & New York: Sheed & Ward.

Marrow, S. 1982. "*Parrhēsia* and the New Testament." *CBQ* 44:431-46.

Marshall, I. H. 1978. *The Gospel of Luke: A Commentary on the Greek Text*. 1978. Grand Rapids: Eerdmans.

McKnight, E. 1988. *Post-Modern Use of the Bible: The Emergence of Reader-Oriented Criticism*. Nashville: Abingdon.

Minear, P. S. 1976. *To Heal and to Reveal: The Prophetic Vocation According to Luke*. New York: Seabury.

——. 1980. "Luke's Use of the Birth Stories." In *Studies in Luke-Acts*, ed. L. Keck & J. Martyn. Philadelphia: Fortress.

Moessner, D. 1983. "Luke 9:1-50: Luke's Preview of the Journey of the Prophet like Moses of Deuteronomy." *JBL* 102:575-605.

——. 1988a. "The 'Leaven of the Pharisees' and 'This Generation': Israel's Rejection of Jesus According to Luke." *Journal for the Study of the New Testament* 34:21-46.

——. 1988b. "Paul in Acts: Preacher of Eschatological Repentance to Israel." *NTS* 34:96-104.

——. 1989. *Lord of the Banquet: The Literary and Theological Significance of the Lukan Travel Narrative*. Minneapolis: Augsburg Fortress.

Moore, S. D. 1989. *Literary Criticism and the Gospels: The Theoretical Challenge*. New Haven & London: Yale Univ.

Moxnes, H. 1988. *The Economy of the Kingdom: Social Conflict and Economic Relations in Luke's Gospel*. Philadelphia: Fortress.

Müller, K. 1979. "Jesus vor Herodes: Eine redaktionsgeschichtliche Untersuchung zu Lk 23, 6-12." In *Zur Geschichte des Urchristentums*, ed. G. Dautzenberg, H. Merklein & K. Muller. Freiburg: Herder.

Munck, J. 1967. *The Acts of the Apostles*. New York: Doubleday.

——. 1977. *Paul and the Salvation of Mankind*. Atlanta: John Knox.

Mussies, G. 1972. *Dio Chrysostom and the New Testament*. Leiden: Brill.

Musurillo, H. A. 1954. *The Acts of the Pagan Martyrs: Acta Alexandrinorum*. Oxford: Clarendon.

Neyrey, J. 1985. *The Passion According to Luke: A Redaction Study of Luke's Soteriology*. New York: Paulist.

Nock, A. D. 1933. *Conversion: The Old and the New in Religion from Alexander the Great to Augustine of Hippo.* Oxford: Clarendon.

Oliver, H. 1964. "The Lucan Birth Stories and the Purpose of Luke-Acts." *NTS* 10:202-226.

O'Toole, R. F. 1984. *The Unity of Luke's Theology: An Analysis of Luke-Acts.* Wilmington, DE: Glazier.

Parsons, M. C. 1987. *The Departure of Jesus in Luke-Acts: The Ascension Narratives in Context.* Sheffield: JSOT.

Perry, B. E. 1967. *The Ancient Romances: A Literary-Historical Account of Their Origins.* Berkeley and Los Angeles: Univ. of California.

——. 1964. *Secundus the Silent Philosopher.* Ithaca, NY: Cornell Univ.

Pervo, R. 1987. *Profit With Delight: The Literary Genre of the Acts of the Apostles.* Philadelphia: Fortress.

Petersen, N. 1978. *Literary Criticism for New Testament Critics.* Philadelphia: Fortress.

Philostratus. 1912. *The Life of Apollonius of Tyana.* Loeb Classical Library. 2 vols. London: Heinemann; Cambridge, MA: Harvard Univ.

Pilgrim, W. 1981. *Good News to the Poor: Wealth and Poverty in Luke-Acts.* Minneapolis: Augsburg.

Plummer, A. 1914. *A Critical and Exegetical Commentary on the Gospel According to St. Luke.* New York: Scribners.

Plutarch. 1960. *The Parallel Lives.* Loeb Classical Library. 10 vols. Cambridge, MA: Harvard Univ.

Powell, M. A. 1990. "The Religious Leaders in Luke: A Literary- Critical Study." *JBL* 109:93-110.

Rabinowitz, P. J. 1987. *Before Reading: Narrative Conventions and the Politics of Interpretation.* Ithaca & London: Cornell Univ.

Rengstorf, K. H. 1958. *Das Evangelium nach Lukas.* Göttingen: Vandenhoeck & Ruprecht.

Rese, M. 1969. *Alttestamentliche Motive in der Christologie des Lukas.* Gütersloh: Mohn.

——. 1975. "Einige Überlegungen zu Lukas XIII, 31-33." In *Jésus aux origines de la christologie*, ed. J. Dupont. Gembloux: Duculot.

Resseguie, J. 1984 "Reader-Response Criticism and the Synoptic Gospels." *Journal of the American Academy of Religion* 52:307-324.

Reumann, J. 1972. "The Quest for the Historical Baptist." In *Understanding the Sacred Text*, ed. J. Reumann. Valley Forge, PA: Judson.

Richard, E. 1983. "Luke—Writer, Theologian, Historian: Research and Orientation of the 1970's." *BTB* 13:3-15.

Richards, I. A. 1936. *The Philosophy of Rhetoric.* Oxford: Oxford Univ.

Richards, I. A. & C. K. Ogden. 1936. *The Meaning of Meaning: A Study of the Influence of Language Upon Thought and of the Science of Symbolism.* New York: Harcourt & Brace.

Richardson, D. 1974. *Peace Child.* Glendale, CA: Regal.

Robbins, V. K. 1983. "Pronouncement Stories and Jesus' Blessing of the Children: A Rhetorical Approach." *Semeia* 29:43-74.

Robinson, J. A. T. 1957-58. "Elijah, John and Jesus: An Essay in Detection." *NTS* 4:263-281.

Said, E. W. 1983. *The World, the Text and the Critic*. Cambridge, MA: Harvard Univ.

Saldarini, A. 1988. *Pharisees, Scribes and Sadducees in Palestinian Society: A Sociological Approach*. Wilmington, DE: Glazier.

Sanders, J. T. 1985. "The Pharisees in Luke-Acts." In *The Living Text: Essays in Honor of Ernest W. Saunders*, ed. D. Groh & R. Jewett. New York: University Press of America.

Sayre, F. 1938. *Diogenes of Sinope: A Study of Greek Cynicism*. Baltimore: Furst.

Schneider, G. 1980. *Die Apostelgeschichte, Kap. 1,1–8,40*. Freiburg: Herder.

Schoeps, H. J. 1950. "Die jüdischen Prophetenmorde." In *Aus frühchristlicher Zeit: Religionsgeschichtliche Untersuchungen*. Tübingen: Mohr (Siebeck).

Scholes, R. 1968. *Elements of Fiction*. New York: Oxford Univ.

Scholes, R. & R. Kellogg. 1966. *The Nature of Narrative*. New York: Oxford Univ.

Schürmann, H. 1969. *Das Lukasevangelium, Kap. 1,1-9,50*. Freiburg: Herder.

Sheely, S. M. 1988. "Narrative Asides and Narrative Authority in Luke-Acts." *BTB* 18:102-107.

Soards, M. L. 1985a. "The Silence of Jesus Before Herod: An Interpretive Suggestion." *Australian Biblical Review* 33:41-45.

——. 1985b. "Tradition, Composition, and Theology in Luke's Account of Jesus Before Herod Antipas." *Biblica* 66:344-63.

Soskice, J. 1985. *Metaphor and Religious Language*. Oxford: Clarendon.

Springer, M. D. 1978. *A Rhetoric of Literary Character: Some Women of Henry James*. Chicago & London: Univ. of Chicago.

Starr, C. 1949. "Epictetus and the Tyrant." *Classical Philology* 44:20-29.

Steele, E. S. 1984. "Luke 11:37-54—A Modified Hellenistic Symposium?" *JBL* 103:379-94.

Steiner, G. 1979. "'Critic/Reader.'" *New Literary History* 10:423-52.

Stern, G. 1931. *Meaning and Change of Meaning: With Special Reference to the English Language*. Bloomington: Indiana Univ.

Sternberg, M. 1985. *The Poetics of Biblical Narrative: Ideological Literature and the Drama of Reading*. Bloomington: Indiana Univ.

Suleiman, S. 1980. "Introduction: Varieties of Audience-Oriented Criticism." In *The Reader in the Text: Essays on Audience and Interpretation*, ed. S. Suleiman & I. Crosman. Princeton: Princeton Univ.

Swaeles, R. 1964. "Jésus, nouvel Élie, dans S. Luc." *Assemblées du Seigneur* 69:41-66.

Talbert, C. H. 1974. *Literary Patterns, Theological Themes, and the Genre of Luke Acts*. Missoula, MT: Scholars.

——. 1983. "Martyrdom in Luke-Acts and the Lukan Social Ethic." In *Political Issues in Luke-Acts*, ed. R. J. Cassidy and P. J. Scharper. Maryknoll, NY: Orbis.

——. 1988. Review of R. C. Tannehill, *The Narrative Unity of Luke-Acts*. *Biblica* 69:135-8.

Tannehill, R. 1972. "The Mission of Jesus According to Luke IV 16-30."

In *Jesus in Nazareth*, ed. W. Eltester. New York: de Gruyter.
——. 1986. *The Narrative Unity of Luke-Acts: A Literary Interpretation*, vol. 1, *The Gospel According to Luke*. Philadelphia: Fortress.
——. 1990. *The Narrative Unity of Luke-Acts: A Literary Interpretation*, vol. 2, *The Acts of the Apostles*. Minneapolis: Fortress.
Thompson, L. L. 1978. *Introducing Biblical Literature: A More Fantastic Country*. Englewood Cliffs, NJ: Prentice-Hall.
Tiede, D. L. 1980. *Prophecy and History in Luke-Acts*. Philadelphia: Fortress.
——. 1986. "'Glory to Thy People Israel': Luke-Acts and the Jews." In *Society of Biblical Literature Seminar Papers*, ed. K. Richards. Atlanta: Scholars.
Tolbert, M. A. 1979. *Perspectives on the Parables: An Approach to Multiple Interpretations*. Philadelphia: Fortress.
——. 1989. *Sowing the Gospel: Mark's World in Literary-Historical Perspective*. Minneapolis: Fortress.
Tompkins, J. 1980. "An Introduction to Reader-Response Criticism." In *Reader-Response Criticism: From Formalism to Post-Structuralism*, ed. J. Tompkins. Baltimore & London: Johns Hopkins Univ.
Toynbee, J. M. C. 1944. "Dictators and Philosophers in the First Century A.D." *Greece and Rome* 13:43-58.
Tyson, J. 1960. "Jesus and Herod Antipas." *JBL* 79:239-246.
——. 1978. "The Opposition to Jesus in the Gospel of Luke." *Perspectives in Religious Studies* 5:144-150.
——. 1983. "Conflict as a Literary Theme in the Gospel of Luke." In *New Synoptic Studies: The Cambridge Gospel Conference and Beyond*, ed. W. R. Farmer. Macon, GA: Mercer Univ.
——. 1984. "The Jewish Public in Luke-Acts." *NTS* 30:574-583.
——. 1987. "The Gentile Mission and the Authority of Scripture in Acts." *NTS* 33:619-631.
——. 1988. *Luke-Acts and the Jewish People: Eight Critical Perspectives*. Minneapolis: Augsburg.
Verrall, A. W. 1908/09. "Christ Before Herod: Luke XXIII 1-16." *Journal of Theological Studies* 10:321-353.
Walaskay, P. 1983. *'And So We Came to Rome': The Political Perspective of St. Luke*. Cambridge: Cambridge Univ.
Walcutt, C. C. 1966. *Man's Changing Mask: Modes and Methods of Characterization in Fiction*. Minneapolis: Univ. of Minnesota.
Wilson, R. 1978-79. "The Bright Chimera: Character as a Literary Term." *Critical Inquiry* 5:725-749.
Wink, W. 1968. *John the Baptist in the Gospel Tradition*. Cambridge: Cambridge Univ.
Ziesler, J. 1978-79. "Luke and the Pharisees." *NTS* 25:146-157.

BTB = *Biblical Theology Bulletin* *CBQ* = *Catholic Biblical Quarterly*
JBL = *Journal of Biblical Literature* *NTS* = *New Testament Studies*

INDEXES

AUTHORS

BIBLICAL REFERENCES

www.ingramcontent.com/pod-product-compliance
Lightning Source LLC
LaVergne TN
LVHW050632100826
845148LV00011B/1842

* 9 7 8 1 7 2 5 2 8 3 5 6 5 *